SHAKESPEARE'S HENRIAD COLLECTION

Richard II, Henry IV, Part 1, Henry IV, Part 2, Henry V

WILLIAM SHAKESPEARE

CONTENTS

RICHARD II

HENRY IV, PART 1

HENRY IV, PART 2

HENRY V

RICHARD II

DRAMATIS PERSONÆ

KING RICHARD THE SECOND.
JOHN of GAUNT, Duke of Lancaster,
EDMUND of LANGLEY, Duke of York,
HENRY, surnamed BOLINGBROKE Duke of Hereford, son to
    John of Gaunt; afterwards KING HENRY IV.
DUKE of AUMERLE, son to the Duke of York.
THOMAS MOWBRAY, Duke of Norfolk.
DUKE OF SURREY.
EARL OF SALISBURY.
LORD BERKLEY.
BUSHY,
BAGOT,
GREEN,
EARL OF NORTHUMBERLAND.
HENRY PERCY, surnamed Hotspur, his son.
LORD ROSS.
LORD WILLOUGHBY.
LORD FITZWATER.
Bishop of Carlisle.
Abbot of Westminster.
Lord Marshal.
SIR STEPHEN SCROOP.
SIR PIERCE OF EXTON.

Captain of a band of Welshmen.
QUEEN to King Richard.
DUCHESS OF YORK.
DUCHESS OF GLOUCESTER.
Lady attending on the Queen.
Lords, Heralds, Officers, Soldiers, two Gardeners, Keeper,
    Messenger, Groom, and other Attendants.

SCENE: England and Wales.

ACT I

SCENE I. LONDON. KING RICHARD'S PALACE

(Enter KING RICHARD, JOHN of GAUNT, with other Nobles and Attendants.)

K. RICH. Old John of Gaunt, time-honour'd Lancaster,
Hast thou, according to thy oath and band,
Brought hither Henry Hereford thy bold son,
Here to make good the boisterous late appeal,
Which then our leisure would not let us hear,₅
Against the Duke of Norfolk, Thomas Mowbray?
GAUNT. I have, my liege.
K. RICH. Tell me, moreover, hast thou sounded him,
If he appeal the duke on ancient malice;
Or worthily, as a good subject should,₁₀
On some known ground of treachery in him?
GAUNT. As near as I could sift him on that argument,
On some apparent danger seen in him
Aim'd at your highness, no inveterate malice.
K. RICH. Then call them to our presence; face to face,₁₅
And frowning brow to brow, ourselves will hear
The accuser and the accused freely speak:
High-stomach'd are they both, and full of ire,

In rage deaf as the sea, hasty as fire.
(ENTER BOLINGBROKE AND MOWBRAY.)
BOLING. Many years of happy days befal$_{20}$
My gracious sovereign, my most loving liege!
MOW. Each day still better other's happiness;
Until the heavens, envying earth's good hap,
Add an immortal title to your crown!
K. RICH. We thank you both: yet one but flatters us,$_{25}$
As well appeareth by the cause you come;
Namely, to appeal each other of high treason.
Cousin of Hereford, what dost thou object
Against the Duke of Norfolk, Thomas Mowbray?
BOLING. First, heaven be the record to my speech!$_{30}$
In the devotion of a subject's love,
Tendering the precious safety of my prince,
And free from other misbegotten hate,
Come I appellant to this princely presence.
Now, Thomas Mowbray, do I turn to thee,$_{35}$
And mark my greeting well; for what I speak
My body shall make good upon this earth,
Or my divine soul answer it in heaven.
Thou art a traitor and a miscreant,
Too good to be so and too bad to live,$_{40}$
Since the more fair and crystal is the sky,
The uglier seem the clouds that in it fly.
Once more, the more to aggravate the note,
With a foul traitor's name stuff I thy throat;
And wish, so please my sovereign, ere I move,$_{45}$
What my tongue speaks my right drawn sword may prove.
MOW. Let not my cold words here accuse my zeal:
'Tis not the trial of a woman's war,
The bitter clamour of two eager tongues,
Can arbitrate this cause betwixt us twain;$_{50}$
The blood is hot that must be cool'd for this:
Yet can I not of such tame patience boast
As to be hush'd and nought at all to say:
First, the fair reverence of your highness curbs me
From giving reins and spurs to my free speech;$_{55}$
Which else would post until it had return'd

These terms of treason doubled down his throat.
Setting aside his high blood's royalty,
And let him be no kinsman to my liege,
I do defy him, and I spit at him;$_{60}$
Call him a slanderous coward and a villain:
Which to maintain I would allow him odds,
And meet him, were I tied to run afoot
Even to the frozen ridges of the Alps,
Or any other ground inhabitable,$_{65}$
Where ever Englishman durst set his foot.
Mean time let this defend my loyalty,
By all my hopes, most falsely doth he lie.
BOLING. Pale trembling coward, there I throw my gage,
Disclaiming here the kindred of the king;$_{70}$
And lay aside my high blood's royalty,
Which fear, not reverence, makes thee to except.
If guilty dread have left thee so much strength
As to take up mine honour's pawn, then stoop:
By that and all the rites of knighthood else,$_{75}$
Will I make good against thee, arm to arm,
What I have spoke, or thou canst worse devise.
MOW. I take it up; and by that sword I swear,
Which gently laid my knighthood on my shoulder,
I'll answer thee in any fair degree,$_{80}$
Or chivalrous design of knightly trial:
And when I mount, alive may I not light,
If I be traitor or unjustly fight!
K. RICH. What doth our cousin lay to Mowbray's charge?
It must be great that can inherit us$_{85}$
So much as of a thought of ill in him.
BOLING. Look, what I speak, my life shall prove it true;
That Mowbray hath received eight thousand nobles
In name of lendings for your highness' soldiers,
The which he hath detain'd for lewd employments,$_{90}$
Like a false traitor and injurious villain.
Besides I say and will in battle prove,
Or here or elsewhere to the furthest verge
That ever was survey'd by English eye,
That all the treasons for these eighteen years$_{95}$

Complotted and contrived in this land
Fetch from false Mowbray their first head and spring.
Further I say and further will maintain
Upon his bad life to make all this good,
That he did plot the Duke of Gloucester's death, 100
Suggest his soon-believing adversaries,
And consequently, like a traitor coward,
Sluiced out his innocent soul through streams of blood:
Which blood, like sacrificing Abel's, cries,
Even from the tongueless caverns of the earth, 105
To me for justice and rough chastisement;
And, by the glorious worth of my descent,
This arm shall do it, or this life be spent.
K. Rich. How high a pitch his resolution soars!
Thomas of Norfolk, what say'st thou to this? 110
Mow. O, let my sovereign turn away his face,
And bid his ears a little while be deaf,
Till I have told this slander of his blood,
How God and good men hate so foul a liar.
K. Rich. Mowbray, impartial are our eyes and ears: 115
Were he my brother, nay, my kingdom's heir,
As he is but my father's brother's son,
Now, by my sceptre's awe, I make a vow,
Such neighbour nearness to our sacred blood
Should nothing privilege him, nor partialize 120
The unstooping firmness of my upright soul:
He is our subject, Mowbray; so art thou:
Free speech and fearless I to thee allow.
Mow. Then, Bolingbroke, as low as to thy heart,
Through the false passage of thy throat, thou liest. 125
Three parts of that receipt I had for Calais
Disbursed I duly to his highness' soldiers;
The other part reserved I by consent,
For that my sovereign liege was in my debt
Upon remainder of a dear account, 130
Since last I went to France to fetch his queen:
Now swallow down that lie. For Gloucester's death,
I slew him not; but to my own disgrace
Neglected my sworn duty in that case.

For you, my noble Lord of Lancaster,$_{135}$
The honourable father to my foe,
Once did I lay an ambush for your life,
A trespass that doth vex my grieved soul;
But ere I last received the sacrament
I did confess it, and exactly begg'd$_{140}$
Your grace's pardon, and I hope I had it.
This is my fault: as for the rest appeal'd,
It issues from the rancour of a villain,
A recreant and most degenerate traitor:
Which in myself I boldly will defend:$_{145}$
And interchangeably hurl down my gage
Upon this overweening traitor's foot,
To prove myself a loyal gentleman
Even in the best blood chamber'd in his bosom.
In haste whereof, most heartily I pray$_{150}$
Your highness to assign our trial day.

K. RICH. Wrath-kindled gentlemen, be ruled by me;
Let's purge this choler without letting blood:
This we prescribe, though no physician;
Deep malice makes too deep incision:$_{155}$
Forget, forgive; conclude and be agreed;
Our doctors say this is no month to bleed.
Good uncle, let this end where it begun;
We'll calm the Duke of Norfolk, you your son.

GAUNT. To be a make-peace shall become my age:$_{160}$
Throw down, my son, the Duke of Norfolk's gage.

K. RICH. And, Norfolk, throw down his.

GAUNT. When, Harry, when?
Obedience bids I should not bid again.

K. RICH. Norfolk, throw down, we bid; there is no boot.

MOW. Myself I throw, dread sovereign, at thy foot.$_{165}$
My life thou shalt command, but not my shame:
The one my duty owes; but my fair name,
Despite of death that lives upon my grave,
To dark dishonour's use thou shalt not have.
I am disgraced, impeach'd and baffled here;$_{170}$
Pierced to the soul with slander's venom'd spear,
The which no balm can cure but his heart-blood

Which breathed this poison.

K. RICH. Rage must be withstood:
Give me his gage: lions make leopards tame.

Mow. Yea, but not change his spots: take but my shame, 175
And I resign my gage. My dear dear lord,
The purest treasure mortal times afford
Is spotless reputation: that away,
Men are but gilded loam or painted clay.
A jewel in a ten-times-barr'd-up chest
Is a bold spirit in a loyal breast. 180
Mine honour is my life; both grow in one;
Take honour from me, and my life is done:
Then, dear my liege, mine honour let me try;
In that I live and for that will I die. 185

K. RICH. Cousin, throw up your gage; do you begin.

BOLING. O, God defend my soul from such deep sin!
Shall I seem crest-fallen in my father's sight?
Or with pale beggar-fear impeach my height
Before this out-dared dastard? Ere my tongue 190
Shall wound my honour with such feeble wrong,
Or sound so base a parle, my teeth shall tear
The slavish motive of recanting fear,
And spit it bleeding in his high disgrace,
Where shame doth harbour, even in Mowbray's face. 195
(Exit Gaunt.)

K. RICH. We were not born to sue, but to command;
Which since we cannot do to make you friends,
Be ready, as your lives shall answer it,
At Coventry, upon Saint Lambert's day:
There shall your swords and lances arbitrate 200
The swelling difference of your settled hate:
Since we can not atone you, we shall see
Justice design the victor's chivalry.
Lord marshal, command our officers at arms
Be ready to direct these home alarms. *(Exeunt.)* 205

SCENE II. THE DUKE OF LANCASTER'S PALACE

(ENTER JOHN OF GAUNT WITH THE DUCHESS OF GLOUCESTER.)

GAUNT. Alas, the part I had in Woodstock's blood
Doth more solicit me than your exclaims,
To stir against the butchers of his life!
But since correction lieth in those hands
Which made the fault that we cannot correct,$_5$
Put we our quarrel to the will of heaven;
Who, when they see the hours ripe on earth,
Will rain hot vengeance on offenders' heads.
DUCH. Finds brotherhood in thee no sharper spur?
Hath love in thy old blood no living fire?$_{10}$
Edward's seven sons, whereof thyself art one,
Were as seven vials of his sacred blood,
Or seven fair branches springing from one root:
Some of those seven are dried by nature's course,
Some of those branches by the Destinies cut;$_{15}$
But Thomas, my dear lord, my life, my Gloucester,
One vial full of Edward's sacred blood,
One flourishing branch of his most royal root,
Is crack'd, and all the precious liquor spilt,
Is hack'd down, and his summer leaves all faded,$_{20}$
By envy's hand and murder's bloody axe.
Ah, Gaunt, his blood was thine! that bed, that womb,
That metal, that self-mould, that fashion'd thee
Made him a man; and though thou livest and breathest,
Yet art thou slain in him: thou dost consent$_{25}$
In some large measure to thy father's death,
In that thou seest thy wretched brother die,
Who was the model of thy father's life.
Call it not patience, Gaunt; it is despair:
In suffering thus thy brother to be slaughter'd.$_{30}$
Thou showest the naked pathway to thy life,
Teaching stern murder how to butcher thee:
That which in mean men we intitle patience
Is pale cold cowardice in noble breasts.

What shall I say? to safeguard thine own life,$_{35}$
The best way is to venge my Gloucester's death.
GAUNT. God's is the quarrel; for God's substitute,
His deputy anointed in His sight,
Hath caused his death: the which if wrongfully,
Let heaven revenge; for I may never lift$_{40}$
An angry arm against His minister.
DUCH. Where then, alas, may I complain myself?
GAUNT. To God, the widow's champion and defence.
DUCH. Why, then, I will. Farewell, old Gaunt.
Thou goest to Coventry, there to behold$_{45}$
Our cousin Hereford and fell Mowbray fight:
O, sit my husband's wrongs on Hereford's spear,
That it may enter butcher Mowbray's breast!
Or, if misfortune miss the first career,
Be Mowbray's sins so heavy in his bosom,$_{50}$
That they may break his foaming courser's back,
And throw the rider headlong in the lists,
A caitiff recreant to my cousin Hereford!
Farewell, old Gaunt: thy sometimes brother's wife
With her companion grief must end her life.$_{55}$
GAUNT. Sister, farewell; I must to Coventry:
As much good stay with thee as go with me!
DUCH. Yet one word more: grief boundeth where it falls,
Not with the empty hollowness, but weight:
I take my leave before I have begun,$_{60}$
For sorrow ends not when it seemeth done.
Commend me to thy brother, Edmund York.
Lo, this is all:—nay, yet depart not so;
Though this be all, do not so quickly go;
I shall remember more. Bid him—ah, what?—$_{65}$
With all good speed at Plashy visit me.
Alack, and what shall good old York there see
But empty lodgings and unfurnish'd walls,
Unpeopled offices, untrodden stones?
And what hear there for welcome but my groans?$_{70}$
Therefore commend me; let him not come there,
To seek out sorrow that dwells every where.
Desolate, desolate, will I hence and die:

The last leave of thee takes my weeping eye. *(Exeunt.)*

SCENE III. THE LISTS AT COVENTRY

(Enter the Lord Marshal and the DUKE of AUMERLE.)

MAR. My Lord Aumerle, is Harry Hereford arm'd?
AUM. Yea, at all points; and longs to enter in.
MAR. The Duke of Norfolk, sprightfully and bold,
Stays but the summons of the appellant's trumpet.
AUM. Why, then, the champions are prepared and stay 5
For nothing but his majesty's approach.
*(The trumpets sound, and the KING enters with his nobles, GAUNT,
BUSHY, BAGOT, GREEN, and others. When they are set, enter
MOWBRAY in arms, defendant, with a Herald.)*
K. RICH. Marshal, demand of yonder champion
The cause of his arrival here in arms:
Ask him his name and orderly proceed
To swear him in the justice of his cause. 10
MAR. In God's name and the king's, say who thou art
And why thou comest thus knightly clad in arms,
Against what man thou comest, and what thy quarrel:
Speak truly, on thy knighthood and thy oath;
As so defend thee heaven and thy valour! 15
MOW. My name is Thomas Mowbray, Duke of Norfolk;
Who hither come engaged by my oath—
Which God defend a knight should violate!—
Both to defend my loyalty and truth
To God, my king and my succeeding issue, 20
Against the Duke of Hereford that appeals me;
And, by the grace of God and this mine arm,
To prove him, in defending of myself,
A traitor to my God, my king, and me:
And as I truly fight, defend me heaven! 25
*(The trumpets sound. Enter BOLINGBROKE, Appellant, in armour, with a
Herald.)*
K. RICH. Marshal, ask yonder knight in arms,
Both who he is and why he cometh hither

Thus plated in habiliments of war,
And formally, according to our law,
Depose him in the justice of his cause.$_{30}$
MAR. What is thy name? and wherefore comest thou hither,
Before King Richard in his royal lists?
Against whom comest thou? and what's thy quarrel?
Speak like a true knight, so defend thee heaven!
BOLING. Harry of Hereford, Lancaster and Derby$_{35}$
Am I; who ready here do stand in arms,
To prove, by God's grace and my body's valour,
In lists, on Thomas Mowbray, Duke of Norfolk,
That he is a traitor, foul and dangerous,
To God of heaven, King Richard and to me;$_{40}$
And as I truly fight, defend me heaven!
MAR. On pain of death, no person be so bold
Or daring-hardy as to touch the lists,
Except the marshal and such officers
Appointed to direct these fair designs.$_{45}$
BOLING. Lord marshal, let me kiss my sovereign's hand,
And bow my knee before his majesty:
For Mowbray and myself are like two men
That vow a long and weary pilgrimage;
Then let us take a ceremonious leave$_{50}$
And loving farewell of our several friends.
MAR. The appellant in all duty greets your highness,
And craves to kiss your hand and take his leave.
K. RICH. We will descend and fold him in our arms.
Cousin of Hereford, as thy cause is right,$_{55}$
So be thy fortune in this royal fight!
Farewell, my blood; which if to-day thou shed,
Lament we may, but not revenge thee dead.
BOLING. O, let no noble eye profane a tear
For me, if I be gored with Mowbray's spear:$_{60}$
As confident as is the falcon's flight
Against a bird, do I with Mowbray fight.
My loving lord, I take my leave of you;
Of you, my noble cousin, Lord Aumerle;
Not sick, although I have to do with death,$_{65}$
But lusty, young, and cheerly drawing breath.

Lo, as at English feasts, so I regreet
The daintiest last, to make the end most sweet:
O thou, the earthly author of my blood,
Whose youthful spirit, in me regenerate, 70
Doth with a twofold vigour lift me up
To reach at victory above my head,
Add proof unto mine armour with thy prayers;
And with thy blessings steel my lance's point,
That it may enter Mowbray's waxen coat, 75
And furbish new the name of John a Gaunt,
Even in the lusty haviour of his son.
GAUNT. God in thy good cause make thee prosperous!
Be swift like lightning in the execution;
And let thy blows, doubly redoubled, 80
Fall like amazing thunder on the casque
Of thy adverse pernicious enemy:
Rouse up thy youthful blood, be valiant and live.
BOLING. Mine innocency and Saint George to thrive!
MOW. However God or fortune cast my lot, 85
There lives or dies, true to King Richard's throne,
A loyal, just and upright gentleman:
Never did captive with a freer heart
Cast off his chains of bondage and embrace
His golden uncontroll'd enfranchisement. 90
More than my dancing soul doth celebrate
This feast of battle with mine adversary.
Most mighty liege, and my companion peers,
Take from my mouth the wish of happy years:
As gentle and as jocund as to jest 95
Go I to fight: truth hath a quiet breast.
K. RICH. Farewell, my lord: securely I espy
Virtue with valour couched in thine eye.
Order the trial, marshal, and begin.
MAR. Harry of Hereford, Lancaster and Derby, 100
Receive thy lance; and God defend the right!
BOLING. Strong as a tower in hope, I cry amen.
MAR. Go bear this lance to Thomas, Duke of Norfolk.
FIRST HER. Harry of Hereford, Lancaster and Derby,
Stands here for God, his sovereign and himself, 105

On pain to be found false and recreant,
To prove the Duke of Norfolk, Thomas Mowbray,
A traitor to his God, his king and him;
And dares him to set forward to the fight.
SEC. HER. Here standeth Thomas Mowbray, Duke of
    Norfolk,$_{110}$
On pain to be found false and recreant,
Both to defend himself and to approve
Henry of Hereford, Lancaster, and Derby,
To God, his sovereign and to him disloyal;
Courageously and with a free desire$_{115}$
Attending but the signal to begin.
MAR. Sound, trumpets; and set forward, combatants.
(A charge sounded.)
Stay, the king hath thrown his warder down.
K. RICH. Let them lay by their helmets and their spears,
And both return back to their chairs again:$_{120}$
Withdraw with us: and let the trumpets sound
While we return these dukes what we decree.
(A long flourish.)
Draw near,
And list what with our council we have done.
For that our kingdom's earth should not be soil'd$_{125}$
With that dear blood which it hath fostered;
And for our eyes do hate the dire aspect
Of civil wounds plough'd up with neighbours' sword;
And for we think the eagle-winged pride
Of sky-aspiring and ambitious thoughts,$_{130}$
With rival-hating envy, set on you
To wake our peace, which in our country's cradle
Draws the sweet infant breath of gentle sleep;
Which so roused up with boisterous untuned drums,
With harsh-resounding trumpets' dreadful bray,$_{135}$
And grating shock of wrathful iron arms,
Might from our quiet confines fright fair peace,
And make us wade even in our kindred's blood;
Therefore, we banish you our territories:
You, cousin Hereford, upon pain of life,$_{140}$
Till twice five summers have enrich'd our fields

Shall not regreet our fair dominions,
But tread the stranger paths of banishment.
BOLING. Your will be done: this must my comfort be,
That sun that warms you here shall shine on me; 145
And those his golden beams to you here lent
Shall point on me and gild my banishment.
K. RICH. Norfolk, for thee remains a heavier doom,
Which I with some unwillingness pronounce:
The sly slow hours shall not determinate 150
The dateless limit of thy dear exile;
The hopeless word of 'never to return'
Breathe I against thee, upon pain of life.
Mow. A heavy sentence, my most sovereign liege,
And all unlook'd for from your highness' mouth: 155
A dearer merit, not so deep a maim
As to be cast forth in the common air,
Have I deserved at your highness' hands.
The language I have learn'd these forty years,
My native English, now I must forego: 160
And now my tongue's use is to me no more
Than an unstringed viol or a harp;
Or like a cunning instrument cased up,
Or, being open, put into his hands
That knows no touch to tune the harmony: 165
Within my mouth you have engaol'd my tongue,
Doubly portcullis'd with my teeth and lips;
And dull unfeeling barren ignorance
Is made my gaoler to attend on me.
I am too old to fawn upon a nurse, 170
Too far in years to be a pupil now:
What is thy sentence then but speechless death,
Which robs my tongue from breathing native breath?
K. RICH. It boots thee not to be compassionate:
After our sentence plaining comes too late. 175
Mow. Then thus I turn me from my country's light,
To dwell in solemn shades of endless night.
K. RICH. Return again, and take an oath with thee.
Lay on our royal sword your banish'd hands;
Swear by the duty that you owe to God— 180

Our part therein we banish with yourselves—
To keep the oath that we administer:
You never shall, so help you truth and God!
Embrace each other's love in banishment;
Nor never look upon each other's face; 185
Nor never write, regreet, nor reconcile
This louring tempest of your home-bred hate;
Nor never by advised purpose meet
To plot, contrive, or complot any ill
'gainst us, our state, our subjects, or our land. 190
Boling. I swear.
Mow. And I, to keep all this.
Boling. Norfolk, so far as to mine enemy:—
By this time, had the king permitted us,
One of our souls had wander'd in the air, 195
Banish'd this frail sepulchre of our flesh,
As now our flesh is banish'd from this land:
Confess thy treasons ere thou fly the realm;
Since thou hast far to go, bear not along
The clogging burthen of a guilty soul. 200
Mow. No, Bolingbroke: if ever I were traitor,
My name be blotted from the book of life,
And I from heaven banish'd as from hence!
But what thou art, God, thou, and I do know;
And all too soon, I fear, the king shall rue. 205
Farewell, my liege. Now no way can I stray;
Save back to England, all the world's my way. *(Exit.)*
K. Rich. Uncle, even in the glasses of thine eyes
I see thy grieved heart: thy sad aspect
Hath from the number of his banish'd years 210
Pluck'd four away. *(To Boling.)* Six frozen winters spent,
Return with welcome home from banishment.
Boling. How long a time lies in one little word!
Four lagging winters and four wanton springs
End in a word: such is the breath of kings. 215
Gaunt. I thank my liege, that in regard of me
He shortens four years of my son's exile:
But little vantage shall I reap thereby;
For, ere the six years that he hath to spend

Can change their moons and bring their times about,$_{220}$
My oil-dried lamp and time-bewasted light
Shall be extinct with age and endless night;
My inch of taper will be burnt and done,
And blindfold death not let me see my son.
K. RICH. Why, uncle, thou hast many years to live.$_{225}$
GAUNT. But not a minute, king, that thou canst give:
Shorten my days thou canst with sullen sorrow,
And pluck nights from me, but not lend a morrow;
Thou canst help time to furrow me with age,
But stop no wrinkle in his pilgrimage;$_{230}$
Thy word is current with him for my death,
But dead, thy kingdom cannot buy my breath.
K. RICH. Thy son is banish'd upon good advice,
Whereto thy tongue a party-verdict gave:
Why at our justice seem'st thou then to lour?$_{235}$
GAUNT. Things sweet to taste prove in digestion sour.
You urged me as a judge; but I had rather
You would have bid me argue like a father.
O, had it been a stranger, not my child,
To smooth his fault I should have been more mild:$_{240}$
A partial slander sought I to avoid,
And in the sentence my own life destroy'd.
Alas, I look'd when some of you should say,
I was too strict to make mine own away;
But you gave leave to my unwilling tongue$_{245}$
Against my will to do myself this wrong.
K. RICH. Cousin, farewell; and, uncle, bid him so:
Six years we banish him, and he shall go.
(Flourish. Exeunt King Richard and train.)
AUM. Cousin, farewell: what presence must not know,
From where you do remain let paper show.$_{250}$
MAR. My lord, no leave take I; for I will ride,
As far as land will let me, by your side.
GAUNT. O, to what purpose dost thou hoard thy words,
That thou return'st no greeting to thy friends?
BOLING. I have too few to take my leave of you,$_{255}$
When the tongue's office should be prodigal
To breathe the abundant dolour of the heart.

GAUNT. Thy grief is but thy absence for a time.

BOLING. Joy absent, grief is present for that time.

GAUNT. What is six winters? they are quickly gone.$_{260}$

BOLING. To men in joy; but grief makes one hour ten.

GAUNT. Call it a travel that thou takest for pleasure.

BOLING. My heart will sigh when I miscall it so,
Which finds it an inforced pilgrimage.

GAUNT. The sullen passage of thy weary steps$_{265}$
Esteem as foil wherein thou art to set
The precious jewel of thy home return.

BOLING. Nay, rather, every tedious stride I make
Will but remember me what a deal of world
I wander from the jewels that I love.$_{270}$
Must I not serve a long apprenticehood
To foreign passages, and in the end,
Having my freedom, boast of nothing else
But that I was a journeyman to grief?

GAUNT. All places that the eye of heaven visits$_{275}$
Are to a wise man ports and happy havens.
Teach thy necessity to reason thus;
There is no virtue like necessity.
Think not the king did banish thee,
But thou the king. Woe doth the heavier sit,$_{280}$
Where it perceives it is but faintly borne.
Go, say I sent thee forth to purchase honour
And not the king exiled thee; or suppose
Devouring pestilence hangs in our air
And thou art flying to a fresher clime:$_{285}$
Look, what thy soul holds dear, imagine it
To lie that way thou go'st, not whence thou comest:
Suppose the singing birds musicians,
The grass whereon thou tread'st the presence strew'd,
The flowers fair ladies, and thy steps no more$_{290}$
Than a delightful measure or a dance;
For gnarling sorrow hath less power to bite
The man that mocks at it and sets it light.

BOLING. O, who can hold a fire in his hand
By thinking on the frosty Caucasus?$_{295}$
Or cloy the hungry edge of appetite

By bare imagination of a feast?
Or wallow naked in December snow
By thinking on fastastic summer's heat?
O, no! the apprehension of the good$_{300}$
Gives but the greater feeling to the worse:
Fell sorrow's tooth doth never rankle more
Than when he bites, but lanceth not the sore.
GAUNT. Come, come, my son, I'll bring thee on thy way:
Had I thy youth and cause, I would not stay.$_{305}$
BOLING. Then, England's ground, farewell; sweet soil, adieu;
My mother, and my nurse, that bears me yet!
Where'er I wander, boast of this I can,
Though banish'd, yet a trueborn Englishman. *(Exeunt.)*

SCENE IV. THE COURT

(Enter the K$_{ING}$, with B$_{AGOT}$ and G$_{REEN}$ at one door; and the D$_{UKE}$ of
A$_{UMERLE}$ at another.)

K. RICH. We did observe. Cousin Aumerle,
How far brought you high Hereford on his way?
AUM. I brought high Hereford, if you call him so,
But to the next highway, and there I left him.
K. RICH. And say, what store of parting tears were shed?$_5$
AUM. Faith, none for me; except the north-east wind,
Which then blew bitterly against our faces,
Awaked the sleeping rheum, and so by chance
Did grace our hollow parting with a tear.
K. RICH. What said our cousin when you parted with him?$_{10}$
AUM. 'Farewell:'
And, for my heart disdained that my tongue
Should so profane the word, that taught me craft
To counterfeit oppression of such grief,
That words seem'd buried in my sorrow's grave.$_{15}$
Marry, would the word 'farewell' have lengthen'd hours
And added years to his short banishment,
He should have had a volume of farewells;
But since it would not, he had none of me.

K. Rich. He is our cousin, cousin; but 'tis doubt, [20]
When time shall call him home from banishment,
Whether our kinsman come to see his friends.
Ourself and Bushy, Bagot here and Green
Observed his courtship to the common people;
How he did seem to dive into their hearts [25]
With humble and familiar courtesy,
What reverence he did throw away on slaves.
Wooing poor craftsmen with the craft of smiles
And patient underbearing of his fortune,
As 'twere to banish their affects with him. [30]
Off goes his bonnet to an oyster-wench;
A brace of draymen bid God speed him well
And had the tribute of his supple knee,
With 'Thanks, my countrymen, my loving friends;'
As were our England in reversion his, [35]
And he our subjects' next degree in hope.
Green. Well, he is gone; and with him go these thoughts.
Now for the rebels which stand out in Ireland,
Expedient manage must be made, my liege,
Ere further leisure yield them further means [40]
For their advantage and your highness' loss.
K. Rich. We will ourself in person to this war:
And, for our coffers, with too great a court
And liberal largess, are grown somewhat light,
We are inforced to farm our royal realm; [45]
The revenue whereof shall furnish us
For our affairs in hand: if that come short,
Our substitutes at home shall have blank charters;
Whereto, when they shall know what men are rich,
They shall subscribe them for large sums of gold [50]
And send them after to supply our wants;
For we will make for Ireland presently.
(Enter Bushy.)
Bushy, what news?
Bushy. Old John of Gaunt is grievous sick, my lord,
Suddenly taken; and hath sent post haste [55]
To entreat your majesty to visit him.
K. Rich. Where lies he?

BUSHY. At Ely House.

K. RICH. Now put it, God, in the physician's mind
To help him to his grave immediately!₆₀
The lining of his coffers shall make coats
To deck our soldiers for these Irish wars.
Come, gentlemen, let's all go visit him:
Pray God we may make haste, and come too late!
*All. Amen. (Exeunt.)*₆₅

ACT II

SCENE I. ELY HOUSE

(Enter JOHN of GAUNT sick, with the DUKE of YORK, &c.)

GAUNT. Will the king come, that I may breathe my last
In wholesome counsel to his unstaid youth?
YORK. Vex not yourself, nor strive not with your breath;
For all in vain comes counsel to his ear.
GAUNT. O, but they say the tongues of dying men$_5$
Enforce attention like deep harmony:
Where words are scarce, they are seldom spent in vain,
For they breathe truth that breathe their words in pain.
He that no more must say is listen'd more
Than they whom youth and ease have taught to glose;$_{10}$
More are men's ends mark'd than their lives before:
The setting sun, and music at the close,
As the last taste of sweets, is sweetest last,
Writ in remembrance more than things long past:
Though Richard my life's counsel would not hear,$_{15}$
My death's sad tale may yet undeaf his ear.
YORK. No; it is stopp'd with other flattering sounds,
As praises, of whose taste the wise are fond,

Lascivious metres, to whose venom sound
The open ear of youth doth always listen;20
Report of fashions in proud Italy,
Whose manners still our tardy apish nation
Limps after in base imitation.
Where doth the world thrust forth a vanity—
So it be new, there's no respect how vile—25
That is not quickly buzz'd into his ears?
Then all too late comes counsel to be heard,
Where will doth mutiny with wit's regard.
Direct not him whose way himself will choose:
'Tis breath thou lack'st, and that breath wilt thou lose.30
GAUNT. Methinks I am a prophet new inspired
And thus expiring do foretell of him:
His rash fierce blaze of riot cannot last,
For violent fires soon burn out themselves;
Small showers last long, but sudden storms are short;35
He tires betimes that spurs too fast betimes;
With eager feeding food doth choke the feeder:
Light vanity, insatiate cormorant,
Consuming means, soon preys upon itself.
This royal throne of kings, this scepter'd isle,40
This earth of majesty, this seat of Mars,
This other Eden, demi-paradise;
This fortress built by Nature for herself
Against infection and the hand of war;
This happy breed of men, this little world,45
This precious stone set in the silver sea,
Which serves it in the office of a wall,
Or as a moat defensive to a house,
Against the envy of less happier lands;
This blessed plot, this earth, this realm, this England,50
This nurse, this teeming womb of royal kings,
Fear'd by their breed and famous by their birth,
Renowned for their deeds as far from home,
For Christian service and true chivalry,
As is the sepulchre in stubborn Jewry55
Of the world's ransom, blessed Mary's Son;
This land of such dear souls, this dear dear land,

Dear for her reputation through the world,
Is now leased out, I die pronouncing it,
Like to a tenement or pelting farm:$_{60}$
England, bound in with the triumphant sea,
Whose rocky shore beats back the envious siege
Of watery Neptune, is now bound in with shame,
With inky blots and rotten parchment bonds:
That England, that was wont to conquer others,$_{65}$
Hath made a shameful conquest of itself.
Ah, would the scandal vanish with my life,
How happy then were my ensuing death!
(ENTER KING RICHARD AND QUEEN, AUMERLE, BUSHY, GREEN,
*   BAGOT, ROSS, AND WILLOUGHBY.)*
YORK. The king is come: deal mildly with his youth;
For young hot colts being raged do rage the more.$_{70}$
QUEEN. How fares our noble uncle, Lancaster?
K. RICH. What comfort, man? how is't with aged Gaunt?
GAUNT. O, how that name befits my composition!
Old Gaunt indeed, and gaunt in being old:
Within me grief hath kept a tedious fast;$_{75}$
And who abstains from meat that is not gaunt?
For sleeping England long time have I watch'd;
Watching breeds leanness, leanness is all gaunt:
The pleasure that some fathers feed upon,
Is my strict fast; I mean, my children's looks;$_{80}$
And therein fasting, hast thou made me gaunt:
Gaunt am I for the grave, gaunt as a grave,
Whose hollow womb inherits nought but bones.
K. RICH. Can sick men play so nicely with their names?
GAUNT. No, misery makes sport to mock itself:$_{85}$
Since thou dost seek to kill my name in me,
I mock my name, great king, to flatter thee.
K. RICH. Should dying men flatter with those that live?
GAUNT. No, no, men living flatter those that die.
K. RICH. Thou, now a-dying, say'st thou flatterest me.$_{90}$
GAUNT. O, no! thou diest, though I the sicker be.
K. RICH. I am in health, I breathe, and see thee ill.
GAUNT. Now, He that made me knows I see thee ill;
Ill in myself to see, and in thee seeing ill.

Thy death-bed is no lesser than thy land$_{95}$
Wherein thou liest in reputation sick;
And thou, too careless patient as thou art,
Commit'st thy anointed body to the cure
Of those physicians that first wounded thee:
A thousand flatterers sit within thy crown,$_{100}$
Whose compass is no bigger than thy head;
And yet, incaged in so small a verge,
The waste is no whit lesser than thy land.
O, had thy grandsire with a prophet's eye
Seen how his son's son should destroy his sons,$_{105}$
From forth thy reach he would have laid thy shame,
Deposing thee before thou wert possess'd,
Which art possess'd now to depose thyself.
Why, cousin, wert thou regent of the world,
It were a shame to let this land by lease;$_{110}$
But for thy world enjoying but this land,
Is it not more than shame to shame it so?
Landlord of England art thou now, not king:
Thy state of law is bondslave to the law;
And thou—
K. RICH. A lunatic lean-witted fool,$_{115}$
Presuming on an ague's privilege,
Barest with thy frozen admonition
Make pale our cheek, chasing the royal blood
With fury from his native residence.
Now, by my seat's right royal majesty,$_{120}$
Wert thou not brother to great Edward's son,
This tongue that runs so roundly in thy head
Should run thy head from thy unreverent shoulders.
GAUNT. O, spare me not, my brother Edward's son,
For that I was his father Edward's son;$_{125}$
That blood already, like the pelican,
Hast thou tapp'd out and drunkenly caroused:
My brother Gloucester, plain well-meaning soul,
Whom fair befal in heaven 'mongst happy souls!
May be a precedent and witness good$_{130}$
That thou respect'st not spilling Edward's blood:
Join with the present sickness that I have;

And thy unkindness be like crooked age,
To crop at once a too long wither'd flower.
Live in thy shame, but die not shame with thee!$_{135}$
These words hereafter thy tormentors be!
Convey me to my bed, then to my grave:
Love they to live that love and honour have.
(Exit, borne off by his Attendants.)
K. RICH. And let them die that age and sullens have;
For both hast thou, and both become the grave.$_{140}$
YORK. I do beseech your majesty, impute his words
To wayward sickliness and age in him:
He loves you, on my life, and holds you dear
As Harry Duke of Hereford, were he here.
K. RICH. Right, you say true: as Hereford's love, so his;$_{145}$
As theirs, so mine; and all be as it is.
(ENTER NORTHUMBERLAND.)
NORTH. My liege, old Gaunt commends him to your majesty.
K. RICH. What says he?
NORTH. Nay, nothing; all is said:
His tongue is now a stringless instrument;
Words life and all, old Lancaster hath spent.$_{150}$
YORK. Be York the next that must be bankrupt so!
Though death be poor, it ends a mortal woe.
K. RICH. The ripest fruit first falls, and so doth he;
His time is spent, our pilgrimage must be.
So much for that. Now for our Irish wars:$_{155}$
We must supplant those rough rug-headed kerns,
Which live like venom where no venom else
But only they have privilege to live.
And for these great affairs do ask some charge,
Towards our assistance we do seize to us$_{160}$
The plate, coin, revenues and moveables,
Whereof our uncle Gaunt did stand possess'd.
YORK. How long shall I be patient? ah, how long
Shall tender duty make me suffer wrong?
Not Gloucester's death, nor Hereford's banishment,$_{165}$
Not Gaunt's rebukes, nor England's private wrongs,
Nor the prevention of poor Bolingbroke
About his marriage, nor my own disgrace,

Have ever made me sour my patient cheek,
Or bend one wrinkle on my sovereign's face. 170
I am the last of noble Edward's sons,
Of whom thy father, Prince of Wales, was first:
In war was never lion raged more fierce,
In peace was never gentle lamb more mild,
Than was that young and princely gentleman. 175
His face thou hast, for even so look'd he,
Accomplish'd with the number of thy hours;
But when he frown'd, it was against the French
And not against his friends; his noble hand
Did win what he did spend and spent not that 180
Which his triumphant father's hand had won;
His hands were guilty of no kindred blood,
But bloody with the enemies of his kin.
O Richard! York is too far gone with grief,
Or else he never would compare between. 185
K. Rich. Why, uncle, what's the matter?
York. O my liege,
Pardon me, if you please; if not, I, pleased
Not to be pardon'd, am content withal.
Seek you to seize and gripe into your hands
The royalties and rights of banish'd Hereford? 190
Is not Gaunt dead, and doth not Hereford live?
Was not Gaunt just, and is not Harry true?
Did not the one deserve to have an heir?
Is not his heir a well-deserving son?
Take Hereford's rights away, and take from time 195
His charters and his customary rights;
Let not to-morrow then ensue to-day:
Be not thyself; for how art thou a king
But by fair sequence and succession?
Now, afore God—God forbid I say true!— 200
If you do wrongfully seize Hereford's rights,
Call in the letters patents that he hath
By his attorneys-general to sue
His livery and deny his offer'd homage,
You pluck a thousand dangers on your head, 205
You lose a thousand well-disposed hearts

And prick my tender patience to those thoughts
Which honour and allegiance cannot think.
K. RICH. Think what you will, we seize into our hands
His plate, his goods, his money and his lands. 210
YORK. I'll not be by the while: my liege, farewell:
What will ensue hereof, there's none can tell;
But by bad courses may be understood
That their events can never fall out good. *(Exit.)*
K. RICH. Go, Bushy, to the Earl of Wiltshire straight: 215
Bid him repair to us to Ely House
To see this business. To-morrow next
We will for Ireland; and 'tis time, I trow:
And we create, in absence of ourself,
Our uncle York lord governor of England; 220
For he is just and always loved us well.
Come on, our queen: to-morrow must we part;
Be merry, for our time of stay is short.
(Flourish. Exeunt King, Queen, Aumerle, Bushy, Green, and Bagot.)
NORTH. Well, lords, the Duke of Lancaster is dead.
ROSS. And living too; for now his son is duke. 225
WILLO. Barely in title, not in revenue.
NORTH. Richly in both, if justice had her right.
ROSS. My heart is great; but it must break with silence,
Ere't be disburden'd with a liberal tongue.
NORTH. Nay, speak thy mind; and let him ne'er speak more 230
That speaks thy words again to do thee harm!
WILLO. Tends that thou wouldst speak to the Duke of
    Hereford?
If it be so, out with it boldly, man;
Quick is mine ear to hear of good towards him.
ROSS. No good at all that I can do for him; 235
Unless you call it good to pity him,
Bereft and gelded of his patrimony.
NORTH. Now, afore God, 'tis shame such wrongs are borne
In him a royal prince and many moe
Of noble blood in this declining land. 240
The king is not himself, but basely led
By flatterers; and what they will inform.
Merely in hate, 'gainst any of us all,

That will the king severely prosecute
'Gainst us, our lives, our children, and our heirs.$_{245}$
Ross. The commons hath he pill'd with grievous taxes,
And quite lost their hearts: the nobles hath he fined
For ancient quarrels, and quite lost their hearts.
WILLO. And daily new exactions are devised,
As blanks, benevolences, and I wot not what:$_{250}$
But what, o' God's name, doth become of this?
NORTH. Wars have not wasted it, for warr'd he hath not,
But basely yielded upon compromise
That which his noble ancestors achieved with blows:
More hath he spent in peace than they in wars.$_{255}$
Ross. The Earl of Wiltshire hath the realm in farm.
WILLO. The king's grown bankrupt, like a broken man.
NORTH. Reproach and dissolution hangeth over him.
Ross. He hath not money for these Irish wars,
His burthenous taxations notwithstanding,$_{260}$
But by the robbing of the banish'd duke.
NORTH. His noble kinsman: most degenerate king!
But, lords, we hear this fearful tempest sing,
Yet seek no shelter to avoid the storm;
We see the wind sit sore upon our sails,$_{265}$
And yet we strike not, but securely perish.
Ross. We see the very wreck that we must suffer;
And unavoided is the danger now,
For suffering so the causes of our wreck.
NORTH. Not so; even through the hollow eyes of death$_{270}$
I spy life peering; but I dare not say
How near the tidings of our comfort is.
WILLO. Nay, let us share thy thoughts, as thou dost ours.
Ross. Be confident to speak, Northumberland:
We three are but thyself; and, speaking so,$_{275}$
Thy words are but as thoughts; therefore, be bold.
NORTH. Then thus: I have from Port le Blanc, a bay
In Brittany, received intelligence
That Harry Duke of Hereford, Rainold Lord Cobham,$_{280}$
That late broke from the Duke of Exeter,
His brother, Archbishop late of Canterbury,
Sir Thomas Erpingham, Sir John Ramston,

Sir John Norbery, Sir Robert Waterton and Francis Quoint,
All these well furnish'd by the Duke of Bretagne$_{285}$
With eight tall ships, three thousand men of war.
Are making hither with all due expedience
And shortly mean to touch our northern shore:
Perhaps they had ere this, but that they stay
The first departing of the king for Ireland.$_{290}$
If then we shall shake off our slavish yoke,
Imp out our drooping country's broken wing,
Redeem from broking pawn the blemish'd crown,
Wipe off the dust that hides our sceptre's gilt
And make high majesty look like itself,$_{295}$
Away with me in post to Ravenspurgh;
But if you faint, as fearing to do so,
Stay and be secret, and myself will go.
Ross. To horse, to horse! urge doubts to them that fear.
Willo. Hold out my horse, and I will first be there.$_{300}$
(Exeunt.)

SCENE II. THE PALACE

(Enter Queen, Bushy, and Bagot.)

Bushy. Madam, your majesty is too much sad.
You promised, when you parted with the king,
To lay aside life-harming heaviness,
And entertain a cheerful disposition.
Queen. To please the king I did; to please myself$_5$
I cannot do it; yet I know no cause
Why I should welcome such a guest as grief,
Save bidding farewell to so sweet a guest
As my sweet Richard: yet again, methinks,
Some unborn sorrow, ripe in fortune's womb,$_{10}$
Is coming towards me, and my inward soul
With nothing trembles: at some thing it grieves,
More than with parting from my lord the king.
Bushy. Each substance of a grief hath twenty shadows,
Which shows like grief itself, but is not so;$_{15}$

For sorrow's eye, glazed with blinding tears,
Divides one thing entire to many objects;
Like perspectives, which, rightly gazed upon,
Show nothing but confusion, eyed awry,
Distinguish form: so your sweet majesty,$_{20}$
Looking awry upon your lord's departure,
Find shapes of grief, more than himself, to wail;
Which, look'd on as it is, is nought but shadows
Of what it is not. Then, thrice-gracious queen,
More than your lord's departure weep not: more's not seen;$_{25}$
Or if it be, 'tis with false sorrow's eye,
Which for things true weeps things imaginary.
QUEEN. It may be so; but yet my inward soul
Persuades me it is otherwise: howe'er it be,
I cannot but be sad; so heavy sad,$_{30}$
As, though on thinking on no thought I think,
Makes me with heavy nothing faint and shrink.
BUSHY. 'Tis nothing but conceit, my gracious lady.
QUEEN. 'Tis nothing less: conceit is still derived
From some forefather grief; mine is not so,$_{35}$
For nothing hath begot my something grief;
Or something hath the nothing that I grieve:
'Tis in reversion that I do possess;
But what it is, that is not yet known; what
I cannot name; 'tis nameless woe, I wot.$_{40}$
(Enter GREEN.)
GREEN. God save your majesty! and well met, gentlemen:
I hope the king is not yet shipp'd for Ireland.
QUEEN. Why hopest thou so? 'tis better hope he is;
For his designs crave haste, his haste good hope:
Then wherefore dost thou hope he is not shipp'd?$_{45}$
GREEN. That he, our hope, might have retired his power,
And driven into despair an enemy's hope,
Who strongly hath set footing in this land:
The banish'd Bolingbroke repeals himself,
And with uplifted arms is safe arrived$_{50}$
At Ravenspurgh.
QUEEN. Now God in heaven forbid!
GREEN. Ah madam, 'tis too true: and that is worse,

The Lord Northumberland, his son young Henry Percy,
The Lords of Ross, Beaumond, and Willoughby,
With all their powerful friends, are fled to him. $_{55}$
BUSHY. Why have you not proclaim'd Northumberland
And all the rest revolted faction traitors?
GREEN. We have: whereupon the Earl of Worcester
Hath broke his staff, resign'd his stewardship,
And all the household servants fled with him $_{60}$
To Bolingbroke.
QUEEN. So, Green, thou art the midwife to my woe,
And Bolingbroke my sorrow's dismal heir:
Now hath my soul brought forth her prodigy,
And I, a gasping new-deliver'd mother, $_{65}$
Have woe to woe, sorrow to sorrow join'd.
BUSHY. Despair not, madam.
QUEEN. Who shall hinder me?
I will despair, and be at enmity
With cozening hope: he is a flatterer,
A parasite, a keeper back of death, $_{70}$
Who gently would dissolve the bands of life,
Which false hope lingers in extremity.
(Enter YORK.)
GREEN. Here comes the Duke of York.
QUEEN. With signs of war about his aged neck;
O, full of careful business are his looks! $_{75}$
Uncle, for God's sake, speak comfortable words.
YORK. Should I do so, I should belie my thoughts:
Comfort's in heaven; and we are on the earth,
Where nothing lives but crosses, cares and grief.
Your husband, he is gone to save far off, $_{80}$
Whilst others come to make him lose at home:
Here am I left to underprop his land,
Who, weak with age, cannot support myself:
Now comes the sick hour that his surfeit made;
Now shall he try his friends that flatter'd him. $_{85}$
(Enter a Servant.)
SERV. My lord, your son was gone before I came.
YORK. He was? Why, so! go all which way it will!
The nobles they are fled, the commons they are cold,

And will, I fear, revolt on Hereford's side.
Sirrah, get thee to Plashy, to my sister Gloucester;$_{90}$
Bid her send me presently a thousand pound:
Hold, take my ring.
SERV. My lord, I had forgot to tell your lordship,
To-day, as I came by, I called there;
But I shall grieve you to report the rest.$_{95}$
YORK. What is't, knave?
SERV. An hour before I came, the duchess died.
YORK. God for his mercy! what a tide of woes
Comes rushing on this woeful land at once!
I know not what to do: I would to God,$_{100}$
So my untruth had not provoked him to it,
The king had cut off my head with my brother's.
What, are there no posts dispatch'd for Ireland?
How shall we do for money for these wars?
Come, sister,—cousin, I would say,—pray, pardon me.$_{105}$
Go, fellow, get thee home, provide some carts
And bring away the armour that is there. *(Exit Servant.)*
Gentlemen, will you go muster men?
If I know how or which way to order these affairs
Thus thrust disorderly into my hands,$_{110}$
Never believe me. Both are my kinsmen:
The one is my sovereign, whom both my oath
And duty bids defend; the other again
Is my kinsman, whom the king hath wrong'd,
Whom conscience and my kindred bids to right.$_{115}$
Well, somewhat we must do. Come, cousin, I'll
Dispose of you.
Gentlemen, go, muster up your men,
And meet me presently at Berkeley.
I should to Plashy too;$_{120}$
But time will not permit: all is uneven,
And every thing is left at six and seven.
(Exeunt York and Queen.)
BUSHY. The wind sits fair for news to go to Ireland,
But none returns. For us to levy power
Proportionable to the enemy$_{125}$
Is all unpossible.

GREEN. Besides, our nearness to the king in love
Is near the hate of those love not the king.
BAGOT. And that's the wavering commons: for their love
Lies in their purses, and whoso empties them$_{130}$
By so much fills their hearts with deadly hate.
BUSHY. Wherein the king stands generally condemn'd.
BAGOT. If judgement lie in them, then so do we,
Because we ever have been near the king.
GREEN. Well, I will for refuge straight to Bristol castle:$_{135}$
The Earl of Wiltshire is already there.
BUSHY. Thither will I with you; for little office
The hateful commons will perform for us,
Except like curs to tear us all to pieces.
Will you go along with us?$_{140}$
BAGOT. No; I will to Ireland to his majesty.
Farewell: if heart's presages be not vain,
We three here part that ne'er shall meet again.
BUSHY. That's as York thrives to beat back Bolingbroke.
GREEN. Alas, poor duke! the task he undertakes$_{145}$
Is numbering sands and drinking oceans dry:
Where one on his side fights, thousands will fly.
Farewell at once, for once, for all, and ever.
BUSHY. Well, we may meet again.
BAGOT. I fear me, never.
(Exeunt.)

SCENE III. WILDS IN GLOUCESTERSHIRE

(Enter Bolingbroke and Northumberland, with Forces.)

BOLING. How far is it, my lord, to Berkeley now?
NORTH. Believe me, noble lord,
I am a stranger here in Gloucestershire:
These high wild hills and rough uneven ways
Draws out our miles, and makes them wearisome;$_5$
And yet your fair discourse hath been as sugar,
Making the hard way sweet and delectable.
But I bethink me what a weary way

From Ravenspurgh to Cotswold will be found
In Ross and Willoughby, wanting your company,$_{10}$
Which, I protest, hath very much beguiled
The tediousness and process of my travel:
But theirs is sweetened with the hope to have
The present benefit which I possess;
And hope to joy is little less in joy$_{15}$
Than hope enjoy'd: by this the weary lords
Shall make their way seem short, as mine hath done
By sight of what I have, your noble company.
BOLING. Of much less value is my company
Than your good words. But who comes here?$_{20}$
(ENTER HENRY PERCY.)
NORTH. It is my son, young Harry Percy,
Sent from my brother Worcester, whencesoever.
Harry, how fares your uncle?
PERCY. I had thought, my lord, to have learn'd his health
    of you.
NORTH. Why, is he not with the queen?$_{25}$
PERCY. No, my good Lord; he hath forsook the court,
Broken his staff of office and dispersed
The household of the king.
NORTH. What was his reason?
He was not so resolved when last we spake together.
PERCY. Because your lordship was proclaimed traitor.$_{30}$
But he, my lord, is gone to Ravenspurgh,
To offer service to the Duke of Hereford,
And sent me over by Berkeley, to discover
What power the Duke of York had levied there;
Then with directions to repair to Ravenspurgh.$_{35}$
NORTH. Have you forgot the Duke of Hereford, boy?
PERCY. No, my good Lord, for that is not forgot
Which ne'er I did remember: to my knowledge,
I never in my life did look on him.
NORTH. Then learn to know him now; this is the duke.$_{40}$
PERCY. My gracious lord, I tender you my service,
Such as it is, being tender, raw and young;
Which elder days shall ripen and confirm
To more approved service and desert.

BOLING. I thank thee, gentle Percy; and be sure$_{45}$
I count myself in nothing else so happy
As in a soul remembering my good friends;
And, as my fortune ripens with thy love,
It shall be still thy true love's recompense:
My heart this covenant makes, my hand thus seals it.$_{50}$
NORTH. How far is it to Berkeley? and what stir
Keeps good old York there with his men of war?
PERCY. There stands the castle, by yon tuft of trees,
Mann'd with three hundred men, as I have heard;
And in it are the Lords of York, Berkeley, and Seymour;$_{55}$
None else of name and noble estimate.
(ENTER ROSS AND WILLOUGHBY.)
NORTH. Here come the Lords of Ross and Willoughby,
Bloody with spurring, fiery-red with haste.
BOLING. Welcome, my lords. I wot your love pursues
A banish'd traitor: all my treasury$_{60}$
Is yet but unfelt thanks, which more enrich'd
Shall be your love and labour's recompense.
ROSS. Your presence makes us rich, most noble lord.
WILLO. And far surmounts our labour to attain it.
BOLING. Evermore thanks, the exchequer of the poor;$_{65}$
Which, till my infant fortune comes to years,
Stands for my bounty. But who comes here?
(ENTER BERKELEY.)
NORTH. It is my Lord of Berkeley, as I guess.
BERK. My Lord of Hereford, my message is to you.
BOLING. My lord, my answer is—to Lancaster;$_{70}$
And I am come to seek that name in England;
And I must find that title in your tongue,
Before I make reply to aught you say.
BERK. Mistake me not, my Lord; 'tis not my meaning
To raze one title of your honour out:$_{75}$
To you, my lord, I come, what lord you will,
From the most gracious regent of this land,
The Duke of York, to know what pricks you on
To take advantage of the absent time
And fright our native peace with self-born arms.$_{80}$
(Enter YORK attended.)

BOLING. I shall not need transport my words by you;
Here comes his grace in person.
My noble uncle! *(Kneels.)*
YORK. Show me thy humble heart, and not thy knee,
Whose duty is deceiveable and false.
BOLING. My gracious uncle—$_{85}$
YORK. Tut, tut!
Grace me no grace, nor uncle me no uncle:
I am no traitor's uncle; and that word 'grace'
In an ungracious mouth is but profane.
Why have those banish'd and forbidden legs$_{90}$
Dared once to touch a dust of England's ground?
But then more 'why?' why have they dared to march
So many miles upon her peaceful bosom,
Frighting her pale-faced villages with war
And ostentation of despised arms?$_{95}$
Comest thou because the anointed king is hence?
Why, foolish boy, the king is left behind,
And in my loyal bosom lies his power.
Were I but now the lord of such hot youth
As when brave Gaunt, thy father, and myself$_{100}$
Rescued the Black Prince, that young Mars of men,
From forth the ranks of many thousand French,
O, then how quickly should this arm of mine,
Now prisoner to the palsy, chastise thee
And minister correction to thy fault!$_{105}$
BOLING. My gracious uncle, let me know my fault:
On what condition stands it and wherein?
YORK. Even in condition of the worst degree,
In gross rebellion and detested treason:
Thou art a banish'd man, and here art come$_{110}$
Before the expiration of thy time,
In braving arms against thy sovereign.
BOLING. As I was banish'd, I was banish'd Hereford:
But as I come, I come for Lancaster.
And, noble uncle, I beseech your grace$_{115}$
Look on my wrongs with an indifferent eye:
You are my father, for methinks in you
I see old Gaunt alive; O, then, my father,

Will you permit that I shall stand condemn'd
A wandering vagabond; my rights and royalties$_{120}$
Pluck'd from my arms perforce and given away
To upstart unthrifts? Wherefore was I born?
If that my cousin king be King of England,
It must be granted I am Duke of Lancaster.
You have a son, Aumerle, my noble cousin;$_{125}$
Had you first died, and he been thus trod down.
He should have found his uncle Gaunt a father,
To rouse his wrongs and chase them to the bay.
I am denied to sue my livery here,
And yet my letters-patents give me leave:$_{130}$
My father's goods are all distrain'd and sold;
And these and all are all amiss employ'd.
What would you have me do? I am a subject,
And I challenge law: attorneys are denied me;
And therefore personally I lay my claim$_{135}$
To my inheritance of free descent.
NORTH. The noble duke hath been too much abused.
Ross. It stands your grace upon to do him right.
WILLO. Base men by his endowments are made great.
YORK. My lords of England, let me tell you this:$_{140}$
I have had feeling of my cousin's wrongs
And laboured all I could to do him right;
But in this kind to come, in braving arms,
Be his own carver and cut out his way,
To find out right with wrong, it may not be;$_{145}$
And you that do abet him in this kind
Cherish rebellion and are rebels all.
NORTH. The noble duke hath sworn his coming is
But for his own; and for the right of that
We all have strongly sworn to give him aid;$_{150}$
And let him ne'er see joy that breaks that oath!
YORK. Well, well, I see the issue of these arms:
I cannot mend it, I must needs confess,
Because my power is weak and all ill left:
But if I could, by Him that gave me life,$_{155}$
I would attach you all and make you stoop
Unto the sovereign mercy of the king;

But since I cannot, be it known to you
I do remain as neuter. So, fare you well;
Unless you please to enter in the castle$_{160}$
And there repose you for this night.
BOLING. An offer, uncle, that we will accept:
But we must win your grace to go with us
To Bristol castle, which they say is held
By Bushy, Bagot and their complices,$_{165}$
The caterpillars of the commonwealth,
Which I have sworn to weed and pluck away.
YORK. It may be I will go with you: but yet I'll pause;
For I am loath to break our country's laws.
Nor friends nor foes, to me welcome you are:$_{170}$
Things past redress are now with me past care. *(Exeunt.)*

SCENE IV. A CAMP IN WALES

(Enter Salisbury and a Welsh Captain.)

CAP. My Lord of Salisbury, we have stay'd ten days,
And hardly kept our countrymen together,
And yet we hear no tidings from the king;
Therefore we will disperse ourselves: farewell.
SAL. Stay yet another day, thou trusty Welshman:$_5$
The king reposeth all his confidence in thee.
CAP. 'Tis thought the king is dead; we will not stay.
The bay-trees in our country are all wither'd
And meteors fright the fixed stars of heaven;
The pale-faced moon looks bloody on the earth$_{10}$
And lean-look'd prophets whisper fearful change;
Rich men look sad and ruffians dance and leap,
The one in fear to lose what they enjoy,
The other to enjoy by rage and war:
These signs forerun the death or fall of kings.$_{15}$
Farewell: our countrymen are gone and fled,
As well assured Richard their king is dead. *(Exit.)*
SAL. Ah, Richard, with the eyes of heavy mind
I see thy glory like a shooting star

Fall to the base earth from the firmament.[20]
Thy sun sets weeping in the lowly west,
Witnessing storms to come, woe and unrest:
Thy friends are fled to wait upon thy foes,
And crossly to thy good all fortune goes. *(Exit.)*

ACT III

SCENE I. BRISTOL. BEFORE THE CASTLE

(Enter BOLINGBROKE, YORK, NORTHUMBERLAND, ROSS, PERCY, WILLOUGHBY, with BUSHY and GREEN, PRISONERS.)

BOLING. Bring forth these men.
Bushy and Green, I will not vex your souls—
Since presently your souls must part your bodies—
With too much urging your pernicious lives,
For 'twere no charity; yet, to wash your blood₅
From off my hands, here in the view of men
I will unfold some causes of your deaths.
You have misled a prince, a royal king,
A happy gentleman in blood and lineaments,
By you unhappied and disfigured clean:₁₀
You have in manner with your sinful hours
Made a divorce betwixt his queen and him,
Broke the possession of a royal bed
And stain'd the beauty of a fair queen's cheeks
With tears drawn from her eyes by your foul wrongs.₁₅
Myself, a prince by fortune of my birth,
Near to the king in blood, and near in love

Till you did make him misinterpret me,
Have stoop'd my neck under your injuries,
And sigh'd my English breath in foreign clouds, 20
Eating the bitter bread of banishment;
Whilst you have fed upon my signories,
Dispark'd my parks and fell'd my forest woods,
From my own windows torn my household coat,
Razed out my imprese, leaving me no sign, 25
Save men's opinions and my living blood,
To show the world I am a gentleman.
This and much more, much more than twice all this,
Condemns you to the death. See them deliver'd over
To execution and the hand of death. 30
BUSHY. More welcome is the stroke of death to me
Than Bolingbroke to England. Lords, farewell.
GREEN. My comfort is that heaven will take our souls
And plague injustice with the pains of hell.
BOLING. My Lord Northumberland, see them dispatch'd. 35
(Exeunt Northumberland and others, with the prisoners.)
Uncle, you say the queen is at your house;
For God's sake, fairly let her be entreated:
Tell her I send to her my kind commends;
Take special care my greetings be deliver'd.
YORK. A gentleman of mine I have dispatch'd 40
With letters of your love to her at large.
BOLING. Thanks, gentle uncle. Come, lords, away,
To fight with Glendower and his complices:
Awhile to work, and after holiday. *(Exeunt.)*

SCENE II. THE COAST OF WALES. A CASTLE IN VIEW.

(Drums: flourish and colours. Enter KING RICHARD, the BISHOP of CARLISLE, AUMERLE, and Soldiers.)

K. RICH. Barkloughly castle call they this at hand?
AUM. Yea, my lord. How brooks your grace the air,
After your late tossing on the breaking seas?
K. RICH. Needs must I like it well: I weep for joy

To stand upon my kingdom once again.$_5$
Dear earth, I do salute thee with my hand,
Though rebels wound thee with their horses' hoofs:
As a long-parted mother with her child
Plays fondly with her tears and smiles in meeting,
So, weeping, smiling, greet I thee, my earth,$_{10}$
And do thee favours with my royal hands.
Feed not thy sovereign's foe, my gentle earth,
Nor with thy sweets comfort his ravenous sense;
But let thy spiders, that suck up thy venom,
And heavy-gaited toads lie in their way,$_{15}$
Doing annoyance to the treacherous feet
Which with usurping steps do trample thee:
Yield stinging nettles to mine enemies;
And when they from thy bosom pluck a flower.
Guard it, I pray thee, with a lurking adder$_{20}$
Whose double tongue may with a mortal touch
Throw death upon thy sovereign's enemies.
Mock not my senseless conjuration, lords:
This earth shall have a feeling and these stones
Prove armed soldiers, ere her native king$_{25}$
Shall falter under foul rebellion's arms.
CAR. Fear not, my lord: that Power that made you king
Hath power to keep you king in spite of all.
The means that heaven yields must be embraced,
And not neglected; else, if heaven would,$_{30}$
And we will not, heaven's offer we refuse,
The proffer'd means of succour and redress.
AUM. He means, my lord, that we are too remiss;
Whilst Bolingbroke, through our security,
Grows strong and great in substance and in power.$_{35}$
K. RICH. Discomfortable cousin! know'st thou not
That when the searching eye of heaven is hid,
Behind the globe, that lights the lower world,
Then thieves and robbers range abroad unseen
In murders and in outrage, boldly here;$_{40}$
But when from under this terrestrial ball
He fires the proud tops of the eastern pines
And darts his light through every guilty hole,

Then murders, treasons and detested sins,
The cloak of night being pluck'd from off their backs, 45
Stand bare and naked, trembling at themselves?
So when this thief, this traitor, Bolingbroke,
Who all this while hath revell'd in the night
Whilst we were wandering with the antipodes,
Shall see us rising in our throne, the east, 50
His treasons will sit blushing in his face,
Not able to endure the sight of day,
But self-affrighted tremble at his sin.
Not all the water in the rough rude sea
Can wash the balm off from an anointed king; 55
The breath of worldly men cannot depose
The deputy elected by the Lord:
For every man that Bolingbroke hath press'd
To lift shrewd steel against our golden crown,
God for his Richard hath in heavenly pay 60
A glorious angel: then, if angels fight,
Weak men must fall, for heaven still guards the right.
(ENTER SALISBURY.)
Welcome, my lord: how far off lies your power?
SAL. Nor near nor farther off, my gracious lord,
Than this weak arm: discomfort guides my tongue 65
And bids me speak of nothing but despair.
One day too late, I fear me, noble lord,
Hath clouded all thy happy days on earth:
O, call back yesterday, bid time return,
And thou shalt have twelve thousand fighting men! 70
To-day, to-day, unhappy day, too late,
O'erthrows thy joys, friends, fortune and thy state:
For all the Welshmen, hearing thou wert dead,
Are gone to Bolingbroke, dispersed and fled.
AUM. Comfort, my liege: why looks your grace so pale? 75
K. RICH. But now the blood of twenty thousand men
Did triumph in my face, and they are fled;
And, till so much blood thither come again,
Have I not reason to look pale and dead?
All souls that will be safe fly from my side, 80
For time hath set a blot upon my pride.

AUM. Comfort, my liege; remember who you are.
K. RICH. I had forgot myself: am I not king?
Awake, thou coward majesty! thou sleepest.
Is not the king's name twenty thousand names? $_{85}$
Arm, arm, my name! a puny subject strikes
At thy great glory. Look not to the ground,
Ye favourites of a king: are we not high?
High be our thoughts: I know my uncle York
Hath power enough to serve our turn. But who comes here? $_{90}$
(ENTER SCROOP.)
SCROOP. More health and happiness betide my liege
Than can my care-tuned tongue deliver him!
K. RICH. Mine ear is open and my heart prepared:
The worst is worldly loss thou canst unfold.
Say, is my kingdom lost? why, 'twas my care; $_{95}$
And what loss is it to be rid of care?
Strives Bolingbroke to be as great as we?
Greater he shall not be; if he serve God,
We'll serve Him too and be his fellow so:
Revolt our subjects? that we cannot mend; $_{100}$
They break their faith to God as well as us:
Cry woe, destruction, ruin and decay;
The worst is death, and death will have his day.
SCROOP. Glad am I that your highness is so arm'd
To bear the tidings of calamity. $_{105}$
Like an unseasonable stormy day,
Which makes the silver rivers drown their shores,
As if the world were all dissolved to tears,
So high above his limits swells the rage
Of Bolingbroke, covering your fearful land $_{110}$
With hard bright steel and hearts harder than steel.
White-beards have arm'd their thin and hairless scalps
Against thy majesty; boys, with women's voices,
Strive to speak big and clap their female joints
In stiff unwieldy arms against thy crown: $_{115}$
Thy very beadsmen learn to bend their bows
Of double-fatal yew against thy state;
Yea, distaff-women manage rusty bills
Against thy seat: both young and old rebel,

And all goes worse than I have power to tell.$_{120}$
K. Rich. Too well, too well thou tell'st a tale so ill.
Where is the Earl of Wiltshire? where is Bagot?
What is become of Bushy? where is Green?
That they have let the dangerous enemy
Measure our confines with such peaceful steps?$_{125}$
If we prevail, their heads shall pay for it:
I warrant they have made peace with Bolingbroke.
Scroop. Peace have they made with him indeed, my lord.
K. Rich. O villains, vipers, damn'd without redemption!
Dogs, easily won to fawn on any man!$_{130}$
Snakes, in my heart-blood warm'd, that sting my heart!
Three Judases, each one thrice worse than Judas!
Would they make peace? terrible hell make war
Upon their spotted souls for this offence!
Scroop. Sweet love, I see, changing his property,$_{135}$
Turns to the sourest and most deadly hate:
Again uncurse their souls; their peace is made
With heads, and not with hands: those whom you curse
Have felt the worst of death's destroying wound
And lie full low, graved in the hollow ground.$_{140}$
Aum. Is Bushy, Green and the Earl of Wiltshire dead?
Scroop. Ay, all of them at Bristol lost their heads.
Aum. Where is the duke my father with his power?
K. Rich. No matter where; of comfort no man speak:
Let's talk of graves, of worms and epitaphs;$_{145}$
Make dust our paper and with rainy eyes
Write sorrow on the bosom of the earth.
Let's choose executors and talk of wills:
And yet not so, for what can we bequeath
Save our deposed bodies to the ground?$_{150}$
Our lands, our lives and all are Bolingbroke's,
And nothing can we call our own but death
And that small model of the barren earth
Which serves as paste and cover to our bones.
For God's sake, let us sit upon the ground$_{155}$
And tell sad stories of the death of kings:
How some have been deposed; some slain in war;
Some haunted by the ghosts they have deposed;

Some poison'd by their wives; some sleeping kill'd;
All murder'd: for within the hollow crown $_{160}$
That rounds the mortal temples of a king
Keeps Death his court and there the antique sits,
Scoffing his state and grinning at his pomp,
Allowing him a breath, a little scene,
To monarchize, be fear'd and kill with looks, $_{165}$
Infusing him with self and vain conceit,
As if this flesh which walls about our life
Were brass impregnable, and humour'd thus
Comes at the last and with a little pin
Bores through his castle wall, and farewell king! $_{170}$
Cover your heads and mock not flesh and blood
With solemn reverence: throw away respect,
Tradition, form and ceremonious duty,
For you have but mistook me all this while:
I live with bread like you, feel want, $_{175}$
Taste grief, need friends: subjected thus,
How can you say to me, I am a king?
CAR. My lord, wise men ne'er sit and wail their woes,
But presently prevent the ways to wail.
To fear the foe, since fear oppresseth strength, $_{180}$
Gives in your weakness strength unto your foe,
And so your follies fight against yourself.
Fear, and be slain; no worse can come to fight:
And fight and die is death destroying death;
Where fearing dying pays death servile breath. $_{185}$
AUM. My father hath a power; inquire of him,
And learn to make a body of a limb.
K. RICH. Thou chidest me well: proud Bolingbroke, I come
To change blows with thee for our day of doom.
This ague fit of fear is over-blown; $_{190}$
An easy task it is to win our own.
Say, Scroop, where lies our uncle with his power?
Speak sweetly, man, although thy looks be sour.
SCROOP. Men judge by the complexion of the sky
The state and inclination of the day: $_{195}$
So may you by my dull and heavy eye,
My tongue hath but a heavier tale to say.

I play the torturer, by small and small
To lengthen out the worst that must be spoken:
Your uncle York is join'd with Bolingbroke,$_{200}$
And all your northern castles yielded up
And all your southern gentlemen in arms
Upon his party.
K. Rich. Thou hast said enough.
Beshrew thee, cousin, which didst lead me forth *(To Aumerle.)*
Of that sweet way I was in to despair!$_{205}$
What say you now? what comfort have we now?
By heaven, I'll hate him everlastingly
That bids me be of comfort any more.
Go to Flint castle: there I'll pine away;
A king, woe's slave, shall kingly woe obey.$_{210}$
That power I have, discharge; and let them go
To ear the land that hath some hope to grow,
For I have none: let no man speak again
To alter this, for counsel is but vain.
Aum. My liege, one word.
K. Rich. He does me double wrong$_{215}$
That wounds me with the flatteries of his tongue.
Discharge my followers: let them hence away,
From Richard's night to Bolingbroke's fair day. *(Exeunt.)*

SCENE III. WALES. BEFORE FLINT CASTLE

*(Enter, with drum and colours, Bolingbroke, York, Northumberland,
Attendants, and forces.)*

Boling. So that by this intelligence we learn
   The Welshmen are dispersed; and Salisbury
   Is gone to meet the king, who lately landed
   With some few private friends upon this coast.
   North. The news is very fair and good, my lord:$_5$
   Richard not far from hence hath hid his head.
   York. It would beseem the Lord Northumberland
   To say 'King Richard': alack the heavy day
   When such a sacred king should hide his head.

NORTH. Your grace mistakes; only to be brief, [10]
Left I his title out.
YORK. The time hath been,
Would you have been so brief with him, he would
Have been so brief with you, to shorten you,
For taking so the head, your whole head's length.
BOLING. Mistake not, uncle, further than you should. [15]
YORK. Take not, good cousin, further than you should,
Lest you mistake the heavens are o'er our heads.
BOLING. I know it, uncle, and oppose not myself
Against their will. But who comes here?

(Enter PERCY.)

Welcome, Harry: what, will not this castle yield? [20]
PERCY. The castle royally is mann'd, my lord,
Against thy entrance.
BOLING. Royally!
Why, it contains no king?
PERCY. Yes, my good lord,
It doth contain a king; King Richard lies [25]
Within the limits of yon lime and stone:
And with him are the Lord Aumerle, Lord Salisbury,
Sir Stephen Scroop, besides a clergyman
Of holy reverence; who, I cannot learn.
NORTH. O, belike it is the Bishop of Carlisle. [30]
BOLING. Noble lords,
Go to the rude ribs of that ancient castle;
Through brazen trumpet send the breath of parley
Into his ruin'd ears, and thus deliver:
Henry Bolingbroke [35]
On both his knees doth kiss King Richard's hand
And sends allegiance and true faith of heart
To his most royal person; hither come
Even at his feet to lay my arms and power,
Provided that my banishment repeal'd [40]
And lands restored again be freely granted:
If not, I'll use the advantage of my power
And lay the summer's dust with showers of blood

Rain'd from the wounds of slaughter'd Englishmen:
The which, how far off from the mind of Bolingbroke$_{45}$
It is, such crimson tempest should bedrench
The fresh green lap of fair King Richard's land,
My stooping duty tenderly shall show.
Go, signify as much, while here we march
Upon the grassy carpet of this plain.$_{50}$
Let's march without the noise of threatening drum,
That from this castle's tatter'd battlements
Our fair appointments may be well perused.
Methinks King Richard and myself should meet
With no less terror than the elements$_{55}$
Of fire and water, when their thundering shock
At meeting tears the cloudy cheeks of heaven.
Be he the fire, I'll be the yielding water:
The rage be his, whilst on the earth I rain
My waters; on the earth, and not on him.$_{60}$
March on, and mark King Richard how he looks.

*(Parle without, and answer within. Then a flourish. Enter on the walls, KING
RICHARD, the BISHOP of CARLISLE, AUMERLE, SCROOP, and SALISBURY.)*

See, see, King Richard doth himself appear,
As doth the blushing discontented sun
From out the fiery portal of the east,
When he perceives the envious clouds are bent$_{65}$
To dim his glory and to stain the track
Of his bright passage to the occident.
YORK. Yet looks he like a king: behold, his eye,
As bright as is the eagle's, lightens forth
Controlling majesty: alack, alack, for woe,$_{70}$
That any harm should stain so fair a show!
K. RICH. We are amazed; and thus long have we stood
To watch the fearful bending of thy knee, *(To North.)*
Because we thought ourself thy lawful king:
And if we be, how dare thy joints forget$_{75}$
To pay their awful duty to our presence?
If we be not, show us the hand of God
That hath dismiss'd us from our stewardship;

For well we know, no hand of blood and bone
Can gripe the sacred handle of our sceptre,₈₀
Unless he do profane, steal, or usurp.
And though you think that all, as you have done,
Have torn their souls by turning them from us,
And we are barren and bereft of friends;
Yet know, my master, God omnipotent,₈₅
Is mustering in his clouds on our behalf
Armies of pestilence; and they shall strike
Your children yet unborn and unbegot,
That lift your vassal hands against my head
And threat the glory of my precious crown.₉₀
Tell Bolingbroke—for yond methinks he stands—
That every stride he makes upon my land
Is dangerous treason: he is come to open
The purple testament of bleeding war;
But ere the crown he looks for live in peace,₉₅
Ten thousand bloody crowns of mothers' sons
Shall ill become the flower of England's face,
Change the complexion of her maid-pale peace
To scarlet indignation and bedew
Her pastures' grass with faithful English blood.₁₀₀
NORTH. The king of heaven forbid our lord the king
Should so with civil and uncivil arms
Be rush'd upon! Thy thrice noble cousin
Harry Bolingbroke doth humbly kiss thy hand;
And by the honourable tomb he swears,₁₀₅
That stands upon your royal grandsire's bones,
And by the royalties of both your bloods,
Currents that spring from one most gracious head,
And by the buried hand of warlike Gaunt,
And by the worth and honour of himself,₁₁₀
Comprising all that may be sworn or said,
His coming hither hath no further scope
Than for his lineal royalties and to beg
Enfranchisement immediate on his knees:
Which on thy royal party granted once,₁₁₅
His glittering arms he will commend to rust,
His barbed steeds to stables, and his heart

To faithful service of your majesty.
This swears he, as he is a prince, is just;
And, as I am a gentleman, I credit him.₁₂₀
K. Rich. Northumberland, say thus the king returns:
His noble cousin is right welcome hither;
And all the number of his fair demands
Shall be accomplish'd without contradiction:
With all the gracious utterance thou hast₁₂₅
Speak to his gentle hearing kind commends.
We do debase ourselves, cousin, do we not, *(To Aumerle.)*
To look so poorly and to speak so fair?
Shall we call back Northumberland, and send
Defiance to the traitor, and so die?₁₃₀
Aum. No, good my lord; let's fight with gentle words
Till time lend friends and friends their helpful swords.
K. Rich. O God, O God! that e'er this tongue of mine,
That laid the sentence of dread banishment
On yon proud man, should take it off again₁₃₅
With words of sooth! O that I were as great
As is my grief, or lesser than my name!
Or that I could forget what I have been,
Or not remember what I must be now!
Swell'st thou, proud heart? I'll give thee scope to beat,₁₄₀
Since foes have scope to beat both thee and me.
Aum. Northumberland comes back from Bolingbroke.
K. Rich. What must the king do now? must he submit?
The king shall do it: must he be deposed?
The king shall be contented: must he lose₁₄₅
The name of king? o' God's name, let it go:
I'll give my jewels for a set of beads,
My gorgeous palace for a hermitage,
My gay apparel for an almsman's gown,
My figured goblets for a dish of wood,₁₅₀
My sceptre for a palmer's walking-staff,
My subjects for a pair of carved saints
And my large kingdom for a little grave,
A little little grave, an obscure grave;
Or I'll be buried in the king's highway,₁₅₅
Some way of common trade, where subjects' feet

May hourly trample on their sovereign's head;
For on my heart they tread now whilst I live;
And buried once, why not upon my head?
Aumerle, thou weep'st, my tender-hearted cousin! 160
We'll make foul weather with despised tears;
Our sighs and they shall lodge the summer corn,
And make a dearth in this revolting land.
Or shall we play the wantons with our woes,
And make some pretty match with shedding tears? 165
As thus, to drop them still upon one place,
Till they have fretted us a pair of graves
Within the earth; and, therein laid,—there lies
Two kinsmen digg'd their graves with weeping eyes.
Would not this ill do well? Well, well, I see 170
I talk but idly, and you laugh at me.
Most mighty prince, my Lord Northumberland,
What says King Bolingbroke? will his majesty
Give Richard leave to live till Richard die?
You make a leg, and Bolingbroke says ay. 175
NORTH. My lord, in the base court he doth attend
To speak with you; may it please you to come down.
K. RICH. Down, down I come; like glistering Phaeton,
Wanting the manage of unruly jades.
In the base court? Base court, where kings grow base, 180
To come at traitors' calls and do them grace.
In the base court? Come down? Down, court! down, king!
For night-owls shriek where mounting larks should sing.

(Exeunt from above.)

BOLING. What says his majesty?
NORTH. Sorrow and grief of heart
Makes him speak fondly, like a frantic man: 185
Yet he is come.

(Enter KING RICHARD and his attendants below.)

BOLING. Stand all apart,
And show fair duty to his majesty. *(He kneels down.)*

My gracious lord,—
K. Rich. Fair cousin, you debase your princely knee[190]
To make the base earth proud with kissing it:
Me rather had my heart might feel your love
Than my unpleased eye see your courtesy.
Up, cousin, up; your heart is up, I know,
Thus high at least, although your knee be low.[195]
Boling. My gracious lord, I come but for mine own.
K. Rich. Your own is yours, and I am yours, and all.
Boling. So far be mine, my most redoubted lord,
As my true service shall deserve your love.
K. Rich. Well you deserve: they well deserve to have,[200]
That know the strong'st and surest way to get.
Uncle, give me your hands: nay, dry your eyes;
Tears show their love, but want their remedies.
Cousin, I am too young to be your father,
Though you are old enough to be my heir.[205]
What you will have, I'll give, and willing too;
For do we must what force will have us do.
Set on towards London, cousin, is it so?
Boling. Yea, my good lord.
K. Rich. Then I must not say no.

(Flourish. Exeunt.)

SCENE IV. LANGLEY. THE DUKE OF YORK'S GARDEN.

(Enter the QUEEN and two Ladies.)

Queen. What sport shall we devise here in this garden,
To drive away the heavy thought of care?
Lady. Madam, we'll play at bowls.
Queen. 'Twill make me think the world is full of rubs,
And that my fortune runs against the bias.[5]
Lady. Madam, we'll dance.
Queen. My legs can keep no measure in delight,
When my poor heart no measure keeps in grief:
Therefore, no dancing, girl; some other sport.

LADY. Madam, we'll tell tales.₁₀

QUEEN. Of sorrow or of joy?

LADY. Of either, madam.

QUEEN. Of neither, girl:

For if of joy, being altogether wanting,

It doth remember me the more of sorrow;

Or if of grief, being altogether had,₁₅

It adds more sorrow to my want of joy:

For what I have I need not to repeat;

And what I want it boots not to complain.

LADY. Madam, I'll sing.

QUEEN. 'Tis well that thou hast cause;

But thou shouldst please me better, wouldst thou weep.₂₀

LADY. I could weep, madam, would it do you good.

QUEEN. And I could sing, would weeping do me good,

And never borrow any tear of thee.

(Enter a Gardener, and two Servants.)

But stay, here come the gardeners:

Let's step into the shadow of these trees.₂₅

My wretchedness unto a row of pins,

They'll talk of state; for every one doth so

Against a change; woe is forerun with woe.

(Queen and Ladies retire.)

GARD. Go, bind thou up yon dangling apricocks,

Which, like unruly children, make their sire₃₀

Stoop with oppression of their prodigal weight:

Give some supportance to the bending twigs.

Go thou, and like an executioner,

Cut off the heads of too fast growing sprays,

That look too lofty in our commonwealth:₃₅

All must be even in our government.

You thus employ'd, I will go root away

The noisome weeds, which without profit suck

The soil's fertility from wholesome flowers.

SERV. Why should we in the compass of a pale₄₀

Keep law and form and due proportion,

Showing, as in a model, our firm estate,

When our sea-walled garden, the whole land,

Is full of weeds; her fairest flowers choked up,

Her fruit-trees all unpruned, her hedges ruin'd,$_{45}$
Her knots disorder'd and her wholesome herbs
Swarming with caterpillars?
GARD. Hold thy peace:
He that hath suffer'd this disorder'd spring
Hath now himself met with the fall of leaf:
The weeds which his broad-spreading leaves did shelter,$_{50}$
That seem'd in eating him to hold him up,
Are pluck'd up root and all by Bolingbroke,
I mean the Earl of Wiltshire, Bushy, Green.
SERV. What, are they dead?
GARD. They are; and Bolingbroke
Hath seized the wasteful king. O, what pity is it$_{55}$
That he had not so trimm'd and dress'd his land
As we this garden! We at time of year
Do wound the bark, the skin of our fruit-trees,
Lest, being over-proud in sap and blood,
With too much riches it confound itself:$_{60}$
Had he done so to great and growing men,
They might have lived to bear and he to taste
Their fruits of duty: superfluous branches
We lop away, that bearing boughs may live:
Had he done so, himself had borne the crown,$_{65}$
Which waste of idle hours hath quite thrown down.
SERV. What, think you then the king shall be deposed?
GARD. Depress'd he is already, and deposed
'Tis doubt he will be: letters came last night
To a dear friend of the good Duke of York's,$_{70}$
That tell black tidings.
QUEEN. O, I am press'd to death through want of speaking!
(Coming forward.)
Thou, old Adam's likeness, set to dress this garden,
How dares thy harsh rude tongue sound this unpleasing news?
What Eve, what serpent, hath suggested thee$_{75}$
To make a second fall of cursed man?
Why dost thou say King Richard is deposed?
Darest thou, thou little better thing than earth,
Divine his downfal? Say, where, when, and how,
Camest thou by this ill tidings? speak, thou wretch.$_{80}$

GARD. Pardon me, madam: little joy have I
To breathe this news; yet what I say is true.
King Richard, he is in the mighty hold
Of Bolingbroke: their fortunes both are weigh'd:
In your lord's scale is nothing but himself,$_{85}$
And some few vanities that make him light;
But in the balance of great Bolingbroke,
Besides himself, are all the English peers,
And with that odds he weighs King Richard down.
Post you to London, and you will find it so;$_{90}$
I speak no more than every one doth know.
QUEEN. Nimble mischance, that art so light of foot,
Doth not thy embassage belong to me,
And am I last that knows it? O, thou think'st
To serve me last, that I may longest keep$_{95}$
Thy sorrow in my breast. Come, ladies, go,
To meet at London London's king in woe.
What, was I born to this, that my sad look
Should grace the triumph of great Bolingbroke?
Gardener, for telling me these news of woe,$_{100}$
Pray God the plants thou graft'st may never grow.
(Exeunt Queen and Ladies.)
GARD. Poor queen! so that thy state might be no worse,
I would my skill were subject to thy curse.
Here did she fall a tear; here in this place
I'll set a bank of rue, sour herb of grace:$_{105}$
Rue, even for ruth, here shortly shall be seen,
In the remembrance of a weeping queen. *(Exeunt.)*

ACT IV

SCENE I. WESTMINSTER HALL

(Enter as to the Parliament, Bolingbroke, Aumerle, Northumberland, Percy, Fitzwater, Surrey, the Bishop of Carlisle, the Abbot of Westminster, and another Lord, Herald, Officers, and Bagot.)

Boling. Call forth Bagot.
Now, Bagot, freely speak thy mind;
What thou dost know of noble Gloucester's death;
Who wrought it with the king, and who perform'd
The bloody office of his timeless end. 5
Bagot. Then set before my face the Lord Aumerle.
Boling. Cousin, stand forth, and look upon that man.
Bagot. My Lord Aumerle, I know your daring tongue
Scorns to unsay what once it hath deliver'd.
In that dead time when Gloucester's death was plotted, 10
I heard you say, 'Is not my arm of length,
That reacheth from the restful English court
As far as Calais, to mine uncle's head?'
Amongst much other talk, that very time,
I heard you say that you had rather refuse 15

The offer of an hundred thousand crowns
Than Bolingbroke's return to England;
Adding withal, how blest this land would be
In this your cousin's death.
AUM. Princes and noble lords,
What answer shall I make to this base man? $_{20}$
Shall I so much dishonour my fair stars,
On equal terms to give him chastisement?
Either I must, or have mine honour soil'd
With the attainder of his slanderous lips.
There is my gage, the manual seal of death, $_{25}$
That marks thee out for hell: I say, thou liest,
And will maintain what thou hast said is false
In thy heart-blood, though being all too base
To stain the temper of my knightly sword.
BOLING. Bagot, forbear; thou shalt not take it up. $_{30}$
AUM. Excepting one, I would he were the best
In all this presence that hath moved me so.
FITZ. If that thy valour stand on sympathy,
There is my gage, Aumerle, in gage to thine:
By that fair sun which shows me where thou stand'st, $_{35}$
I heard thee say, and vauntingly thou spakest it,
That thou wert cause of noble Gloucester's death.
If thou deny'st it twenty times, thou liest;
And I will turn thy falsehood to thy heart,
Where it was forged, with my rapier's point. $_{40}$
AUM. Thou darest not, coward, live to see that day.
FITZ. Now, by my soul, I would it were this hour.
AUM. Fitzwater, thou art damn'd to hell for this.
PERCY. Aumerle, thou liest; his honour is as true
In this appeal as thou art all unjust; $_{45}$
And that thou art so, there I throw my gage,
To prove it on thee to the extremest point
Of mortal breathing: seize it, if thou darest.
AUM. An if I do not, may my hands rot off
And never brandish more revengeful steel $_{50}$
Over the glittering helmet of my foe!
Another Lord. I task the earth to the like, forsworn Aumerle;
And spur thee on with full as many lies

As may be holloa'd in thy treacherous ear
From sun to sun: there is my honour's pawn;[55]
Engage it to the trial, if thou darest.
Aum. Who sets me else? by heaven, I'll throw at all:
I have a thousand spirits in one breast,
To answer twenty thousand such as you.
Surrey. My Lord Fitzwater, I do remember well[60]
The very time Aumerle and you did talk.
Fitz. 'Tis very true: you were in presence then;
And you can witness with me this is true.
Surrey. As false, by heaven, as heaven itself is true.
Fitz. Surrey, thou liest.
Surrey. Dishonourable boy![65]
That lie shall lie so heavy on my sword,
That it shall render vengeance and revenge
Till thou the lie-giver and that lie do lie
In earth as quiet as thy father's skull:
In proof whereof, there is my honour's pawn;[70]
Engage it to the trial, if thou darest.
Fitz. How fondly dost thou spur a forward horse!
If I dare eat, or drink, or breathe, or live,
I dare meet Surrey in a wilderness,
And spit upon him, whilst I say he lies,[75]
And lies, and lies: there is my bond of faith,
To tie thee to my strong correction.
As I intend to thrive in this new world,
Aumerle is guilty of my true appeal:
Besides, I heard the banish'd Norfolk say,[80]
That thou, Aumerle, didst send two of thy men
To execute the noble duke at Calais.
Aum. Some honest Christian trust me with a gage,
That Norfolk lies: here do I throw down this,
If he may be repeal'd, to try his honour.[85]
Boling. These differences shall all rest under gage
Till Norfolk be repeal'd: repeal'd he shall be,
And, though mine enemy, restored again
To all his lands and signories: when he's return'd,
Against Aumerle we will enforce his trial.[90]
Car. That honourable day shall ne'er be seen.

Many a time hath banish'd Norfolk fought
For Jesu Christ in glorious Christian field,
Streaming the ensign of the Christian cross
Against black pagans, Turks, and Saracens;95
And toil'd with works of war, retired himself
To Italy; and there at Venice gave
His body to that pleasant country's earth,
And his pure soul unto his captain Christ,
Under whose colours he had fought so long.100
BOLING. Why, bishop, is Norfolk dead?
CAR. As surely as I live, my lord.
BOLING. Sweet peace conduct his sweet soul to the bosom
Of good old Abraham! Lords appellants,
Your differences shall all rest under gage105
Till we assign you to your days of trial.
(Enter YORK, attended.)
YORK. Great Duke of Lancaster, I come to thee
From plume-pluck'd Richard; who with willing soul
Adopts thee heir, and his high sceptre yields
To the possession of thy royal hand:110
Ascend his throne, descending now from him;
And long live Henry, fourth of that name!
BOLING. In God's name, I'll ascend the regal throne.
CAR. Marry, God forbid!
Worst in this royal presence may I speak,115
Yet best beseeming me to speak the truth.
Would God that any in this noble presence
Were enough noble to be upright judge
Of noble Richard! then true noblesse would
Learn him forbearance from so foul a wrong.120
What subject can give sentence on his king?
And who sits here that is not Richard's subject?
Thieves are not judged but they are by to hear,
Although apparent guilt be seen in them;
And shall the figure of God's majesty,125
His captain, steward, deputy, elect,
Anointed, crowned, planted many years,
Be judged by subject and inferior breath,
And he himself not present? O, forfend it, God,

That in a Christian climate souls refined$_{130}$
Should show so heinous, black, obscene a deed!
I speak to subjects, and a subject speaks,
Stirr'd up by God, thus boldly for his king.
My Lord of Hereford here, whom you call king,
Is a foul traitor to proud Hereford's king:$_{135}$
And if you crown him, let me prophesy;
The blood of English shall manure the ground,
And future ages groan for this foul act;
Peace shall go sleep with Turks and infidels,
And in this seat of peace tumultuous wars$_{140}$
Shall kin with kin and kind with kind confound;
Disorder, horror, fear and mutiny
Shall here inhabit, and this land be call'd
The field of Golgotha and dead men's skulls.
O, if you raise this house against this house,$_{145}$
It will the woefullest division prove
That ever fell upon this cursed earth.
Prevent it, resist it, let it not be so,
Lest child, child's children, cry against you 'woe!'
NORTH. Well have you argued, sir; and, for your pains,$_{150}$
Of capital treason we arrest you here.
My Lord of Westminster, be it your charge
To keep him safely till his day of trial.
May it please you, lords, to grant the commons' suit.
BOLING. Fetch hither Richard, that in common view$_{155}$
He may surrender; so we shall proceed
Without suspicion.
YORK. I will be his conduct. *(Exit.)*
BOLING. Lords, you that here are under our arrest,
Procure your sureties for your days of answer.
Little are we beholding to your love,$_{160}$
And little look'd for at your helping hands.
(Re-enter YORK, with RICHARD, and Officers bearing the regalia.)
K. RICH. Alack, why am I sent for to a king,
Before I have shook off the regal thoughts
Wherewith I reign'd? I hardly yet have learn'd
To insinuate, flatter, bow, and bend my limbs:$_{165}$
Give sorrow leave awhile to tutor me

To this submission. Yet I well remember
The favours of these men: were they not mine?
Did they not sometime cry, 'all hail!' to me?
So Judas did to Christ: but he, in twelve, 170
Found truth in all but one; I, in twelve thousand, none.
God save the king! Will no man say amen?
Am I both priest and clerk? well then, amen.
God save the king! although I be not he;
And yet, amen, if heaven do think him me. 175
To do what service am I sent for hither?
YORK. To do that office of thine own good will
Which tired majesty did make thee offer,
The resignation of thy state and crown
To Henry Bolingbroke. 180
K. RICH. Give me the crown. Here, cousin, seize the crown;
Here cousin;
On this side my hand, and on that side yours.
Now is this golden crown like a deep well
That owes two buckets, filling one another, 185
The emptier ever dancing in the air,
The other down, unseen and full of water:
That bucket down and full of tears am I,
Drinking my griefs, whilst you mount up on high.
BOLING. I thought you had been willing to resign. 190
K. RICH. My crown I am; but still my griefs are mine:
You may my glories and my state depose,
But not my griefs; still am I king of those.
BOLING. Part of your cares you give me with your crown.
K. RICH. Your cares set up do not pluck my cares down. 195
My care is loss of care, by old care done;
Your care is gain of care, by new care won:
The cares I give, I have, though given away;
They tend the crown, yet still with me they stay.
BOLING. Are you contented to resign the crown? 200
K. RICH. Ay, no; no, ay; for I must nothing be;
Therefore no no, for I resign to thee.
Now mark me, how I will undo myself:
I give this heavy weight from off my head
And this unwieldy sceptre from my hand, 205

The pride of kingly sway from out my heart;
With mine own tears I wash away my balm,
With mine own hands I give away my crown,
With mine own tongue deny my sacred state,
With mine own breath release all duty's rites: $_{210}$
All pomp and majesty I do forswear;
My manors, rents, revenues I forego;
My acts, decrees, and statutes I deny:
God pardon all oaths that are broke to me!
God keep all vows unbroke that swear to thee! $_{215}$
Make me, that nothing have, with nothing grieved,
And thou with all pleased, that hast all achieved!
Long mayst thou live in Richard's seat to sit,
And soon lie Richard in an earthy pit!
God save King Harry, unking'd Richard says, $_{220}$
And send him many years of sunshine days!
What more remains?
NORTH. No more, but that you read
These accusations and these grievous crimes
Committed by your person and your followers
Against the state and profit of this land; $_{225}$
That, by confessing them, the souls of men
May deem that you are worthily deposed.
K. RICH. Must I do so? and must I ravel out
My weaved-up folly? Gentle Northumberland,
If thy offences were upon record, $_{230}$
Would it not shame thee in so fair a troop
To read a lecture of them? If thou wouldst,
There shouldst thou find one heinous article,
Containing the deposing of a king
And cracking the strong warrant of an oath, $_{235}$
Mark'd with a blot, damn'd in the book of heaven:
Nay, all of you that stand and look upon,
Whilst that my wretchedness doth bait myself,
Though some of you with Pilate wash your hands
Showing an outward pity; yet you Pilates $_{240}$
Have here deliver'd me to my sour cross,
And water cannot wash away your sin.
NORTH. My lord, dispatch; read o'er these articles.

K. RICH. Mine eyes are full of tears, I cannot see:
And yet salt water blinds them not so much$_{245}$
But they can see a sort of traitors here.
Nay, if I turn mine eyes upon myself,
I find myself a traitor with the rest;
For I have given here my soul's consent
To undeck the pompous body of a king;$_{250}$
Made glory base and sovereignty a slave,
Proud majesty a subject, state a peasant.
NORTH. My lord,—
K. RICH. No lord of thine, thou haught insulting man,
Nor no man's lord; I have no name, no title,$_{255}$
No, not that name was given me at the font,
But 'tis usurp'd: alack the heavy day,
That I have worn so many winters out,
And know not now what name to call myself!
O that I were a mockery king of snow,$_{260}$
Standing before the sun of Bolingbroke,
To melt myself away in water-drops!
Good king, great king, and yet not greatly good,
An if my word be sterling yet in England,
Let it command a mirror hither straight,$_{265}$
That it may show me what a face I have,
Since it is bankrupt of his majesty.
BOLING. Go some of you and fetch a looking-glass.
(Exit an attendant.)
NORTH. Read o'er this paper while the glass doth come.
K. RICH. Fiend, thou torment'st me ere I come to hell!$_{270}$
BOLING. Urge it no more, my Lord Northumberland.
NORTH. The commons will not then be satisfied.
K. RICH. They shall be satisfied: I'll read enough,
When I do see the very book indeed
Where all my sins are writ, and that's myself.$_{275}$
(Re-enter Attendant, with a glass.)
Give me the glass, and therein will I read.
No deeper wrinkles yet? hath sorrow struck
So many blows upon this face of mine,
And made no deeper wounds? O flattering glass,
Like to my followers in prosperity,$_{280}$

Thou dost beguile me! Was this face the face
That every day under his household roof
Did keep ten thousand men? was this the face
That, like the sun, did make beholders wink?
Was this the face that faced so many follies,$_{285}$
And was at last out-faced by Bolingbroke?
A brittle glory shineth in this face:
As brittle as the glory is the face;
(Dashes the glass against the ground.)
For there it is, crack'd in a hundred shivers.
Mark, silent king, the moral of this sport,$_{290}$
How soon my sorrow hath destroy'd my face.
BOLING. The shadow of your sorrow hath destroy'd
The shadow of your face.
K. RICH. Say that again.
The shadow of my sorrow! ha! let's see:
'Tis very true, my grief lies all within;$_{295}$
And these external manners of laments
Are merely shadows to the unseen grief,
That swells with silence in the tortured soul;
There lies the substance: and I thank thee, king,
For thy great bounty, that not only givest$_{300}$
Me cause to wail but teachest me the way
How to lament the cause. I'll beg one boon,
And then be gone and trouble you no more.
Shall I obtain it?
BOLING. Name it, fair cousin.
K. RICH. 'Fair cousin'? I am greater than a king:$_{305}$
For when I was a king, my flatterers
Were then but subjects; being now a subject,
I have a king here to my flatterer.
Being so great, I have no need to beg.
BOLING. Yet ask.$_{310}$
K. RICH. And shall I have?
BOLING. You shall.
K. RICH. Then give me leave to go.
BOLING. Whither?
K. RICH. Whither you will, so I were from your sights.$_{315}$
BOLING. Go, some of you convey him to the Tower.

K. RICH. O, good! convey? conveyers are you all,
That rise thus nimbly by a true king's fall.
(Exeunt King Richard, some Lords, and a Guard.)
BOLING. On Wednesday next we solemnly set down
Our coronation: lords, prepare yourselves.320
*(Exeunt all except the Bishop of Carlisle, the Abbot of Westminster, and
    Aumerle.)*
ABBOT. A woeful pageant have we here beheld.
CAR. The woe's to come; the children yet unborn
Shall feel this day as sharp to them as thorn.
AUM. You holy clergymen, is there no plot
To rid the realm of this pernicious blot?325
ABBOT. My lord,
Before I freely speak my mind herein,
You shall not only take the sacrament
To bury mine intents, but also to effect
Whatever I shall happen to devise.330
I see your brows are full of discontent,
Your hearts of sorrow and your eyes of tears:
Come home with me to supper; and I'll lay
A plot shall show us all a merry day. *(Exeunt.)*

ACT V

SCENE I. LONDON. A STREET LEADING TO THE TOWER.

(Enter QUEEN and Ladies.)

QUEEN. This way the king will come; this is the way
To Julius Cæsar's ill-erected tower,
To whose flint bosom my condemned lord
Is doom'd a prisoner by proud Bolingbroke:
Here let us rest, if this rebellious earth₅
Have any resting for her true king's queen.
(Enter RICHARD and Guard.)
But soft, but see, or rather do not see,
My fair rose wither: yet look up, behold,
That you in pity may dissolve to dew,
And wash him fresh again with true-love tears.₁₀
Ah, thou, the model where old Troy did stand,
Thou map of honour, thou King Richard's tomb,
And not King Richard; thou most beauteous inn,
Why should hard-favour'd grief be lodged in thee,
When triumph is become an alehouse guest?₁₅
K. RICH. Join not with grief, fair woman, do not so,

To make my end too sudden: learn, good soul,
To think our former state a happy dream;
From which awaked, the truth of what we are
Shows us but this: I am sworn brother, sweet, 20
To grim Necessity, and he and I
Will keep a league till death. Hie thee to France
And cloister thee in some religious house:
Our holy lives must win a new world's crown,
Which our profane hours here have stricken down. 25
QUEEN. What, is my Richard both in shape and mind
Transform'd and weaken'd? hath Bolingbroke deposed
Thine intellect? hath he been in thy heart?
The lion dying thrusteth forth his paw,
And wounds the earth, if nothing else, with rage 30
To be o'erpower'd; and wilt thou, pupil-like,
Take thy correction mildly, kiss the rod,
And fawn on rage with base humility,
Which art a lion and a king of beasts?
K. RICH. A king of beasts, indeed; if aught but beasts. 35
I had been still a happy king of men.
Good sometime queen, prepare thee hence for France:
Think I am dead, and that even here thou takest,
As from my death-bed, thy last living leave.
In winter's tedious nights sit by the fire 40
With good old folks and let them tell thee tales
Of woeful ages long ago betid;
And ere thou bid good night, to quit their griefs,
Tell thou the lamentable tale of me
And send the hearers weeping to their beds: 45
For why, the senseless brands will sympathize
The heavy accent of thy moving tongue
And in compassion weep the fire out;
And some will mourn in ashes, some coal-black,
For the deposing of a rightful king. 50
(ENTER NORTHUMBERLAND AND OTHERS.)
NORTH. My lord, the mind of Bolingbroke is changed;
You must to Pomfret, not unto the Tower.
And, madam, there is order ta'en for you;
With all swift speed you must away to France.

K. Rich. Northumberland, thou ladder wherewithal[55]
The mounting Bolingbroke ascends my throne,
The time shall not be many hours of age
More than it is, ere foul sin gathering head
Shall break into corruption: thou shalt think,
Though he divide the realm, and give thee half,[60]
It is too little, helping him to all;
And he shall think that thou, which know'st the way
To plant unrightful kings, wilt know again,
Being ne'er so little urged, another way
To pluck him headlong from the usurped throne.[65]
The love of wicked men converts to fear;
That fear to hate, and hate turns one or both
To worthy danger and deserved death.
North. My guilt be on my head, and there an end.
Take leave and part; for you must part forthwith.[70]
K. Rich. Doubly divorced! Bad men, you violate
A twofold marriage; 'twixt my crown and me,
And then betwixt me and my married wife.
Let me unkiss the oath 'twixt thee and me;
And yet not so, for with a kiss 'twas made.[75]
Part us, Northumberland; I towards the north,
Where shivering cold and sickness pines the clime;
My wife to France: from whence, set forth in pomp,
She came adorned hither like sweet May,
Sent back like Hallowmas or short'st of day.[80]
Queen. And must we be divided? must we part?
K. Rich. Ay, hand from hand, my love, and heart from heart.
Queen. Banish us both and send the king with me.
North. That were some love but little policy.
Queen. Then whither he goes, thither let me go.[85]
K. Rich. So two, together weeping, make one woe.
Weep thou for me in France, I for thee here;
Better far off than near, be ne'er the near.
Go, count thy way with sighs; I mine with groans.
Queen. So longest way shall have the longest moans.[90]
K. Rich. Twice for one step I'll groan, the way being short,
And piece the way out with a heavy heart.
Come, come, in wooing sorrow let's be brief,

Since, wedding it, there is such length in grief:
One kiss shall stop our mouths, and dumbly part;$_{95}$
Thus give I mine, and thus take I thy heart.
QUEEN. Give me mine own again; 'twere no good part
To take on me to keep and kill thy heart.
So, now I have mine own again, be gone,
That I may strive to kill it with a groan.$_{100}$
K. RICH. We make woe wanton with this fond delay:
Once more, adieu; the rest let sorrow say. *(Exeunt.)*

SCENE II. THE DUKE OF YORK'S PALACE

(Enter YORK and his DUCHESS.)

DUCH. My lord, you told me you would tell the rest,
When weeping made you break the story off
Of our two cousins coming into London.
YORK. Where did I leave?
DUCH. At that sad stop, my lord,
Where rude misgovern'd hands from windows' tops$_5$
Threw dust and rubbish on King Richard's head.
YORK. Then, as I said, the duke, great Bolingbroke,
Mounted upon a hot and fiery steed
Which his aspiring rider seem'd to know,
With slow but stately pace kept on his course,$_{10}$
Whilst all tongues cried 'God save thee, Bolingbroke!'
You would have thought the very windows spake,
So many greedy looks of young and old
Through casements darted their desiring eyes
Upon his visage, and that all the walls$_{15}$
With painted imagery had said at once
'Jesu preserve thee! welcome, Bolingbroke!'
Whilst he, from the one side to the other turning,
Bareheaded, lower than his proud steed's neck,
Bespake them thus; 'I thank you, countrymen:'$_{20}$
And thus still doing, thus he pass'd along.
DUCH. Alack, poor Richard! where rode he the whilst?
YORK. As in a theatre, the eyes of men,

After a well-graced actor leaves the stage,
Are idly bent on him that enters next,$_{25}$
Thinking his prattle to be tedious;
Even so, or with much more contempt, men's eyes
Did scowl on gentle Richard; no man cried 'God save him!'
No joyful tongue gave him his welcome home:
But dust was thrown upon his sacred head;$_{30}$
Which with such gentle sorrow he shook off,
His face still combating with tears and smiles,
The badges of his grief and patience,
That had not God, for some strong purpose, steel'd
The hearts of men, they must perforce have melted$_{35}$
And barbarism itself have pitied him.
But heaven hath a hand in these events,
To whose high will we bound our calm contents.
To Bolingbroke are we sworn subjects now,
Whose state and honour I for aye allow.$_{40}$
DUCH. Here comes my son Aumerle.
YORK. Aumerle that was;
But that is lost for being Richard's friend,
And, madam, you must call him Rutland now:
I am in parliament pledge for his truth
And lasting fealty to the new made king.$_{45}$
(ENTER AUMERLE.)
DUCH. Welcome, my son: who are the violets now
That strew the green lap of the new come spring?
AUM. Madam, I know not, nor I greatly care not:
God knows I had as lief be none as one.
YORK. Well, bear you well in this new spring of time,$_{50}$
Lest you be cropp'd before you come to prime.
What news from Oxford? hold those justs and triumphs?
AUM. For aught I know, my lord, they do.
YORK. You will be there, I know.
AUM. If God prevent not, I purpose so.$_{55}$
YORK. What seal is that, that hangs without thy bosom?
Yea, look'st thou pale? let me see the writing.
AUM. My lord, 'tis nothing.
YORK. No matter, then, who see it:
I will be satisfied; let me see the writing.

AUM. I do beseech your grace to pardon me:$_{60}$
It is a matter of small consequence,
Which for some reasons I would not have seen.
YORK. Which for some reasons, sir, I mean to see.
I fear, I fear,—
DUCH. What should you fear?
'Tis nothing but some band, that he is enter'd into$_{65}$
For gay apparel 'gainst the triumph day.
YORK. Bound to himself! what doth he with a bond
That he is bound to? Wife, thou art a fool.
Boy, let me see the writing.
AUM. I do beseech you, pardon me; I may not show it.$_{70}$
YORK. I will be satisfied; let me see it, I say.
(He plucks it out of his bosom and reads it.)
Treason! foul treason! Villain! traitor! slave!
DUCH. What is the matter, my lord?
YORK. Ho! who is within there?
(Enter a Servant.)
Saddle my horse.
God for his mercy, what treachery is here!$_{75}$
DUCH. Why, what is it, my lord?
YORK. Give me my boots, I say; saddle my horse.
(Exit Servant.)
Now, by mine honour, by my life, by my troth,
I will appeach the villain.
DUCH. What is the matter?
YORK. Peace, foolish woman.$_{80}$
DUCH. I will not peace. What is the matter, Aumerle?
AUM. Good mother, be content; it is no more
Than my poor life must answer.
DUCH. Thy life answer!
YORK. Bring me my boots: I will unto the king.
(Re-enter Servant with boots.)
DUCH. Strike him, Aumerle. Poor boy, thou art amazed.$_{85}$
Hence, villain! never more come in my sight.
YORK. Give me my boots, I say.
DUCH. Why, York, what wilt thou do?
Wilt thou not hide the trespass of thine own?
Have we more sons? or are we like to have?$_{90}$

Is not my teeming date drunk up with time?
And wilt thou pluck my fair son from mine age,
And rob me of a happy mother's name?
Is he not like thee? is he not thine own?
YORK. Thou fond mad woman,$_{95}$
Wilt thou conceal this dark conspiracy?
A dozen of them here have ta'en the sacrament,
And interchangeably set down their hands,
To kill the king at Oxford.
DUCH. He shall be none;
We'll keep him here: then what is that to him?$_{100}$
YORK. Away, fond woman! were he twenty times my son,
I would appeach him.
DUCH. Hadst thou groan'd for him
As I have done, thou wouldst be more pitiful.
But now I know thy mind; thou dost suspect
That I have been disloyal to thy bed,$_{105}$
And that he is a bastard, not thy son:
Sweet York, sweet husband, be not of that mind:
He is as like thee as a man may be,
Not like to me, or any of my kin,
And yet I love him.
YORK. Make way, unruly woman! *(Exit.)*$_{110}$
DUCH. After, Aumerle! mount thee upon his horse;
Spur post, and get before him to the king,
And beg thy pardon ere he do accuse thee.
I'll not be long behind; though I be old,
I doubt not but to ride as fast as York:$_{115}$
And never will I rise up from the ground
Till Bolingbroke have pardon'd thee. Away, be gone!
(Exeunt.)

SCENE III. A ROYAL PALACE

(Enter BOLINGBROKE, PERCY, and other Lords.)

BOLING. Can no man tell me of my unthrifty son?
'Tis full three months since I did see him last:

If any plague hang over us, 'tis he.
I would to God, my lords, he might be found:
Inquire at London, 'mongst the taverns there, 5
For there, they say, he daily doth frequent,
With unrestrained loose companions,
Even such, they say, as stand in narrow lanes,
And beat our watch, and rob our passengers;
Which he, young wanton and effeminate boy, 10
Takes on the point of honour to support
So dissolute a crew.
PERCY. My lord, some two days since I saw the prince,
And told him of those triumphs held at Oxford.
BOLING. And what said the gallant? 15
PERCY. His answer was, he would unto the stews,
And from the common'st creature pluck a glove,
And wear it as a favour; and with that
He would unhorse the lustiest challenger.
BOLING. As dissolute as desperate; yet through both 20
I see some sparks of better hope, which elder years
May happily bring forth. But who comes here?
(ENTER AUMERLE.)
AUM. Where is the king?
BOLING. What means our cousin, that he stares and looks
So wildly? 25
AUM. God save your grace! I do beseech your majesty,
To have some conference with your grace alone.
BOLING. Withdraw yourselves, and leave us here alone.
(Exeunt Percy and Lords.)
What is the matter with our cousin now?
AUM. For ever may my knees grow to the earth, 30
My tongue cleave to my roof within my mouth,
Unless a pardon ere I rise or speak.
BOLING. Intended or committed was this fault?
If on the first, how heinous e'er it be,
To win thy after-love I pardon thee. 35
AUM. Then give me leave that I may turn the key,
That no man enter till my tale be done.
BOLING. Have thy desire.
YORK. *(Within)* My liege, beware; look to thyself;

Thou hast a traitor in thy presence there.$_{40}$
BOLING. Villain, I'll make thee safe. *(Drawing.)*
AUM. Stay thy revengeful hand; thou hast no cause to fear.
YORK. *(Within)* Open the door, secure, foolhardy king:
Shall I for love speak treason to thy face?
Open the door, or I will break it open.$_{45}$
(Enter YORK.)
BOLING. What is the matter, uncle? speak;
Recover breath; tell us how near is danger,
That we may arm us to encounter it.
YORK. Peruse this writing here, and thou shalt know
The treason that my haste forbids me show.$_{50}$
AUM. Remember, as thou read'st, thy promise pass'd:
I do repent me; read not my name there;
My heart is not confederate with my hand.
YORK. It was, villain, ere thy hand did set it down.
I tore it from the traitor's bosom, king;$_{55}$
Fear, and not love, begets his penitence:
Forget to pity him, lest thy pity prove
A serpent that will sting thee to the heart.
BOLING. O heinous, strong and bold conspiracy!
O loyal father of a treacherous son!$_{60}$
Thou sheer, immaculate and silver fountain,
From whence this stream through muddy passages
Hath held his current and denied himself!
Thy overflow of good converts to bad,
And thy abundant goodness shall excuse$_{65}$
This deadly blot in thy digressing son.
YORK. So shall my virtue be his vice's bawd;
And he shall spend mine honour with his shame,
As thriftless sons their scraping fathers' gold.
Mine honour lives when his dishonour dies,$_{70}$
Or my shamed life in his dishonour lies:
Thou kill'st me in his life; giving him breath,
The traitor lives, the true man's put to death.
DUCH. *(Within)* What ho, my liege! for God's sake, let me in.
BOLING. What shrill-voiced suppliant makes this eager cry.$_{75}$
DUCH. A woman, and thy aunt, great king; 'tis I.
Speak with me, pity me, open the door:

A beggar begs that never begg'd before.
BOLING. Our scene is alter'd from a serious thing,
And now changed to 'The Beggar and the King.'₈₀
My dangerous cousin, let your mother in:
I know she is come to pray for your foul sin.
YORK. If thou do pardon, whosoever pray,
More sins for this forgiveness prosper may.
This fester'd joint cut off, the rest rest sound;₈₅
This let alone will all the rest confound.
(ENTER DUCHESS.)
DUCH. O king, believe not this hard-hearted man!
Love loving not itself none other can.
YORK. Thou frantic woman, what dost thou make here?
Shall thy old dugs once more a traitor rear?₉₀
DUCH. Sweet York, be patient. Hear me, gentle liege. *(Kneels.)*
BOLING. Rise up, good aunt.
DUCH. Not yet, I thee beseech:
For ever will I walk upon my knees,
And never see day that the happy sees,
Till thou give joy; until thou bid me joy,₉₅
By pardoning Rutland, my transgressing boy.
AUM. Unto my mother's prayers I bend my knee.
YORK. Against them both my true joints bended be.
Ill mayst thou thrive, if thou grant any grace!
DUCH. Pleads he in earnest? look upon his face;₁₀₀
His eyes do drop no tears, his prayers are in jest;
His words come from his mouth, ours from our breast:
He prays but faintly and would be denied;
We pray with heart and soul and all beside:
His weary joints would gladly rise, I know;₁₀₅
Our knees shall kneel till to the ground they grow:
His prayers are full of false hypocrisy;
Ours of true zeal and deep integrity.
Our prayers do out-pray his; then let them have
That mercy which true prayer ought to have.₁₁₀
BOLING. Good aunt, stand up.
DUCH. Nay, do not say, 'stand up;'
Say 'pardon' first, and afterwards 'stand up.'
An if I were thy nurse, thy tongue to teach,

'Pardon' should be the first word of thy speech.
I never long'd to hear a word till now;$_{115}$
Say 'pardon,' king; let pity teach thee how:
The word is short, but not so short as sweet;
No word like 'pardon' for kings' mouths so meet.
YORK. Speak it in French, king; say, 'pardonne moi.'
DUCH. Dost thou teach pardon pardon to destroy?$_{120}$
Ah, my sour husband, my hard-hearted lord,
That set'st the word itself against the word!
Speak 'pardon' as 'tis current in our land;
The chopping French we do not understand.
Thine eye begins to speak, set thy tongue there:$_{125}$
Or in thy piteous heart plant thou thine ear;
That hearing how our plaints and prayers do pierce,
Pity may move thee 'pardon' to rehearse.
BOLING. Good aunt, stand up.
DUCH. I do not sue to stand;
Pardon is all the suit I have in hand.$_{130}$
BOLING. I pardon him, as God shall pardon me.
DUCH. O happy vantage of a kneeling knee!
Yet am I sick for fear: speak it again;
Twice saying 'pardon' doth not pardon twain,
But makes one pardon strong.
BOLING. With all my heart$_{135}$
I pardon him.
DUCH. A god on earth thou art.
BOLING. But for our trusty brother-in-law, and the abbot,
With all the rest of that consorted crew,
Destruction straight shall dog them at the heels.
Good uncle, help to order several powers$_{140}$
To Oxford, or where'er these traitors are:
They shall not live within this world, I swear,
But I will have them, if I once know where.
Uncle, farewell: and, cousin too, adieu:
Your mother well hath pray'd, and prove you true.$_{145}$
DUCH. Come, my old son: I pray God make thee new.
(Exeunt.)

SCENE IV. THE SAME

(Enter Exton and Servant.)

EXTON. Didst thou not mark the king, what words he spake,
'Have I no friend will rid me of this living fear?'
Was it not so?
SER. These were his very words.
EXTON. 'Have I no friend?' quoth he: he spake it twice.
And urged it twice together, did he not? 5
SER. He did.
EXTON. And speaking it, he wistly look'd on me;
As who should say, 'I would thou wert the man
That would divorce this terror from my heart;'
Meaning the king at Pomfret. Come, let's go: 10
I am the king's friend, and will rid his foe. *(Exeunt.)*

SCENE V. POMFRET CASTLE

(Enter King Richard.)

K. RICH. I have been studying how I may compare
This prison where I live unto the world:
And for because the world is populous
And here is not a creature but myself,
I cannot do it; yet I'll hammer it out. 5
My brain I'll prove the female to my soul,
My soul the father; and these two beget
A generation of still-breeding thoughts,
And these same thoughts people this little world,
In humours like the people of this world, 10
For no thought is contented. The better sort,
As thoughts of things divine, are intermix'd
With scruples and do set the word itself
Against the word:
As thus, 'Come, little ones,' and then again, 15
'It is as hard to come as for a camel
To thread the postern of a small needle's eye.'

Thoughts tending to ambition, they do plot
Unlikely wonders; how these vain weak nails
May tear a passage through the flinty ribs$_{20}$
Of this hard world, my ragged prison walls,
And, for they cannot, die in their own pride.
Thoughts tending to content flatter themselves
That they are not the first of fortune's slaves,
Nor shall not be the last; like silly beggars$_{25}$
Who sitting in the stocks refuge their shame,
That many have and others must sit there;
And in this thought they find a kind of ease,
Bearing their own misfortunes on the back
Of such as have before endured the like.$_{30}$
Thus play I in one person many people,
And none contented: sometimes am I king;
Then treasons make me wish myself a beggar,
And so I am: then crushing penury
Persuades me I was better when a king;$_{35}$
Then am I king'd again: and by and by
Think that I am unking'd by Bolingbroke,
And straight am nothing: but whate'er I be,
Nor I nor any man that but man is
With nothing shall be pleased, till he be eased$_{40}$
With being nothing. Music do I hear? *(Music.)*
Ha, ha! keep time: how sour sweet music is,
When time is broke and no proportion kept!
So is it in the music of men's lives.
And here have I the daintiness of ear$_{45}$
To check time broke in a disorder'd string;
But for the concord of my state and time
Had not an ear to hear my true time broke.
I wasted time, and now doth time waste me;
For now hath time made me his numbering clock:$_{50}$
My thoughts are minutes; and with sighs they jar
Their watches on unto mine eyes, the outward watch,
Whereto my finger, like a dial's point,
Is pointing still, in cleansing them from tears.
Now sir, the sound that tells what hour it is$_{55}$
Are clamorous groans, which strike upon my heart,

Which is the bell: so sighs and tears and groans
Show minutes, times, and hours: but my time
Runs, posting on in Bolingbroke's proud joy,
While I stand fooling here, his Jack o' the clock.$_{60}$
This music mads me; let it sound no more;
For though it have holp madmen to their wits,
In me it seems it will make wise men mad.
Yet blessing on his heart that gives it me!
For 'tis a sign of love; and love to Richard$_{65}$
Is a strange brooch in this all-hating world.
(Enter a Groom of the Stable.)
GROOM. Hail, royal prince!
K. RICH. Thanks, noble peer;
The cheapest of us is ten groats too dear.
What art thou? and how comest thou hither,
Where no man never comes, but that sad dog$_{70}$
That brings me food to make misfortune live?
GROOM. I was a poor groom of thy stable, king,
When thou wert king; who, travelling towards York,
With much ado at length have gotten leave
To look upon my sometimes royal master's face.$_{75}$
O, how it yearn'd my heart when I beheld
In London streets, that coronation-day,
When Bolingbroke rode on roan Barbary,
That horse that thou so often hast bestrid,
That horse that I so carefully have dress'd!$_{80}$
K. RICH. Rode he on Barbary? Tell me, gentle friend,
How went he under him?
GROOM. So proudly as if he disdain'd the ground.
K. RICH. So proud that Bolingbroke was on his back!
That jade hath eat bread from my royal hand;$_{85}$
This hand hath made him proud with clapping him.
Would he not stumble? would he not fall down,
Since pride must have a fall, and break the neck
Of that proud man that did usurp his back?
Forgiveness, horse! why do I rail on thee,$_{90}$
Since thou, created to be awed by man,
Wast born to bear? I was not made a horse;
And yet I bear a burthen like an ass,

Spurr'd, gall'd and tired by jauncing Bolingbroke.
(Enter Keeper, with a dish.)
KEEP. Fellow, give place; here is no longer stay.₉₅
K. RICH. If thou love me, 'tis time thou wert away.
GROOM. What my tongue dares not, that my heart shall say.
(Exit.)
KEEP. My lord, will't please you to fall to?
K. RICH. Taste of it first, as thou art wont to do.
KEEP. My lord, I dare not: sir Pierce of Exton, who₁₀₀
lately came from the king, commands the contrary.
K. RICH. The devil take Henry of Lancaster and thee!
Patience is stale, and I am weary of it. *(Beats the Keeper.)*
KEEP. Help, help, help!
(Enter EXTON and Servants, armed.)
K. RICH. How now! what means death in this rude assault?₁₀₅
Villain, thy own hand yields thy death's instrument.
(Snatching an axe from a Servant and killing him.)
Go thou, and fill another room in hell.
(He kills another. Then Exton strikes him down.)
That hand shall burn in never-quenching fire
That staggers thus my person. Exton, thy fierce hand
Hath with the king's blood stain'd the king's own land.₁₁₀
Mount, mount, my soul! thy seat is up on high;
Whilst my gross flesh sinks downward, here to die. *(Dies.)*
EXTON. As full of valour as of royal blood:
Both have I spill'd; O would the deed were good!
For now the devil, that told me I did well,₁₁₅
Says that this deed is chronicled in hell.
This dead king to the living king I'll bear:
Take hence the rest, and give them burial here. *(Exeunt.)*

SCENE VI. WINDSOR CASTLE

(Flourish. Enter BOLINGBROKE, YORK, with other Lords, and Attendants.)

BOLING. Kind uncle York, the latest news we hear
Is that the rebels have consumed with fire
Our town of Cicester in Gloucestershire;

But whether they be ta'en or slain we hear not.
(ENTER NORTHUMBERLAND.)
Welcome, my lord: what is the news? 5
NORTH. First, to thy sacred state wish I all happiness.
The next news is, I have to London sent
The heads of Oxford, Salisbury, Blunt, and Kent:
The manner of their taking may appear
At large discoursed in this paper here. 10
BOLING. We thank thee, gentle Percy, for thy pains;
And to thy worth will add right worthy gains.
(ENTER FITZWATER.)
FITZ. My lord, I have from Oxford sent to London
The heads of Brocas and Sir Bennet Seely,
Two of the dangerous consorted traitors 15
That sought at Oxford thy dire overthrow.
BOLING. Thy pains, Fitzwater, shall not be forgot;
Right noble is thy merit, well I wot.
(ENTER PERCY, AND THE BISHOP OF CARLISLE.)
PERCY. The grand conspirator, Abbot of Westminster,
With clog of conscience and sour melancholy 20
Hath yielded up his body to the grave;
But here is Carlisle living, to abide
Thy kingly doom and sentence of his pride.
BOLING. Carlisle, this is your doom:
Choose out some secret place, some reverend room, 25
More than thou hast, and with it joy thy life;
So as thou livest in peace, die free from strife:
For though mine enemy thou hast ever been,
High sparks of honour in thee have I seen.
(Enter EXTON, with persons bearing a coffin.)
EXTON. Great king, within this coffin I present 30
Thy buried fear: herein all breathless lies
The mightiest of thy greatest enemies,
Richard of Bordeaux, by me hither brought.
BOLING. Exton, I thank thee not; for thou hast wrought
A deed of slander, with thy fatal hand, 35
Upon my head and all this famous land.
EXTON. From your own mouth, my lord, did I this deed.
BOLING. They love not poison that do poison need,

Nor do I thee: though I did wish him dead,
I hate the murderer, love him murdered.$_{40}$
The guilt of conscience take thou for thy labour,
But neither my good word nor princely favour:
With Cain go wander thorough shades of night,
And never show thy head by day nor light.
Lords, I protest, my soul is full of woe,$_{45}$
That blood should sprinkle me to make me grow:
Come, mourn with me for that I do lament,
And put on sullen black incontinent:
I'll make a voyage to the Holy Land,
To wash this blood off from my guilty hand:$_{50}$
March sadly after; grace my mournings here;
In weeping after this untimely bier. *(Exeunt.)*

HENRY IV, PART 1

DRAMATIS PERSONÆ

KING HENRY the Fourth.
HENRY, Prince of Wales,
JOHN of Lancaster,
EARL OF WESTMORELAND.
SIR WALTER BLUNT.
THOMAS PERCY, Earl of Worcester.
HENRY PERCY, Earl of Northumberland.
HENRY PERCY, surnamed HOTSPUR, his son.
EDMUND MORTIMER, Earl of March.
RICHARD SCROOP, Archbishop of York.
ARCHIBALD, EARL OF DOUGLAS.
OWEN GLENDOWER.
SIR RICHARD VERNON.
SIR JOHN FALSTAFF.
SIR MICHAEL, a friend to the Archbishop of York.
POINS.
GADSHILL.
PETO.
BARDOLPH.
LADY PERCY, wife to Hotspur, and sister to Mortimer.
LADY MORTIMER, daughter to Glendower, and wife to
    Mortimer.

Mistress Quickly, hostess of a tavern in Eastcheap.
Lords, Officers, Sheriff, Vintner, Chamberlain, Drawers, two
    Carriers, Travellers, and Attendants.

Scene: England.

ACT I

SCENE I. LONDON. THE PALACE.

(Enter King Henry, Lord John of Lancaster, *the* Earl of Westmoreland, Sir Walter Blunt, *and others.*)

KING. So shaken as we are, so wan with care,
Find we a time for frighted peace to pant,
And breathe short-winded accents of new broils
To be commenced in stronds afar remote.
No more the thirsty entrance of this soil$_5$
Shall daub her lips with her own children's blood;
No more shall trenching war channel her fields,
Nor bruise her flowerets with the armed hoofs
Of hostile paces: those opposed eyes,
Which, like the meteors of a troubled heaven,$_{10}$
All of one nature, of one substance bred,
Did lately meet in the intestine shock
And furious close of civil butchery
Shall now, in mutual well-beseeming ranks,
March all one way and be no more opposed$_{15}$
Against acquaintance, kindred and allies:
The edge of war, like an ill-sheathed knife,

No more shall cut his master. Therefore, friends,
As far as to the sepulchre of Christ,
Whose soldier now, under whose blessed cross$_{20}$
We are impressed and engaged to fight,
Forthwith a power of English shall we levy;
Whose arms were moulded in their mothers' womb
To chase these pagans in those holy fields
Over whose acres walk'd those blessed feet$_{25}$
Which fourteen hundred years ago were nail'd
For our advantage on the bitter cross.
But this our purpose now is twelve month old,
And bootless 'tis to tell you we will go:
Therefore we meet not now. Then let me hear$_{30}$
Of you, my gentle cousin Westmoreland,
What yesternight our council did decree
In forwarding this dear expedience.
WEST. My liege, this haste was hot in question,
And many limits of the charge set down$_{35}$
But yesternight: when all athwart there came
A post from Wales loaden with heavy news;
Whose worst was, that the noble Mortimer,
Leading the men of Herefordshire to fight
Against the irregular and wild Glendower,$_{40}$
Was by the rude hands of that Welshman taken,
A thousand of his people butchered;
Upon whose dead corpse there was such misuse,
Such beastly shameless transformation,
By those Welshwomen done, as may not be$_{45}$
Without much shame retold or spoken of.
KING. It seems then that the tidings of this broil
Brake off our business for the Holy Land.
WEST. This match'd with other did, my gracious lord;
For more uneven and unwelcome news$_{50}$
Came from the north and thus it did import:
On Holy-rood day, the gallant Hotspur there,
Young Harry Percy, and brave Archibald,
That ever-valiant and approved Scot,
At Holmedon met,$_{55}$
Where they did spend a sad and bloody hour;

As by discharge of their artillery,
And shape of likelihood, the news was told;
For he that brought them, in the very heat
And pride of their contention did take horse, $_{60}$
Uncertain of the issue any way.
KING. Here is a dear, a true industrious friend,
Sir Walter Blunt, new lighted from his horse,
Stain'd with the variation of each soil
Betwixt that Holmedon and this seat of ours; $_{65}$
And he hath brought us smooth and welcome news.
The Earl of Douglas is discomfited:
Ten thousand bold Scots, two and twenty knights,
Balk'd in their own blood did Sir Walter see
On Holmedon's plains. Of prisoners, Hotspur took $_{70}$
Mordake the Earl of Fife, and eldest son
To beaten Douglas; and the Earl of Athol,
Of Murray, Angus, and Menteith:
And is not this an honourable spoil?
A gallant prize? ha, cousin, is it not? $_{75}$
WEST. In faith,
It is a conquest for a prince to boast of.
KING. Yea, there thou makest me sad and makest me sin
In envy that my Lord Northumberland
Should be the father to so blest a son, $_{80}$
A son who is the theme of honour's tongue;
Amongst a grove, the very straightest plant;
Who is sweet Fortune's minion and her pride:
Whilst I, by looking on the praise of him,
See riot and dishonour stain the brow $_{85}$
Of my young Harry. O that it could be proved
That some night-tripping fairy had exchanged
In cradle-clothes our children where they lay,
And call'd mine Percy, his Plantagenet!
Then would I have his Harry, and he mine. $_{90}$
But let him from my thoughts. What think you, coz,
Of this young Percy's pride? the prisoners,
Which he in this adventure hath surprised,
To his own use he keeps; and sends me word,
I shall have none but Mordake Earl of Fife. $_{95}$

WEST. This is his uncle's teaching: this is Worcester,
Malevolent to you in all aspects;
Which makes him prune himself, and bristle up
The crest of youth against your dignity.
KING. But I have sent for him to answer this; 100
And for this cause awhile we must neglect
Our holy purpose to Jerusalem.
Cousin, on Wednesday next our council we
Will hold at Windsor; so inform the lords:
But come yourself with speed to us again; 105
For more is to be said and to be done
Than out of anger can be uttered.
WEST. I will, my liege. *(Exeunt.)*

SCENE II. LONDON. AN APARTMENT OF THE PRINCE'S.

(ENTER THE PRINCE OF WALES AND FALSTAFF.)

FAL. Now, Hal, what time of day is it, lad?
PRINCE. Thou art so fat-witted, with drinking of old
sack and unbuttoning thee after supper and sleeping upon
benches after noon, that thou hast forgotten to demand
that truly which thou wouldst truly know. What a devil 5
hast thou to do with the time of the day? Unless hours
were cups of sack and minutes capons and clocks the
tongues of bawds and dials the signs of leaping-houses
and the blessed sun himself a fair hot wench in flame-coloured
taffeta, I see no reason why thou shouldst be so 10
superfluous to demand the time of the day.
FAL. Indeed, you come near me now, Hal; for we that
take purses go by the moon and the seven stars, and not
by Phœbus, he, 'that wandering knight so fair.' And, I
prithee, sweet wag, when thou art king, as, God save 15
thy grace,—majesty I should say, for grace thou wilt have
none,—
PRINCE. What, none?
FAL. No, by my troth, not so much as will serve to

be prologue to an egg and butter.$_{20}$

PRINCE. Well, how then? come, roundly, roundly.

FAL. Marry, then, sweet wag, when thou art king, let
not us that are squires of the night's body be called thieves
of the day's beauty: let us be Diana's foresters, gentlemen
of the shade, minions of the moon; and let men say we$_{25}$
be men of good government, being governed, as the sea
is, by our noble and chaste mistress the moon, under whose
countenance we steal.

PRINCE. Thou sayest well, and it holds well too; for
the fortune of us that are the moon's men doth ebb and$_{30}$
flow like the sea, being governed, as the sea is, by the
moon. As, for proof, now: a purse of gold most resolutely
snatched on Monday night and most dissolutely spent on
Tuesday morning; got with swearing 'Lay by' and spent
with crying 'Bring in;' now in as low an ebb as the foot of$_{35}$
the ladder and by and by in as high a flow as the ridge of
the gallows.

FAL. By the Lord, thou sayest true, lad. And is not
my hostess of the tavern a most sweet wench?

PRINCE. As the honey of Hybla, my old lad of the$_{40}$
castle. And is not a buff jerkin a most sweet robe of
durance?

FAL. How now, how now, mad wag! what, in thy
quips and thy quiddities? what a plague have I to do with
a buff jerkin?$_{45}$

PRINCE. Why, what a pox have I to do with my hostess
of the tavern?

FAL. Well, thou hast called her to a reckoning many
a time and oft.

PRINCE. Did I ever call for thee to pay thy part?$_{50}$

FAL. No; I'll give thee thy due, thou hast paid all
there.

PRINCE. Yea, and elsewhere, so far as my coin would
stretch; and where it would not, I have used my credit.

FAL. Yea, and so used it that, were it not here apparent$_{55}$
that thou art heir apparent—But, I prithee, sweet
wag, shall there be gallows standing in England when thou
art king? and resolution thus fobbed as it is with the rusty

curb of old father antic the law? Do not thou, when thou
art king, hang a thief.$_{60}$
PRINCE. No; thou shalt.
FAL. Shall I? O rare! By the Lord, I'll be a brave
judge.
PRINCE. Thou judgest false already: I mean, thou
shalt have the hanging of the thieves and so become a$_{65}$
rare hangman.
FAL. Well, Hal, well; and in some sort it jumps with
my humour as well as waiting in the court, I can tell you.
PRINCE. For obtaining of suits?
FAL. Yea, for obtaining of suits, whereof the hangman$_{70}$
hath no lean wardrobe. 'Sblood, I am as melancholy as a
gib cat or a lugged bear.
PRINCE. Or an old lion, or a lover's lute.
FAL. Yea, or the drone of a Lincolnshire bagpipe.
PRINCE. What sayest thou to a hare, or the melancholy$_{75}$
of Moor-ditch?
FAL. Thou hast the most unsavoury similes and art
indeed the most comparative, rascalliest, sweet young
PRINCE. But, Hal, I prithee, trouble me no more with
vanity. I would to God thou and I knew where a commodity$_{80}$
of good names were to be bought. An old lord of
the council rated me the other day in the street about you,
sir, but I marked him not; and yet he talked very
wisely, but I regarded him not; and yet he talked wisely,
and in the street too.$_{85}$
PRINCE. Thou didst well; for wisdom cries out in the
streets, and no man regards it.
FAL. O, thou hast damnable iteration and art indeed
able to corrupt a saint. Thou hast done much harm upon
me, Hal; God forgive thee for it! Before I knew thee,$_{90}$
Hal, I knew nothing; and now am I, if a man should
speak truly, little better than one of the wicked. I must
give over this life, and I will give it over: by the Lord, an
I do not, I am a villain: I'll be damned for never a king's
son in Christendom.$_{95}$
PRINCE. Where shall we take a purse to-morrow, Jack?
FAL. 'Zounds, where thou wilt, lad; I'll make one; an

I do not, call me villain and baffle me.

PRINCE. I see a good amendment of life in thee; from
praying to purse-taking.₁₀₀

FAL. Why, Hal, 'tis my vocation, Hal; 'tis no sin for
a man to labour in his vocation.

(Enter POINS.)

Poins! Now shall we know if Gadshill have set a match.
O, if men were to be saved by merit, what hole in hell
were hot enough for him? This is the most omnipotent₁₀₅
villain that ever cried 'Stand' to a true man.

PRINCE. Good morrow, Ned.

POINS. Good morrow, sweet Hal. What says Monsieur
Remorse? what says Sir John Sack and Sugar?
Jack! how agrees the devil and thee about thy soul, that₁₁₀
thou soldest him on Good-Friday last for a cup of Madeira
and a cold capon's leg?

PRINCE. Sir John stands to his word, the devil shall
have his bargain; for he was never yet a breaker of proverbs:
he will give the devil his due.₁₁₅

POINS. Then art thou damned for keeping thy word
with the devil.

PRINCE. Else he had been damned for cozening the
devil.

POINS. But, my lads, my lads, to-morrow morning, by₁₂₀
four o'clock, early at Gadshill! there are pilgrims going to
Canterbury with rich offerings, and traders riding to London
with fat purses: I have vizards for you all; you have
horses for yourselves: Gadshill lies to-night in Rochester:
I have bespoke supper to-morrow night in Eastcheap: we₁₂₅
may do it as secure as sleep. If you will go, I will stuff
your purses full of crowns; if you will not, tarry at home
and be hanged.

FAL. Hear ye, Yedward; if I tarry at home and go
not, I'll hang you for going.₁₃₀

POINS. You will, chops?

FAL. Hal, wilt thou make one?

PRINCE. Who, I rob? I a thief? not I, by my faith.

FAL. There's neither honesty, manhood, nor good fellowship
in thee, nor thou earnest not of the blood royal, if₁₃₅

thou darest not stand for ten shillings.

PRINCE. Well then, once in my days I'll be a madcap.

FAL. Why, that's well said.

PRINCE. Well, come what will, I'll tarry at home.

FAL. By the Lord, I'll be a traitor then, when thou $_{140}$
art king.

PRINCE. I care not.

POINS. Sir John, I prithee, leave the prince and me
alone: I will lay him down such reasons for this adventure
that he shall go. $_{145}$

FAL. Well, God give thee the spirit of persuasion and
him the ears of profiting, that what thou speakest may
move and what he hears may be believed, that the true
prince may, for recreation sake, prove a false thief; for the
poor abuses of the time want countenance. Farewell: you $_{150}$
shall find me in Eastcheap.

PRINCE. Farewell, thou latter spring! farewell, Allhallown
summer! (Exit Falstaff.)

POINS. Now, my good sweet honey lord, ride with us
to-morrow: I have a jest to execute that I cannot manage $_{155}$
alone. Falstaff, Bardolph, Peto and Gadshill shall rob
those men that we have already waylaid; yourself and I
will not be there; and when they have the booty, if you
and I do not rob them, cut this head off from my shoulders.

PRINCE. How shall we part with them in setting $_{160}$
forth?

POINS. Why, we will set forth before or after them, and
appoint them a place of meeting, wherein it is at our pleasure
to fail, and then will they adventure upon the exploit
themselves; which they shall have no sooner achieved, but $_{165}$
we'll set upon them.

PRINCE. Yea, but 'tis like that they will know us by
our horses, by our habits and by every other appointment,
to be ourselves.

POINS. Tut! our horses they shall not see; I'll tie $_{170}$
them in the wood; our vizards we will change after we
leave them: and, sirrah, I have cases of buckram for the
nonce, to immask our noted outward garments.

PRINCE. Yea, but I doubt they will be too hard for us.

POINS. Well, for two of them, I know them to be as$_{175}$
true-bred cowards as ever turned back; and for the third,
if he fight longer than he sees reason, I'll forswear arms.
The virtue of this jest will be, the incomprehensible lies
that this same fat rogue will tell us when we meet at supper:
how thirty, at least, he fought with; what wards, what$_{180}$
blows, what extremities he endured; and in the reproof of
this lies the jest.
PRINCE. Well, I'll go with thee: provide us all things
necessary and meet me to-morrow night in Eastcheap;
there I'll sup. Farewell.$_{185}$
POINS. Farewell, my lord. *(Exit.)*
PRINCE. I know you all, and will awhile uphold
The unyoked humour of your idleness:
Yet herein will I imitate the sun,
Who doth permit the base contagious clouds$_{190}$
To smother up his beauty from the world,
That, when he please again to be himself,
Being wanted, he may be more wonder'd at,
By breaking through the foul and ugly mists
Of vapours that did seem to strangle him.$_{195}$
If all the year were playing holidays,
To sport would be as tedious as to work;
But when they seldom come, they wish'd for come,
And nothing pleaseth but rare accidents.
So, when this loose behaviour I throw off$_{200}$
And pay the debt I never promised,
By how much better than my word I am,
By so much shall I falsify men's hopes;
And like bright metal on a sullen ground,
My reformation, glittering o'er my fault,$_{205}$
Shall show more goodly and attract more eyes
Than that which hath no foil to set it off.
I'll so offend, to make offence a skill;
Redeeming time when men think least I will. *(Exit.)*

SCENE III. LONDON. THE PALACE

*(ENTER THE KING, NORTHUMBERLAND, WORCESTER, HOTSPUR, SIR
WALTER BLUNT, WITH OTHERS.)*

KING. My blood hath been too cold and temperate,
Unapt to stir at these indignities,
And you have found me; for accordingly
You tread upon my patience: but be sure
I will from henceforth rather be myself,$_5$
Mighty and to be fear'd, than my condition;
Which hath been smooth as oil, soft as young down,
And therefore lost that title of respect
Which the proud soul ne'er pays but to the proud.
WOR. Our house, my sovereign liege, little deserves$_{10}$
The scourge of greatness to be used on it;
And that same greatness too which our own hands
Have holp to make so portly.
North. My lord,—
KING. Worcester, get thee gone; for I do see$_{15}$
Danger and disobedience in thine eye:
O, sir, your presence is too bold and peremptory,
And majesty might never yet endure
The moody frontier of a servant brow.
You have good leave to leave us: when we need$_{20}$
Your use and counsel, we shall send for you. *(Exit Wor.)*
You were about to speak. *(To North.)*
NORTH. Yea, my good lord.
Those prisoners in your highness' name demanded,
Which Harry Percy here at Holmedon took,
Were, as he says, not with such strength denied$_{25}$
As is deliver'd to your majesty:
Either envy, therefore, or misprision
Is guilty of this fault and not my son.
HOT. My liege, I did deny no prisoners.
But I remember, when the fight was done,$_{30}$
When I was dry with rage and extreme toil,
Breathless and faint, leaning upon my sword,

Came there a certain lord, neat, and trimly dress'd,
Fresh as a bridegroom; and his chin new reap'd
Show'd like a stubble-land at harvest-home;$_{35}$
He was perfumed like a milliner;
And 'twixt his finger and his thumb he held
A pouncet-box, which ever and anon
He gave his nose and took 't away again;
Who therewith angry, when it next came there,$_{40}$
Took it in snuff; and still he smiled and talk'd,
And as the soldiers bore dead bodies by,
He call'd them untaught knaves, unmannerly,
To bring a slovenly unhandsome corse
Betwixt the wind and his nobility.$_{45}$
With many holiday and lady terms
He question'd me; amongst the rest, demanded
My prisoners in your majesty's behalf.
I then, all smarting with my wounds being cold,
To be so pester'd with a popinjay,$_{50}$
Out of my grief and my impatience,
Answer'd neglectingly I know not what,
He should, or he should not; for he made me mad
To see him shine so brisk and smell so sweet
And talk so like a waiting-gentlewoman$_{55}$
Of guns and drums and wounds,—God save the mark!—
And telling me the sovereign'st thing on earth
Was parmaceti for an inward bruise;
And that it was great pity, so it was,
This villanous salt-petre should be digg'd$_{60}$
Out of the bowels of the harmless earth,
Which many a good tall fellow had destroy'd
So cowardly; and but for these vile guns,
He would himself have been a soldier.
This bald unjointed chat of his, my lord,$_{65}$
I answer'd indirectly, as I said;
And I beseech you, let not his report
Come current for an accusation
Betwixt my love and your high majesty.
BLUNT. The circumstance consider'd, good my lord,$_{70}$
Whate'er Lord Harry Percy then had said

To such a person and in such a place,
At such a time, with all the rest re-told,
May reasonably die and never rise
To do him wrong or any way impeach$_{75}$
What then he said, so he unsay it now.
KING. Why, yet he doth deny his prisoners,
But with proviso and exception,
That we at our own charge shall ransom straight
His brother-in-law, the foolish Mortimer;$_{80}$
Who, on my soul, hath wilfully betray'd
The lives of those that he did lead to fight
Against that great magician, damn'd Glendower,
Whose daughter, as we hear, the Earl of March
Hath lately married. Shall our coffers, then,$_{85}$
Be emptied to redeem a traitor home?
Shall we buy treason? and indent with fears,
When they have lost and forfeited themselves?
No, on the barren mountains let him starve;
For I shall never hold that man my friend$_{90}$
Whose tongue shall ask me for one penny cost
To ransom home revolted Mortimer.
HOT. Revolted Mortimer!
He never did fall off, my sovereign liege,
But by the chance of war: to prove that true$_{95}$
Needs no more but one tongue for all those wounds,
Those mouthed wounds, which valiantly he took,
When on the gentle Severn's sedgy bank,
In single opposition, hand to hand,
He did confound the best part of an hour$_{100}$
In changing hardiment with great Glendower:
Three times they breathed and three times did they drink,
Upon agreement, of swift Severn's flood;
Who then, affrighted with their bloody looks,
Ran fearfully among the trembling reeds,$_{105}$
And hid his crisp head in the hollow bank
Bloodstained with these valiant combatants.
Never did base and rotten policy
Colour her working with such deadly wounds;
Nor never could the noble Mortimer$_{110}$

Receive so many, and all willingly:
Then let not him be slander'd with revolt.
KING. Thou dost belie him, Percy, thou dost belie him;
He never did encounter with Glendower:
I tell thee,$_{115}$
He durst as well have met the devil alone
As Owen Glendower for an enemy.
Art thou not ashamed? But, sirrah, henceforth
Let me not hear you speak of Mortimer:
Send me your prisoners with the speediest means,$_{120}$
Or you shall hear in such a kind from me
As will displease you. My Lord Northumberland,
We license your departure with your son.
Send us your prisoners, or you will hear of it.
(Exeunt King Henry, Blunt, and train.)
HOT. An if the devil come and roar for them,$_{125}$
I will not send them: I will after straight
And tell him so; for I will ease my heart,
Albeit I make a hazard of my head.
NORTH. What, drunk with choler? stay and pause awhile:
Here comes your uncle.
(RE-ENTER WORCESTER.)
HOT. Speak of$_{130}$
'Zounds, I will speak of him; and let my soul
Want mercy, if I do not join with him:
Yea, on his part I'll empty all these veins,
And shed my dear blood drop by drop in the dust,
But I will lift the down-trod Mortimer$_{135}$
As high in the air as this unthankful king,
As this ingrate and canker'd Bolingbroke.
NORTH. Brother, the king hath made your nephew mad.
WOR. Who struck this heat up after I was gone?
HOT. He will, forsooth, have all my prisoners;$_{140}$
And when I urged the ransom once again
Of my wife's brother, then his cheek look'd pale,
And on my face he turn'd an eye of death,
Trembling even at the name of Mortimer.
WOR. I cannot blame him: was not he proclaim'd$_{145}$
By Richard that dead is the next of blood?

NORTH. He was; I heard the proclamation:
And then it was when the unhappy king,—
Whose wrongs in us God pardon!—did set forth
Upon his Irish expedition; 150
From whence he intercepted did return
To be deposed and shortly murdered.
WOR. And for whose death we in the world's wide mouth
Live scandalized and foully spoken of.
HOT. But, soft, I pray you; did King Richard then 155
Proclaim my brother Edmund Mortimer
Heir to the crown?
NORTH. He did; myself did hear it.
HOT. Nay, then I cannot blame his cousin king,
That wish'd him on the barren mountains starve.
But shall it be, that you, that set the crown 160
Upon the head of this forgetful man
And for his sake wear the detested blot
Of murderous subornation, shall it be,
That you a world of curses undergo,
Being the agents, or base second means, 165
The cords, the ladder, or the hangman rather?
O, pardon me that I descend so low,
To show the line and the predicament
Wherein you range under this subtle king;
Shall it for shame be spoken in these days, 170
Or fill up chronicles in time to come,
That men of your nobility and power
Did gage them both in an unjust behalf,
As both of you—God pardon it!—have done,
To put down Richard, that sweet lovely rose, 175
And plant this thorn, this canker, Bolingbroke?
And shall it in more shame be further spoken,
That you are fool'd, discarded and shook off
By him for whom these shames ye underwent?
No; yet time serves wherein you may redeem 180
Your banish'd honours and restore yourselves
Into the good thoughts of the world again,
Revenge the jeering and disdain'd contempt
Of this proud king, who studies day and night

To answer all the debt he owes to you$_{185}$
Even with the bloody payment of your deaths:
Therefore, I say,—
WOR. Peace, cousin, say no more:
And now I will unclasp a secret book,
And to your quick-conceiving discontents
I'll read you matter deep and dangerous,$_{190}$
As full of peril and adventurous spirit
As to o'er-walk a current roaring loud
On the unsteadfast footing of a spear.
HOT. If he fall in, good night! or sink or swim:
Send danger from the east unto the west,$_{195}$
So honour cross it from the north to south,
And let them grapple: O, the blood more stirs
To rouse a lion than to start a hare!
NORTH. Imagination of some great exploit
Drives him beyond the bounds of patience.$_{200}$
HOT. By heaven, methinks it were an easy leap,
To pluck bright honour from the pale-faced moon,
Or dive into the bottom of the deep,
Where fathom-line could never touch the ground,
And pluck up drowned honour by the locks;$_{205}$
So he that doth redeem her thence might wear
Without corrival all her dignities:
But out upon this half-faced fellowship!
WOR. He apprehends a world of figures here,
But not the form of what he should attend.$_{210}$
Good cousin, give me audience for a while.
HOT. I cry you mercy.
WOR. Those same noble Scots
That are your prisoners,—
HOT. I'll keep them all;
By God, he shall not have a Scot of them;
No, if a Scot would save his soul, he shall not:$_{215}$
I'll keep them, by this hand.
WOR. You start away
And lend no ear unto my purposes.
Those prisoners you shall keep.
HOT. Nay, I will; that's flat:

He said he would not ransom Mortimer;
Forbad my tongue to speak of Mortimer;$_{220}$
But I will find him when he lies asleep,
And in his ear I'll holla 'Mortimer!'
Nay,
I'll have a starling shall be taught to speak
Nothing but 'Mortimer,' and give it him,$_{225}$
To keep his anger still in motion.
WOR. Hear you, cousin; a word.
HOT. All studies here I solemnly defy,
Save how to gall and pinch this Bolingbroke:
And that same sword-and-buckler Prince of Wales,$_{230}$
But that I think his father loves him not
And would be glad he met with some mischance,
I would have him poison'd with a pot of ale.
WOR. Farewell, kinsman: I'll talk to you
When you are better temper'd to attend.$_{235}$
NORTH. Why, what a wasp-stung and impatient fool
Art thou to break into this woman's mood,
Tying thine ear to no tongue but thine own!
HOT. Why, look you, I am whipp'd and scourged with rods,
Nettled, and stung with pismires, when I hear$_{240}$
Of this vile politician, Bolingbroke.
In Richard's time,—what do you call the place?—
A plague upon it, it is in Gloucestershire;
'Twas where the madcap duke his uncle kept.
His uncle York; where I first bow'd my knee$_{245}$
Unto this king of smiles, this Bolingbroke,—
'Sblood!—
When you and he came back from Ravenspurgh.
NORTH. At Berkley-castle.
HOT. You say true:$_{250}$
Why, what a candy deal of courtesy
This fawning greyhound then did proffer me!
Look, 'when his infant fortune came to age,'
And 'gentle Harry Percy,' and 'kind cousin;'
O, the devil take such cozeners! God forgive me!$_{255}$
Good uncle, tell your tale; I have done.
WOR. Nay, if you have not, to it again;

We will stay your leisure.
Hot. I have done, i' faith.
Wor. Then once more to your Scottish prisoners.
Deliver them up without their ransom straight,$_{260}$
And make the Douglas' son your only mean
For powers in Scotland; which, for divers reasons
Which I shall send you written, be assured,
Will easily be granted. You, my lord, *(To Northumberland.)*
Your son in Scotland being thus employ'd,$_{265}$
Shall secretly into the bosom creep
Of that same noble prelate, well beloved,
The archbishop.
Hot. Of York, is it not?
Wor. True; who bears hard$_{270}$
His brother's death at Bristol, the Lord Scroop.
I speak not this in estimation,
As what I think might be, but what I know
Is ruminated, plotted and set down,
And only stays but to behold the face$_{275}$
Of that occasion that shall bring it on.
Hot. I smell it: upon my life, it will do well.
North. Before the game is a-foot, thou still let'st slip.
Hot. Why, it cannot choose but be a noble plot:
And then the power of Scotland and of York,$_{280}$
To join with Mortimer, ha?
Wor. And so they shall.
Hot. In faith, it is exceedingly well aim'd.
Wor. And 'tis no little reason bids us speed,
To save our heads by raising of a head;
For, bear ourselves as even as we can,$_{285}$
The king will always think him in our debt,
And think we think ourselves unsatisfied,
Till he hath found a time to pay us home:
And see already how he doth begin
To make us strangers to his looks of love.$_{290}$
Hot. He does, he does: we'll be revenged on him.
Wor. Cousin, farewell: no further go in this
Than I by letters shall direct your course.
When time is ripe, which will be suddenly,

I'll steal to Glendower and Lord Mortimer;₂₉₅
Where you and Douglas and our powers at once,
As I will fashion it, shall happily meet,
To bear our fortunes in our own strong arms,
Which now we hold at much uncertainty.
NORTH. Farewell, good brother: we shall thrive, I trust.₃₀₀
HOT. Uncle, adieu: O, let the hours be short
Till fields and blows and groans applaud our sport! *(Exeunt.)*

ACT II

SCENE I. ROCHESTER. AN INN YARD.

(Enter a Carrier with a lantern in his hand.)

First Car. Heigh-ho! an it be not four by the day,
I'll be hanged: Charles' wain is over the new chimney, and
yet our horse not packed. What, ostler!
Host. *(Within)* Anon, anon.
First Car. I prithee, Tom, beat Cut's saddle, put a 5
few flocks in the point; poor jade, is wrung in the withers
out of all cess.
(Enter another Carrier.)
Sec. Car. Peas and beans are as dank here as a dog,
and that is the next way to give poor jades the bots: this
house is turned upside down since Robin Ostler died. 10
First Car. Poor fellow, never joyed since the price of
oats rose; it was the death of him.
Sec. Car. I think this be the most villanous house in
all London road for fleas: I am stung like a tench.
First Car. Like a tench! by the mass, there is ne'er a 15
king christen could be better bit than I have been since
the first cock.

SEC. CAR. Why, they will allow us ne'er a jordan, and then we leak in your chimney; and your chamber-lie breeds fleas like a loach.$_{20}$

FIRST CAR. What, ostler! come away and be hanged! come away.

SEC. CAR. I have a gammon of bacon and two razes of ginger, to be delivered as far as Charing-cross.

FIRST CAR. God's body! the turkeys in my pannier are$_{25}$ quite starved. What, ostler! A plague on thee! hast thou never an eye in thy head? canst not hear? An 'twere not as good deed as drink, to break the pate on thee, I am a very villain. Come, and be hanged! hast no faith in thee?

(ENTER GADSHILL.)

GADS. Good morrow, carriers. What's o'clock?$_{30}$

FIRST CAR. I think it be two o'clock.

GADS. I prithee, lend me thy lantern, to see my gelding in the stable.

FIRST CAR. Nay, by God, soft; I know a trick worth two of that, i' faith.$_{35}$

GADS. I pray thee, lend me thine.

SEC. CAR. Ay, when? canst tell? Lend me thy lantern, quoth he? marry, I'll see thee hanged first.

GADS. Sirrah carrier, what time do you mean to come to London?$_{40}$

SEC. CAR. Time enough to go to bed with a candle, I warrant thee. Come, neighbour Mugs, we'll call up the gentlemen: they will along with company, for they have *great charge. (Exeunt Carriers.)*

GADS. What, ho! chamberlain!$_{45}$

CHAM. *(Within)* At hand, quoth pick-purse.

GADS. That's even as fair as—at hand, quoth the chamberlain; for thou variest no more from picking of purses than giving direction doth from labouring; thou layest the plot how.$_{50}$

(Enter Chamberlain.)

CHAM. Good morrow, Master Gadshill. It holds current that I told you yesternight: there's a franklin in the wild of Kent hath brought three hundred marks with him in gold: I heard him tell it to one of his company last

night at supper; a kind of auditor; one that hath abundance$_{55}$
of charge too, God knows what. They are up already, and
call for eggs and butter: they will away presently.

GADS. Sirrah, if they meet not with Saint Nicholas'
clerks, I'll give thee this neck.

CHAM. No, I'll none of it: I pray thee, keep that for$_{60}$
the hangman; for I know thou worshippest Saint Nicholas
as truly as a man of falsehood may.

GADS. What talkest thou to me of the hangman? if I
hang, I'll make a fat pair of gallows; for if I hang, old Sir
John hangs with me, and thou knowest he is no starveling$_{65}$
Tut! there are other Trojans that thou dreamest
not of, the which for sport sake are content to do the
    profession
some grace; that would, if matters should be looked
into, for their own credit sake, make all whole. I am joined
with no foot-land rakers, no long-staff sixpenny strikers,$_{70}$
none of these mad mustachio purple-hued malt-worms; but
with nobility and tranquillity, burgomasters and great oneyers,
such as can hold in, such as will strike sooner than
speak, and speak sooner than drink, and drink sooner than
pray: and yet, 'zounds, I lie; for they pray continually to$_{75}$
their saint, the commonwealth; or rather, not pray to her,
but prey on her, for they ride up and down on her and
make her their boots.

CHAM. What, the commonwealth their boots? will she
hold out water in foul way?$_{80}$

GADS. She will, she will; justice hath liquored her.
We steal as in a castle, cock-sure; we have the receipt of
fern-seed, we walk invisible.

CHAM. Nay, by my faith, I think you are more beholding
to the night than to fern-seed for your walking invisible.$_{85}$

GADS. Give me thy hand: thou shalt have a share in
our purchase, as I am a true man.

CHAM. Nay, rather let me have it, as you are a false
thief.

GADS. Go to; 'homo' is a common name to all men.$_{90}$
Bid the ostler bring my gelding out of the stable. Farewell,
you muddy knave. *(Exeunt.)*

SCENE II. THE HIGHWAY, NEAR GADSHILL

(ENTER PRINCE HENRY AND POINS.)

POINS. Come, shelter, shelter: I have removed Falstaff's
horse, and he frets like a gummed velvet.
PRINCE. Stand close.
(ENTER FALSTAFF.)
FAL. Poins! Poins, and be hanged! Poins!
PRINCE. Peace, ye fat-kidneyed rascal! what a brawling$_5$
dost thou keep!
FAL. Where's Poins, Hal?
PRINCE. He is walked up to the top of the hill: I'll go
seek him.
FAL. I am accursed to rob in that thief's company: the$_{10}$
rascal hath removed my horse, and tied him I know not
where. If I travel but four foot by the squier further afoot,
I shall break my wind. Well, I doubt not but to die a fair
death for all this, if I 'scape hanging for killing that rogue.
I have forsworn his company hourly any time this two and$_{15}$
twenty years, and yet I am bewitched with the rogue's
company. If the rascal have not given me medicines to
make me love him, I'll be hanged; it could not be else; I
have drunk medicines. Poins! Hal! a plague upon you
both! Bardolph! Peto! I'll starve ere I'll rob a foot further.$_{20}$
An 'twere not as good a deed as drink, to turn true
man and to leave these rogues, I am the veriest varlet that
ever chewed with a tooth. Eight yards of uneven ground
is threescore and ten miles afoot with me; and the stony-
hearted
villains know it well enough: a plague upon it$_{25}$
when thieves cannot be true one to another! *(They whistle.)*
Whew! A plague upon you all! Give me my horse, you
rogues; give me my horse, and be hanged!
PRINCE. Peace, ye fat-guts! lie down; lay thine ear
close to the ground and list if thou canst hear the tread of$_{30}$
travellers.
FAL. Have you any levers to lift me up again, being

down? 'Sblood, I'll not bear mine own flesh so far afoot
again for all the coin in thy father's exchequer. What a
plague mean ye to colt me thus?$_{35}$

PRINCE. Thou liest; thou art not colted, thou art uncolted.

FAL. I prithee, good Prince Hal, help me to my horse,
good king's son.

PRINCE. Out, ye rogue! shall I be your ostler?$_{40}$

FAL. Go, hang thyself in thine own heir-apparent garters!
If I be ta'en, I'll peach for this. An I have not ballads made
on you all and sung to filthy tunes, let a cup of sack be my
poison: when a jest is so forward, and afoot too! I hate it.

(ENTER GADSHILL, BARDOLPH AND PETO WITH HIM.)

GADS. Stand.$_{45}$

FAL. So I do, against my will.

POINS. O, 'tis our setter: I know his voice. Bardolph,
what news?

BARD. Case ye, case ye; on with your vizards: there's
money of the king's coming down the hill; 'tis going to the$_{50}$
king's exchequer.

FAL. You lie, ye rogue; 'tis going to the king's tavern.

GADS. There's enough to make us all.

FAL. To be hanged.

PRINCE. Sirs, you four shall front them in the narrow$_{55}$
lane; Ned Poins and I will walk lower: if they 'scape from
your encounter, then they light on us.

PETO. How many be there of them?

GADS. Some eight or ten.

FAL. 'Zounds, will they not rob us?$_{60}$

PRINCE. What, a coward, Sir John Paunch?

FAL. Indeed, I am not John of Gaunt, your grandfather;
but yet no coward, Hal.

PRINCE. Well, we leave that to the proof.

POINS. Sirrah Jack, thy horse stands behind the hedge:$_{65}$
when thou needest him, there thou shalt find him. Farewell,
and stand fast.

FAL. Now cannot I strike him, if I should be hanged.

PRINCE. Ned, where are our disguises?

POINS. Here, hard by: stand close.$_{70}$

(Exeunt Prince and Poins.)

FAL. Now, my masters, happy man be his dole, say I:
every man to his business.

(Enter the Travellers.)

FIRST TRAV. Come, neighbour: the boy shall lead our
horses down the hill; we'll walk afoot awhile, and ease
our legs.75

THIEVES. Stand!

TRAVELLERS. Jesus bless us!

FAL. Strike; down with them; cut the villains' throats:
ah! whoreson caterpillars! bacon-fed knaves! they hate us
youth: down with them; fleece them.80

TRAVELLERS. O, we are undone, both we and ours for ever!

FAL. Hang ye, gorbellied knaves, are ye undone? No,
ye fat chuffs; I would your store were here! On, bacons,
on! What, ye knaves! young men must live. You are
grandjurors, are ye? we'll jure ye, 'faith.85

(Here they rob them and bind them. Exeunt.)

(RE-ENTER PRINCE HENRY AND POINS.)

PRINCE. The thieves have bound the true men. Now
could thou and I rob the thieves and go merrily to London,
it would be argument for a week, laughter for a
month and a good jest for ever.

POINS. Stand close; I hear them coming.90

(Enter the Thieves again.)

FAL. Come, my masters, let us share, and then to
horse before day. An the Prince and Poins be not two
arrant cowards, there's no equity stirring: there's no more
valour in that Poins than in a wild-duck.

PRINCE. Your money!95

POINS. Villains!

(As they are sharing, the Prince and Poins set upon them; they all run
away; and Falstaff, after a blow or two, runs away too, leaving the
booty behind them.)

PRINCE. Got with much ease. Now merrily to horse:
The thieves are all scatter'd and possess'd with fear
So strongly that they dare not meet each other;
Each takes his fellow for an officer.100
Away, good Ned. Falstaff sweats to death,
And lards the lean earth as he walks along:

Were 't not for laughing, I should pity him.
POINS. How the rogue roar'd! *(Exeunt.)*

SCENE III. WARKWORTH CASTLE

(ENTER HOTSPUR SOLUS, READING A LETTER.)

HOT. 'But, for mine own part, my lord, I could be well
    contented
to be there, in respect of the love I bear your house.' He
could be contented: why is he not, then? In respect of
the love he bears our house: he shows in this, he loves
his own barn better than he loves our house. Let me₅
see some more. 'The purpose you undertake is
    dangerous;'—why,
that's certain: 'tis dangerous to take a cold, to sleep, to
drink; but I tell you, my lord fool, out of this nettle,
danger, we pluck this flower, safety. 'The purpose you
    undertake
is dangerous; the friends you have named uncertain; the time₁₀
itself unsorted; and your whole plot too light for the coun-
    terpoise
of so great an opposition.' Say you so, say you so? I say
unto you again, you are a shallow cowardly hind, and you
lie. What a lack-brain is this! By the Lord, our plot is
a good plot as ever was laid; our friends true and constant:₁₅
a good plot, good friends, and full of expectation;
an excellent plot, very good friends. What a frosty-spirited
rogue is this! Why, my lord of York commends the plot
and the general course of the action. 'Zounds, an I were
now by this rascal, I could brain him with his lady's fan.₂₀
Is there not my father, my uncle, and myself? lord
Edmund Mortimer, my lord of York, and Owen Glendower?
is there not besides the Douglas? have I not all
their letters to meet me in arms by the ninth of the next
month? and are they not some of them set forward already?₂₅
What a pagan rascal is this! an infidel! Ha! you shall
see now in very sincerity of fear and cold heart, will he to

the king, and lay open all our proceedings. O, I could
divide myself, and go to buffets, for moving such a dish of
skim milk with so honourable an action! Hang him! let$_{30}$
him tell the king: we are prepared. I will set forward
to-night.
(ENTER LADY PERCY.)
How now, Kate! I must leave you within these two hours.
LADY. O, my good Lord, why are you thus alone?
For what offence have I this fortnight been$_{35}$
A banish'd woman from my Harry's bed?
Tell me, sweet lord, what is 't that takes from thee
Thy stomach, pleasure, and thy golden sleep?
Why dost thou bend thine eyes upon the earth,
And start so often when thou sit'st alone?$_{40}$
Why hast thou lost the fresh blood in thy cheeks;
And given my treasures and my rights of thee
To thick-eyed musing and cursed melancholy?
In thy faint slumbers I by thee have watch'd,
And heard thee murmur tales of iron wars;$_{45}$
Speak terms of manage to thy bounding steed;
Cry 'Courage! to the field!' And thou hast talk'd
Of sallies and retires, of trenches, tents,
Of palisadoes, frontiers, parapets,
Of basilisks, of cannon, culverin,$_{50}$
Of prisoners' ransom, and of soldiers slain,
And all the currents of a heady fight.
Thy spirit within thee hath been so at war
And thus hath so bestirred thee in thy sleep,
That beads of sweat have stood upon thy brow,$_{55}$
Like bubbles in a late-disturbed stream;
And in thy face strange motions have appear'd,
Such as we see when men restrain their breath
On some great sudden hest. O, what portents are these?
Some heavy business hath my lord in hand,$_{60}$
And I must know it, else he loves me not.
HOT. What, ho!
(Enter Servant.)
Is Gilliams with the packet gone?
SERV. He is, my lord, an hour ago.

Hot. Hath Butler brought those horses from the sheriff?
Serv. One horse, my lord, he brought even now. [65]
Hot. What horse? a roan, a crop-ear, is it not?
Serv. It is, my lord.
Hot. That roan shall be my throne.
Well, I will back him straight: O esperance!
Bid Butler lead him forth into the park. *(Exit Servant.)*
Lady. But hear you, my lord. [70]
Hot. What say'st thou, my lady?
Lady. What is it carries you away?
Hot. Why, my horse, my love, my horse.
Lady. Out, you mad-headed ape!
A weasel hath not such a deal of spleen [75]
As you are toss'd with. In faith,
I'll know your business, Harry, that I will.
I fear my brother Mortimer doth stir
About his title, and hath sent for you
To line his enterprize: but if you go,⸺ [80]
Hot. So far afoot, I shall be weary, love.
Lady. Come, come, you paraquito, answer me
Directly unto this question that I ask:
In faith, I'll break thy little finger, Harry,
An if thou wilt not tell me all things true. [85]
Hot. Away,
Away, you trifler! Love! I love thee not,
I care not for thee, Kate: this is no world
To play with mammets and to tilt with lips:
We must have bloody noses and crack'd crowns, [90]
And pass them current too. God's me, my horse!
What say'st thou, Kate? what would'st thou have with me?
Lady. Do you not love me? do you not, indeed?
Well, do not then; for since you love me not,
I will not love myself. Do you not love me? [95]
Nay, tell me if you speak in jest or no.
Hot. Come, wilt thou see me ride?
And when I am o' horseback, I will swear
I love thee infinitely. But hark you, Kate;
I must not have you henceforth question me [100]
Whither I go, nor reason whereabout:

Whither I must, I must; and, to conclude,
This evening must I leave you, gentle Kate.
I know you wise, but yet no farther wise
Than Harry Percy's wife: constant you are,₁₀₅
But yet a woman: and for secrecy,
No lady closer; for I well believe
Thou wilt not utter what thou dost not know;
And so far will I trust thee, gentle Kate.
LADY. How! so far?₁₁₀
HOT. Not an inch further. But hark you, Kate:
Whither I go, thither shall you go too;
To-day will I set forth, to-morrow you.
Will this content you, Kate?
LADY. It must of force. *(Exeunt.)*

SCENE IV. THE BOAR'S-HEAD TAVERN, EASTCHEAP

(ENTER THE PRINCE, AND POINS.)

PRINCE. Ned, prithee, come out of that fat room, and
lend me thy hand to laugh a little.
POINS. Where hast been, Hal?
PRINCE. With three or four loggerheads amongst three
or fourscore hogsheads. I have sounded the very base-string₅
of humility. Sirrah, I am sworn brother to a leash
of drawers; and can call them all by their christen
names, as Tom, Dick, and Francis. They take it already
upon their salvation, that though I be but Prince of Wales,
yet I am the king of courtesy; and tell me flatly I am no₁₀
proud Jack, like Falstaff, but a Corinthian, a lad of mettle,
a good boy, by the Lord, so they call me, and when I am
king of England, I shall command all the good lads in
Eastcheap. They call drinking deep, dyeing scarlet; and
when you breathe in your watering, they cry 'hem!' and₁₅
bid you play it off. To conclude, I am so good a proficient
in one quarter of an hour, that I can drink with any
tinker in his own language during my life. I tell thee,
Ned, thou hast lost much honour, that thou wert not with

me in this action. But, sweet Ned,—to sweeten which $_{20}$
name of Ned, I give thee this pennyworth of sugar,
clapped even now into my hand by an under-skinker, one
that never spake other English in his life than 'Eight
shillings and sixpence,' and 'You are welcome,' with this
shrill addition, 'Anon, anon, sir! Score a pint of bastard $_{25}$
in the Half-moon,' or so. But, Ned, to drive away the
time till Falstaff come, I prithee, do thou stand in some
by-room, while I question my puny drawer to what end he
gave me the sugar; and do thou never leave calling
'Francis,' that his tale to me may be nothing but 'Anon.' $_{30}$
Step aside, and I'll show thee a precedent.

POINS. Francis!

PRINCE. Thou art perfect.

POINS. *Francis! (Exit Poins.)*

(ENTER FRANCIS.)

FRAN. Anon, anon, sir. Look down into the Pomgarnet, $_{35}$
Ralph.

PRINCE. Come hither, Francis.

FRAN. My lord?

PRINCE. How long hast thou to serve, Francis?

FRAN. Forsooth, five years, and as much as to— $_{40}$

POINS. *(Within) Francis!*

FRAN. Anon, anon, sir.

PRINCE. Five year! by'r lady, a long lease for the
clinking of pewter. But, Francis, darest thou be so valiant
as to play the coward with thy indenture and show it a $_{45}$
fair pair of heels and run from it?

FRAN. O Lord, sir, I'll be sworn upon all the books in
England, I could find in my heart.

POINS. *(Within) Francis!*

FRAN. Anon, sir. $_{50}$

PRINCE. How old art thou, Francis?

FRAN. Let me see—about Michaelmas next I shall be—

POINS. *(Within) Francis!*

FRAN. Anon, sir. Pray stay a little, my lord.

PRINCE. Nay, but hark you, Francis: for the sugar $_{55}$
thou gavest me, 'twas a pennyworth, was't not?

FRAN. O Lord, I would it had been two!

PRINCE. I will give thee for it a thousand pound: ask
me when thou wilt, and thou shalt have it.
POINS. *(Within)* Francis! 60
FRAN. Anon, anon.
PRINCE. Anon, Francis? No, Francis; but to-morrow,
Francis; or Francis, o' Thursday; or indeed, Francis,
when thou wilt. But, Francis!
FRAN. My lord? 65
PRINCE. Wilt thou rob this leathern jerkin, crystal-button,
not-pated, agate-ring, puke-stocking, caddis-garter,
smooth-tongue, Spanish-pouch,—
FRAN. O lord, sir, who do you mean?
PRINCE. Why, then, your brown bastard is your only 70
drink; for look you, Francis, your white canvas doublet
will sully: in Barbary, sir, it cannot come to so much.
FRAN. What, sir?
POINS. *(Within)* Francis!
PRINCE. Away, you rogue! dost thou not hear them 75
call?
*(Here they both call him; the drawer stands amazed, not knowing which
way to go.)*
(Enter Vintner.)
VINT. What, standest thou still, and hearest such a
calling? Look to the guests within. *(Exit Francis.)* My
lord, old Sir John, with half-a-dozen more, are at the door:
shall I let them in? 80
PRINCE. Let them alone awhile, and then open the
door. *(Exit Vintner.)* Poins!
(Re-enter POINS.)
POINS. Anon, anon, sir.
PRINCE. Sirrah, Falstaff and the rest of the thieves are
at the door: shall we be merry? 85
POINS. As merry as crickets, my lad. But hark ye;
what cunning match have you made with this jest of the
drawer? come, what's the issue?
PRINCE. I am now of all humours that have showed
themselves humours since the old days of goodman Adam 90
to the pupil age of this present twelve o'clock at midnight.
(Re-enter FRANCIS.)

What's o'clock, Francis?

FRAN. Anon, anon, sir. *(Exit.)*

PRINCE. That ever this fellow should have fewer
words than a parrot, and yet the son of a woman! His
     industry[95]
is up-stairs and down-stairs; his eloquence the
parcel of a reckoning. I am not yet of Percy's mind, the
Hotspur of the north; he that kills me some six or seven
dozen of Scots at a breakfast, washes his hands, and says
to his wife 'Fie upon this quiet life! I want work.' 'O[100]
my sweet Harry,' says she, 'how many hast thou killed to-day?'
'Give my roan horse a drench,' says he; and answers
'Some fourteen,' an hour after; 'a trifle, a trifle.' I
prithee, call in Falstaff: I'll play Percy, and that damned
brawn shall play Dame Mortimer his wife. 'Rivo!' says[105]
the drunkard. Call in ribs, call in tallow.

*(ENTER FALSTAFF, GADSHILL, BARDOLPH, AND PETO; FRANCIS
     FOLLOWING WITH WINE.)*

POINS. Welcome, Jack: where hast thou been?

FAL. A plague of all cowards, I say, and a vengeance
too! marry, and amen! Give me a cup of sack, boy.
Ere I lead this life long, I'll sew nether stocks and mend[110]
them and foot them too. A plague of all cowards! Give
me a cup of sack, rogue. Is there no virtue extant? *(He drinks.)*

PRINCE. Didst thou never see Titan kiss a dish of
butter? pitiful-hearted Titan, that melted at the sweet tale
of the sun's! if thou didst, then behold that compound.[115]

FAL. You rogue, here's lime in this sack too: there is
nothing but roguery to be found in villanous man: yet
a coward is worse than a cup of sack with lime in it. A
villanous coward! Go thy ways, old Jack; die when thou
wilt, if manhood, good manhood, be not forgot upon the[120]
face of the earth, then am I a shotten herring. There live
not three good men unhanged in England; and one of
them is fat, and grows old: God help the while! a bad
world, I say. I would I were a weaver; I could sing
psalms or any thing. A plague of all cowards, I say still.[125]

PRINCE. How now, wool-sack! what mutter you?

FAL. A king's son! If I do not beat thee out of thy

kingdom with a dagger of lath, and drive all thy subjects
afore thee like a flock of wild-geese, I'll never wear hair on
my face more. You Prince of Wales!$_{130}$

PRINCE. Why, you whoreson round man, what's the
matter?

FAL. Are not you a coward? answer me to that: and
Poins there?

POINS. 'Zounds, ye fat paunch, an ye call me coward,$_{135}$
by the Lord, I'll stab thee.

FAL. I call thee coward! I'll see thee damned ere I
call thee coward: but I would give a thousand pound I
could run as fast as thou canst. You are straight enough
in the shoulders, you care not who sees your back: call you$_{140}$
that backing of your friends? A plague upon such backing!
give me them that will face me. Give me a cup of
sack: I am a rogue, if I drunk to-day.

PRINCE. O villain! thy lips are scarce wiped since thou
drunkest last.$_{145}$

FAL. All's one for that. *(He drinks.)* A plague of all
cowards, still say I.

PRINCE. What's the matter?

FAL. What's the matter! there be four of us here have
ta'en a thousand pound this day morning.$_{150}$

PRINCE. Where is it, Jack? where is it?

FAL. Where is it! taken from us it is: a hundred upon
poor four of us.

PRINCE. What, a hundred, man?

FAL. I am a rogue, if I were not at half-sword with a$_{155}$
dozen of them two hours together. I have 'scaped by miracle.
I am eight times thrust through the doublet, four
through the hose; my buckler cut through and through;
my sword hacked like a hand-saw—ecce signum! I never
dealt better since I was a man: all would not do. A$_{160}$
plague of all cowards! Let them speak: if they speak
more or less than truth, they are villains and the sons of
darkness.

PRINCE. Speak, sirs; how was it?

GADS. We four set upon some dozen—$_{165}$

FAL. Sixteen at least, my lord.

GADS. And bound them.

PETO. No, no, they were not bound.

FAL. You rogue, they were bound, every man of them; or I am a Jew else, an Ebrew Jew.[170]

GADS. As we were sharing, some six or seven fresh men set upon us—

FAL. And unbound the rest, and then come in the other.

PRINCE. What, fought you with them all?[175]

FAL. All! I know not what you call all; but if I fought not with fifty of them, I am a bunch of radish: if there were not two or three and fifty upon poor old Jack, then am I no two-legged creature.

PRINCE. Pray God you have not murdered some of[180] them.

FAL. Nay, that's past praying for: I have peppered two of them; two I am sure I have paid, two rogues in buckram suits. I tell thee what, Hal, if I tell thee a lie, spit in my face, call me horse. Thou knowest my old[185] ward; here I lay, and thus I bore my point. Four rogues in buckram let drive at me—

PRINCE. What, four? thou saidst but two even now.

FAL. Four, Hal; I told thee four.

POINS. Ay, ay, he said four.[190]

FAL. These four came all a-front, and mainly thrust at me. I made me no more ado but took all their seven points in my target, thus.

PRINCE. Seven? why, there were but four even now.

FAL. In buckram?[195]

POINS. Ay, four, in buckram suits.

FAL. Seven, by these hilts, or I am a villain else.

PRINCE. Prithee, let him alone; we shall have more anon.

FAL. Dost thou hear me, Hal?[200]

PRINCE. Ay, and mark thee too, Jack.

FAL. Do so, for it is worth the listening to. These nine in buckram that I told thee of—

PRINCE. So, two more already.

FAL. Their points being broken,—[205]

POINS. Down fell their hose.

FAL. Began to give me ground: but I followed me
close, came in foot and hand; and with a thought seven of
the eleven I paid.

PRINCE. O monstrous! eleven buckram men grown out$_{210}$
of two!

FAL. But, as the devil would have it, three misbegotten
knaves in Kendal green came at my back and let drive at
me; for it was so dark, Hal, that thou couldst not see thy
hand.$_{215}$

PRINCE. These lies are like their father that begets
them; gross as a mountain, open, palpable. Why, thou
clay-brained guts, thou knotty-pated fool, thou whoreson,
obscene, greasy tallow-catch,—

FAL. What, art thou mad? art thou mad? is not the$_{220}$
truth the truth?

PRINCE. Why, how couldst thou know these men in
Kendal green, when it was so dark thou couldst not see
thy hand? come, tell us your reason: what sayest thou to
this?$_{225}$

POINS. Come, your reason, Jack, your reason.

FAL. What, upon compulsion? 'Zounds, an I were at
the strappado, or all the racks in the world, I would not
tell you on compulsion. Give you a reason on compulsion!
if reasons were as plentiful as blackberries, I would give no$_{230}$
man a reason upon compulsion, I.

PRINCE. I'll be no longer guilty of this sin; this sanguine
coward, this bed-presser, this horse-back-breaker,
this huge hill of flesh,—

FAL. 'Sblood, you starveling, you elf-skin, you dried$_{235}$
neat's tongue, you bull's pizzle, you stock-fish! O for
breath to utter what is like thee! you tailor's-yard, you
sheath, you bow-case, you vile standing-tuck,—

PRINCE. Well, breathe awhile, and then to it again:
and when thou hast tired thyself in base comparisons, hear$_{240}$
me speak but this.

POINS. Mark, Jack.

PRINCE. We two saw you four set on four and bound
them, and were masters of their wealth. Mark now, how

a plain tale shall put you down. Then did we two set on[245]
you four; and, with a word, out-faced you from your prize,
and have it; yea, and can show it you here in the house:
and, Falstaff, you carried your guts away as nimbly, with
as quick dexterity, and roared for mercy and still run and
roared, as ever I heard bull-calf. What a slave art thou, to[250]
hack thy sword as thou hast done, and then say it was in
fight! What trick, what device, what starting-hole, canst
thou now find out to hide thee from this open and apparent
shame?

POINS. Come, let's hear, Jack; what trick hast thou[255]
now?

FAL. By the Lord, I knew ye as well as he that made
ye. Why, hear you, my masters: was it for me to kill the
heir-apparent? should I turn upon the true prince? why,
thou knowest I am as valiant as Hercules: but beware
 instinct;[260]
the lion will not touch the true prince. Instinct is
a great matter; I was now a coward on instinct. I shall
think the better of myself and thee during my life; I for
a valiant lion, and thou for a true prince. But, by the
Lord, lads, I am glad you have the money. Hostess, clap[265]
to the doors: watch to-night, pray to-morrow. Gallants,
lads, boys, hearts of gold, all the titles of good fellowship
come to you! What, shall we be merry? shall we have a
play extempore?

PRINCE. Content; and the argument shall be thy[270]
running away.

FAL. Ah, no more of that, Hal, an thou lovest me!
(Enter Hostess.)

HOST. O Jesu, my lord the prince!

PRINCE. How now, my lady the hostess! what sayest
thou to me?[275]

HOST. Marry, my lord, there is a nobleman of the
court at door would speak with you: he says he comes
from your father.

PRINCE. Give him as much as will make him a royal
man, and send him back again to my mother.[280]

FAL. What manner of man is he?

HOST. An old man.

FAL. What doth gravity out of his bed at midnight?
Shall I give him his answer?

PRINCE. Prithee, do, Jack.₂₈₅

FAL. 'Faith, and I'll send him packing. *(Exit.)*

PRINCE. Now, sirs: by'r lady, you fought fair; so did
you, Peto; so did you, Bardolph: you are lions too, you
ran away upon instinct, you will not touch the true prince;
no, fie!₂₉₀

BARD. Faith, I ran when I saw others run.

PRINCE. Faith, tell me now in earnest, how came Falstaff's
sword so hacked?

PETO. Why, he hacked it with his dagger, and said he
would swear truth out of England but he would make you₂₉₅
believe it was done in fight, and persuaded us to do the like.

BARD. Yea, and to tickle our noses with spear-grass to
make them bleed, and then to beslubber our garments
with it and swear it was the blood of true men. I did
that I did not this seven year before, I blushed to hear his₃₀₀
monstrous devices.

PRINCE. O villain, thou stolest a cup of sack eighteen
years ago, and wert taken with the manner, and ever since
thou hast blushed extempore. Thou hadst fire and sword
on thy side, and yet thou rannest away: what instinct₃₀₅
hadst thou for it?

BARD. My lord, do you see these meteors? do you
behold these exhalations?

PRINCE. *I do.*

BARD. What think you they portend?₃₁₀

PRINCE. Hot livers and cold purses.

BARD. Choler, my lord, if rightly taken.

PRINCE. No, if rightly taken, halter.

(Re-enter FALSTAFF.)

Here comes lean Jack, here comes bare-bone. How now,
my sweet creature of bombast! How long is't ago, Jack,₃₁₅
since thou sawest thine own knee?

FAL. My own knee! when I was about thy years, Hal,
I was not an eagle's talon in the waist; I could have crept
into any alderman's thumb-ring: a plague of sighing and

grief! it blows a man up like a bladder. There's villanous [320]
news abroad: here was Sir John Bracy from your father;
you must to the court in the morning. That same mad
fellow of the north, Percy, and he of Wales, that gave
Amamon the bastinado and made Lucifer cuckold and
swore the devil his true liegeman upon the cross of a Welsh [325]
hook—what a plague call you him?

POINS. O, Glendower.

FAL. Owen, Owen, the same; and his son-in-law Mortimer,
and old Northumberland, and that sprightly Scot
of Scots, Douglas, that runs o' horseback up a hill [330]
perpendicular,—

PRINCE. He that rides at high speed and with his
pistol kills a sparrow flying.

FAL. You have hit it.

PRINCE. So did he never the sparrow. [335]

FAL. Well, that rascal hath good mettle in him; he
will not run.

PRINCE. Why, what a rascal art thou then, to praise
him so for running!

FAL. O' horseback, ye cuckoo; but afoot he will not [340]
budge a foot.

PRINCE. Yes, Jack, upon instinct.

FAL. I grant ye, upon instinct. Well, he is there too,
and one Mordake, and a thousand blue-caps more: Worcester
is stolen away to-night; thy father's beard is turned [345]
white with the news: you may buy land now as cheap as
stinking mackerel.

PRINCE. Why, then, it is like, if there come a hot
June and this civil buffeting hold, we shall buy maidenheads
as they buy hob-nails, by the hundreds. [350]

FAL. By the mass, lad, thou sayest true; it is like we
shall have good trading that way. But tell me, Hal, art not
thou horrible afeard? thou being heir-apparent, could the
world pick thee out three such enemies again as that fiend
Douglas, that spirit Percy, and that devil Glendower? art [355]
thou not horribly afraid? doth not thy blood thrill at it?

PRINCE. Not a whit, i' faith; I lack some of thy instinct.

FAL. Well, thou wilt be horribly chid to-morrow when

thou comest to thy father: if thou love me, practise an
answer.360
PRINCE. Do thou stand for my father, and examine
me upon the particulars of my life.
FAL. Shall I? content: this chair shall be my state,
this dagger my sceptre, and this cushion my crown.
PRINCE. Thy state is taken for a joined-stool, thy365
golden sceptre for a leaden dagger, and thy precious rich
crown for a pitiful bald crown!
FAL. Well, an the fire of grace be not quite out of
thee, now shalt thou be moved. Give me a cup of sack to
make my eyes look red, that it may be thought I have370
wept; for I must speak in passion, and I will do it in King
Cambyses' vein.
PRINCE. Well, here is my leg.
FAL. And here is my speech. Stand aside, nobility.
HOST. O Jesu, this is excellent sport, i' faith!375
FAL. Weep not, sweet queen; for trickling tears are vain.
HOST. O, the father, how he holds his countenance!
FAL. For God's sake, lords, convey my tristful queen;
For tears do stop the flood-gates of her eyes.
HOST. O Jesu, he doth it as like one of these harlotry380
players as ever I see!
FAL. Peace, good pint-pot; peace, good tickle-brain.
Harry, I do not only marvel where thou spendest thy time,
but also how thou art accompanied: for though the camomile,
the more it is trodden on the faster it grows, yet385
youth, the more it is wasted the sooner it wears. That thou
art my son, I have partly thy mother's word, partly my
own opinion, but chiefly a villanous trick of thine eye and
a foolish hanging of thy nether lip, that doth warrant me.
If then thou be son to me, here lies the point; why, being390
son to me, art thou so pointed at? Shall the blessed sun
of heaven prove a micher and eat blackberries? a question
not to be asked. Shall the son of England prove a thief
and take purses? a question to be asked. There is a thing,
Harry, which thou hast often heard of and it is known to395
many in our land by the name of pitch: this pitch, as ancient
writers do report, doth defile; so doth the company thou

keepest: for, Harry, now I do not speak to thee in drink
but in tears, not in pleasure but in passion, not in words
only, but in woes also: and yet there is a virtuous man$_{400}$
whom I have often noted in thy company, but I know not
his name.

PRINCE. What manner of man, an it like your majesty?

FAL. A goodly portly man, i' faith, and a corpulent; of
a cheerful look, a pleasing eye and a most noble carriage;$_{405}$
and, as I think, his age some fifty, or, by'r lady, inclining to
three score; and now I remember me, his name is Falstaff:
if that man should be lewdly given, he deceiveth me; for,
Harry, I see virtue in his looks. If then the tree may be
known by the fruit, as the fruit by the tree, then,$_{410}$
peremptorily I speak it, there is virtue in that Falstaff: him keep
with, the rest banish. And tell me now, thou naughty
varlet, tell me, where hast thou been this month?

PRINCE. Dost thou speak like a king? Do thou stand
for me, and I'll play my father.$_{415}$

FAL. Depose me? if thou dost it half so gravely, so
majestically, both in word and matter, hang me up by the
heels for a rabbit-sucker or a poulter's hare.

PRINCE. Well, here I am set.

FAL. And here I stand: judge, my masters.$_{420}$

PRINCE. Now, Harry, whence come you?

FAL. My noble lord, from Eastcheap.

PRINCE. The complaints I hear of thee are grievous.

FAL. 'Sblood, my lord, they are false: nay, I'll tickle ye
for a young prince, i' faith.$_{425}$

PRINCE. Swearest thou, ungracious boy? henceforth
ne'er look on me. Thou art violently carried away from
grace: there is a devil haunts thee in the likeness of an old
fat man; a tun of man is thy companion. Why dost thou
converse with that trunk of humours, that bolting-hutch of$_{430}$
beastliness, that swollen parcel of dropsies, that huge bombard
of sack, that stuffed cloak-bag of guts, that roasted
Manningtree ox with the pudding in his belly, that
reverend vice, that grey iniquity, that father ruffian, that
vanity in years? Wherein is he good, but to taste sack$_{435}$
and drink it? wherein neat and cleanly, but to carve a capon

and eat it? wherein cunning, but in craft? wherein crafty,
but in villany? wherein villanous, but in all things? wherein
worthy, but in nothing?

FAL. I would your grace would take me with you:₄₄₀
whom means your grace?

PRINCE. That villanous abominable misleader of youth,
Falstaff, that old white-bearded Satan.

FAL. My lord, the man I know.

PRINCE. I know thou dost.₄₄₅

FAL. But to say I know more harm in him than in myself,
were to say more than I know. That he is old, the
more the pity, his white hairs do witness it; but that he is,
saving your reverence, a whoremaster, that I utterly deny.
If sack and sugar be a fault, God help the wicked! if to be₄₅₀
old and merry be a sin, then many an old host that I know
is damned: if to be fat be to be hated, then Pharaoh's lean
kine are to be loved. No, my good lord; banish Peto,
banish Bardolph, banish Poins: but for sweet Jack Falstaff,
kind Jack Falstaff, true Jack Falstaff, valiant Jack Falstaff,₄₅₅
and therefore more valiant, being, as he is, old Jack Falstaff,
banish not him thy Harry's company, banish not him
thy Harry's company: banish plump Jack, and banish all
the world.

PRINCE. I do, I will. (*A knocking-heard.*)₄₆₀
(*Exeunt Hostess, Francis, and Bardolph.*)
(*Re-enter BARDOLPH, running.*)

BARD. O, my lord, my lord! the sheriff with a most
monstrous watch is at the door.

FAL. Out, ye rogue! Play out the play: I have much
to say in the behalf of that Falstaff.
(*Re-enter the Hostess.*)

HOST. O Jesu, my lord, my lord!—₄₆₅

PRINCE. Heigh, heigh! the devil rides upon a
fiddlestick: what's the matter?

HOST. The sheriff and all the watch are at the door:
they are come to search the house. Shall I let them in?

FAL. Dost thou hear, Hal? never call a true piece of gold₄₇₀
a counterfeit: thou art essentially mad, without seeming so.

PRINCE. And thou a natural coward, without instinct.

FAL. I deny your major: if you will deny the sheriff, so;
if not, let him enter: if I become not a cart as well as another
man, a plague on my bringing up! I hope I shall as$_{475}$
soon be strangled with a halter as another.

PRINCE. Go, hide thee behind the arras: the rest walk
up above. Now, my masters, for a true face and good
conscience.

FAL. Both which I have had: but their date is out, and$_{480}$
therefore I'll hide me.

PRINCE. Call in the sheriff.

(Exeunt all except the Prince and Peto.)
(Enter Sheriff and the Carrier.)

Now, master sheriff, what is your will with me?

SHER. First, pardon me, my lord. A hue and cry
Hath follow'd certain men unto this house.$_{485}$

PRINCE. What men?

SHER. One of them is well known, my gracious lord,
A gross fat man.

CAR. As fat as butter.

PRINCE. The man, I do assure you, is not here;
For I myself at this time have employ'd him.$_{490}$
And, sheriff, I will engage my word to thee
That I will, by to-morrow dinner-time,
Send him to answer thee, or any man,
For any thing he shall be charged withal:
And so let me entreat you leave the house.$_{495}$

SHER. I will, my lord. There are two gentlemen
Have in this robbery lost three hundred marks.

PRINCE. It may be so: if he have robb'd these men,
He shall be answerable; and so farewell.

SHER. Good night, my noble lord.$_{500}$

PRINCE. I think it is good morrow, is it not?

SHER. Indeed, my lord, I think it be two o'clock.

(Exeunt Sheriff and Carrier.)

PRINCE. This oily rascal is known as well as Paul's.
Go, call him forth.

PETO. Falstaff!—Fast asleep behind the arras, and$_{505}$
snorting like a horse.

PRINCE. Hark, how hard he fetches breath. Search

his pockets. (He searcheth his pockets, and findeth certain
papers.) What hast thou found?
PETO. Nothing but papers, my lord. 510
PRINCE. Let's see what they be: read them.
PETO. *(reads)* Item, A capon, 2s. 2d.
Item, Sauce, 4d.
Item, Sack, two gallons, 5s. 8d.
Item, Anchovies and sack after supper, 2s. 6d. 515
Item, Bread, ob.
PRINCE. O monstrous! but one half-pennyworth of bread
to this intolerable deal of sack! What there is else, keep
close; we'll read it at more advantage: there let him sleep
till day. I'll to the court in the morning. We must all to 520
the wars, and thy place shall be honourable. I'll procure
this fat rogue a charge of foot; and I know his death will
be a march of twelve-score. The money shall be paid back
again with advantage. Be with me betimes in the morning;
and so, good morrow, Peto. *(Exeunt.)* 525
PETO. Good morrow, good my lord.

ACT III

(Enter Hotspur, Worcester, Mortimer, and Glendower.)

Mort. These promises are fair, the parties sure,
And our induction full of prosperous hope.
Hot. Lord Mortimer, and cousin Glendower,
Will you sit down?
And uncle Worcester: a plague upon it!₅
I have forgot the map.
Glend. No, here it is.
Sit, cousin Percy; sit, good cousin Hotspur,
For by that name as oft as Lancaster
Doth speak of you, his cheek looks pale and with
A rising sigh he wisheth you in heaven.₁₀
Hot. And you in hell, as oft as lie hears Owen
Glendower spoke of.
Glend. I cannot blame him: at my nativity
The front of heaven was full of fiery shapes,
Of burning cressets; and at my birth₁₅
The frame and huge foundation of the earth
Shaked like a coward.

Hot. Why, so it would have done at the same season,
if your mother's cat had but kittened, though yourself had
never been born.$_{20}$
Glend. I say the earth did shake when I was born.
Hot. And I say the earth was not of my mind,
If you suppose as fearing you it shook.
Glend. The heavens were all on fire, the earth did tremble.
Hot. O, then the earth shook to see the heavens on fire,$_{25}$
And not in fear of your nativity.
Diseased nature oftentimes breaks forth
In strange eruptions; oft the teeming earth
Is with a kind of colic pinch'd and vex'd
By the imprisoning of unruly wind$_{30}$
Within her womb; which, for enlargement striving,
Shakes the old beldam earth and topples down
Steeples and moss-grown towers. At your birth
Our grandam earth, having this distemperature,
In passion shook.
Glend. Cousin, of many men$_{35}$
I do not bear these crossings. Give me leave
To tell you once again that at my birth
The front of heaven was full of fiery shapes,
The goats ran from the mountains, and the herds
Were strangely clamorous to the frighted fields.$_{40}$
These signs have mark'd me extraordinary;
And all the courses of my life do show
I am not in the roll of common men.
Where is he living, clipp'd in with the sea
That chides the banks of England, Scotland, Wales,$_{45}$
Which calls me pupil, or hath read to me?
And bring him out that is but woman's son
Can trace me in the tedious ways of art
And hold me pace in deep experiments.
Hot. I think there's no man speaks better Welsh.$_{50}$
I'll to dinner.
Mort. Peace, cousin Percy; you will make him mad.
Glend. I can call spirits from the vasty deep.
Hot. Why, so can I, or so can any man;
But will they come when you do call for them?$_{55}$

GLEND. Why, I can teach you, cousin, to command
The devil.
HOT. And I can teach thee, coz, to shame the devil
By telling truth: tell truth, and shame the devil.
If thou have power to raise him, bring him hither,$_{60}$
And I 'll be sworn I have power to shame him hence.
O, while you live, tell truth, and shame the devil!
MORT. Come, come, no more of this unprofitable chat.
GLEND. Three times hath Henry Bolingbroke made head
Against my power; thrice from the banks of Wye$_{65}$
And sandy-bottom'd Severn have I sent him
Bootless home and weather-beaten back.
HOT. Home without boots, and in foul weather too!
How 'scapes he agues, in the devil's name?
GLEND. Come, here's the map: shall we divide our right$_{70}$
According to our threefold order ta'en?
MORT. The archdeacon hath divided it
Into three limits very equally:
England, from Trent and Severn hitherto,
By south and east is to my part assign'd:$_{75}$
All westward, Wales beyond the Severn shore.
And all the fertile land within that bound.
To Owen Glendower: and, dear coz, to you
The remnant northward, lying off from Trent.
And our indentures tripartite are drawn;$_{80}$
Which being sealed interchangeably,
A business that this night may execute,
To-morrow, cousin Percy, you and I
And my good Lord of Worcester will set forth
To meet your father and the Scottish power,$_{85}$
As is appointed us, at Shrewsbury.
My father Glendower is not ready yet,
Nor shall we need his help these fourteen days.
Within that space you may have drawn together
Your tenants, friends, and neighbouring gentlemen.$_{90}$
GLEND. A shorter time shall send me to you, lords:
And in my conduct shall your ladies come;
From whom you now must steal and take no leave,
For there will be a world of water shed

Upon the parting of your wives and you.$_{95}$
HOT. Methinks my moiety, north from Burton here,
In quantity equals not one of yours:
See how this river comes me cranking in,
And cuts me from the best of all my land
A huge half-moon, a monstrous cantle out.$_{100}$
I'll have the current in this place damm'd up;
And here the smug and silver Trent shall run
In a new channel, fair and evenly;
It shall not wind with such a deep indent,
To rob me of so rich a bottom here.$_{105}$
GLEND. Not wind? it shall, it must; you see it doth.
MORT. Yea, but
Mark how he bears his course, and runs me up
With like advantage on the other side;
Gelding the opposed continent as much$_{110}$
As on the other side it takes from you.
WOR. Yea, but a little charge will trench him here
And on this north side win this cape of land;
And then he runs straight and even.
HOT. I'll have it so: a little charge will do it.$_{115}$
GLEND. I'll not have it alter'd.
HOT. Will not you?
GLEND. No, nor you shall not.
HOT. Who shall say me nay?
GLEND. Why, that will I.
HOT. Let me not understand you, then; speak it in
Welsh.$_{120}$
GLEND. I can speak English, lord, as well as you;
For I was train'd up in the English court;
Where, being but young, I framed to the harp
Many an English ditty lovely well
And gave the tongue a helpful ornament,$_{125}$
A virtue that was never seen in you.
HOT. Marry,
And I am glad of it with all my heart:
I had rather be a kitten and cry mew
Than one of these same metre ballad-mongers;$_{130}$
I had rather hear a brazen canstick turn'd,

Or a dry wheel grate on the axle-tree;
And that would set my teeth nothing on edge,
Nothing so much as mincing poetry:
'Tis like the forced gait of a shuffling nag. 135
GLEND. Come, you shall have Trent turn'd.
HOT. I do not care: I'll give thrice so much land
To any well-deserving friend;
But in the way of bargain, mark ye me,
I'll cavil on the ninth part of a hair. 140
Are the indentures drawn? shall we be gone?
GLEND. The moon shines fair; you may away by night:
I'll haste the writer, and withal
Break with your wives of your departure hence:
I am afraid my daughter will run mad, 145
So much she doteth on her Mortimer. *(Exit.)*
MORT. Fie, cousin Percy! how you cross my father!
HOT. I cannot choose: sometime he angers me
With telling me of the moldwarp and the ant,
Of the dreamer Merlin and his prophecies, 150
And of a dragon and a finless fish,
A clip-wing'd griffin and a moulten raven,
A couching lion and a ramping cat,
And such a deal of skimble-skamble stuff
As puts me from my faith. I tell you what,— 155
He held me last night at least nine hours
In reckoning up the several devils' names
That were his lackeys: I cried 'hum,' and 'well, go to,'
But mark'd him not a word. O, he is as tedious
As a tired horse, a railing wife; 160
Worse than a smoky house: I had rather live
With cheese and garlic in a windmill, far,
Than feed on cates and have him talk to me
In any summer-house in Christendom.
MORT. In faith, he is a worthy gentleman, 165
Exceedingly well read, and profited
In strange concealments, valiant as a lion
And wondrous affable and as bountiful
As mines of India. Shall I tell you, cousin?
He holds your temper in a high respect 170

And curbs himself even of his natural scope
When you come 'cross his humour; faith, he does:
I warrant you, that man is not alive
Might so have tempted him as you have done,
Without the taste of danger and reproof: 175
But do not use it oft, let me entreat you.
WOR. In faith, my lord, you are too wilful-blame;
And since your coming hither have done enough
To put him quite beside his patience.
You must needs learn, lord, to amend this fault: 180
Though sometimes it show greatness, courage, blood,—
And that's the dearest grace it renders you,—
Yet oftentimes it doth present harsh rage,
Defect of manners, want of government,
Pride, haughtiness, opinion and disdain: 185
The least of which haunting a nobleman
Loseth men's hearts and leaves behind a stain
Upon the beauty of all parts besides,
Beguiling them of commendation.
HOT. Well, I am school'd: good manners be your speed! 190
Here come our wives, and let us take our leave.
(Re-enter GLENDOWER with the ladies.)
MORT. This is the deadly spite that angers me;
My wife can speak no English, I no Welsh.
GLEND. My daughter weeps: she will not part with you;
She'll be a soldier too, she'll to the wars. 195
MORT. Good father, tell her that she and my aunt Percy
Shall follow in your conduct speedily.
one that no persuasion can do good upon.
(The lady speaks in Welsh.)
MORT. I understand thy looks: that pretty Welsh 200
Which thou pour'st down from these swelling heavens
I am too perfect in; and, but for shame,
In such a parley should I answer thee.
(The lady speaks again in Welsh.)
I understand thy kisses and thou mine,
And that's a feeling disputation: 205
But I will never be a truant, love,
Till I have learn'd thy language; for thy tongue

Makes Welsh as sweet as ditties highly penn'd,
Sung by a fair queen in a summer's bower,
With ravishing division, to her lute.$_{210}$
GLEND. Nay, if you melt, then will she run mad.
(The lady speaks again in Welsh.)
MORT. O, I am ignorance itself in this!
GLEND. She bids you on the wanton rushes lay you down
And rest your gentle head upon her lap,
And she will sing the song that pleaseth you$_{215}$
And on your eyelids crown the god of sleep,
Charming your blood with pleasing heaviness,
Making such difference 'twixt wake and sleep
As is the difference betwixt day and night
The hour before the heavenly-harness'd team$_{220}$
Begins his golden progress in the east.
MORT. With all my heart I'll sit and hear her sing:
By that time will our book, I think, be drawn.
GLEND. Do so;
And those musicians that shall play to you$_{225}$
Hang in the air a thousand leagues from hence,
And straight they shall be here: sit, and attend.
HOT. Come, Kate, thou art perfect in lying down:
come, quick, quick, that I may lay my head in thy lap.
LADY P. Go, ye giddy goose.$_{230}$
(The music plays.)
HOT. Now I perceive the devil understands Welsh;
And 'tis no marvel he is so humorous.
By'r lady, he is a good musician.
LADY P. Then should you be nothing but musical, for
you are altogether governed by humours. Lie still, ye$_{235}$
thief, and hear the lady sing in Welsh.
HOT. I had rather hear Lady, my brach, howl in Irish.
LADY P. Wouldst thou have thy head broken?
HOT. *No.*
LADY P. Then be still.$_{240}$
HOT. Neither; 'tis a woman's fault.
LADY P. Now God help thee!
HOT. To the Welsh lady's bed.
LADY P. What's that?

HOT. Peace! she sings.$_{245}$
(Here the lady sings a Welsh song.)
HOT. Come, Kate, I'll have your song too.
LADY P. Not mine, in good sooth.
HOT. Not yours, in good sooth! Heart! you swear
like a comfit-maker's wife. 'Not you, in good sooth,' and
'as true as I live,' and 'as God shall mend me,' and 'as$_{250}$
sure as day,'
And givest such sarcenet surety for thy oaths,
As if thou never walk'st further than Finsbury.
Swear me, Kate, like a lady as thou art,
A good mouth-filling oath, and leave 'in sooth,'$_{255}$
And such protest of pepper-gingerbread,
To velvet-guards and Sunday-citizens.
Come, sing.
LADY P. I will not sing.
HOT. 'Tis the next way to turn tailor, or be red-breast$_{260}$
teacher. An the indentures be drawn, I'll away within these
two hours; and so, come in when ye will. *(Exit.)*
GLEND. Come, come, Lord Mortimer; you are as slow
As hot Lord Percy is on fire to go.
By this our book is drawn; we'll but seal,$_{265}$
And then to horse immediately.
MORT. With all my heart. *(Exeunt.)*

SCENE II. LONDON. THE PALACE

(Enter the KING, PRINCE of WALES, and others.)

KING. Lords, give us leave; the Prince of Wales and I
Must have some private conference: but be near at hand,
For we shall presently have need of you. *(Exeunt Lords.)*
I know not whether God will have it so,
For some displeasing service I have done,$_5$
That, in his secret doom, out of my blood
He'll breed revengement and a scourge for me;
But thou dost in thy passages of life
Make me believe that thou art only mark'd

For the hot vengeance and the rod of heaven$_{10}$
To punish my mistreadings. Tell me else,
Could such inordinate and low desires,
Such poor, such bare, such lewd, such mean attempts,
Such barren pleasures, rude society,
As thou art match'd withal and grafted to,$_{15}$
Accompany the greatness of thy blood
And hold their level with thy princely heart?
PRINCE. So please your majesty, I would I could
Quit all offences with as clear excuse
As well as I am doubtless I can purge$_{20}$
Myself of many I am charged withal:
Yet such extenuation let me beg,
As, in reproof of many tales devised,
Which oft the ear of greatness needs must hear,
By smiling pick-thanks and base newsmongers,$_{25}$
I may, for some things true, wherein my youth
Hath faulty wander'd and irregular,
Find pardon on my true submission.
KING. God pardon thee! yet let me wonder, Harry,
At thy affections, which do hold a wing$_{30}$
Quite from the flight of all thy ancestors.
Thy place in council thou hast rudely lost,
Which by thy younger brother is supplied,
And art almost an alien to the hearts
Of all the court and princes of my blood:$_{35}$
The hope and expectation of thy time
Is ruin'd, and the soul of every man
Prophetically do forethink thy fall.
Had I so lavish of my presence been,
So common-hackney'd in the eyes of men,$_{40}$
So stale and cheap to vulgar company,
Opinion, that did help me to the crown,
Had still kept loyal to possession
And left me in reputeless banishment,
A fellow of no mark nor likelihood.$_{45}$
By being seldom seen, I could not stir
But like a comet I was wonder'd at;
That men would tell their children 'This is he;'

Others would say 'Where, which is Bolingbroke?'
And then I stole all courtesy from heaven, $_{50}$
And dress'd myself in such humility
That I did pluck allegiance from men's hearts,
Loud shouts and salutations from their mouths,
Even in the presence of the crowned king.
Thus did I keep my person fresh and new; $_{55}$
My presence, like a robe pontifical,
Ne'er seen but wonder'd at: and so my state,
Seldom but sumptuous, showed like a feast
And wan by rareness such solemnity.
The skipping king, he ambled up and down $_{60}$
With shallow jesters and rash bavin wits,
Soon kindled and soon burnt; carded his state,
Mingled his royalty with capering fools,
Had his great name profaned with their scorns
And gave his countenance, against his name, $_{65}$
To laugh at gibing boys and stand the push
Of every beardless vain comparative,
Grew a companion to the common streets,
Enfeoff'd himself to popularity;
That, being daily swallow'd by men's eyes, $_{70}$
They surfeited with honey and began
To loathe the taste of sweetness, whereof a little
More than a little is by much too much.
So when he had occasion to be seen,
He was but as the cuckoo is in June, $_{75}$
Heard, not regarded; seen, but with such eyes
As, sick and blunted with community,
Afford no extraordinary gaze,
Such as is bent on sun-like majesty
When it shines seldom in admiring eyes; $_{80}$
But rather drowzed and hung their eyelids down,
Slept in his face and render'd such aspect
As cloudy men use to their adversaries,
Being with his presence glutted, gorged and full.
And in that very line, Harry, standest thou; $_{85}$
For thou hast lost thy princely privilege
With vile participation: not an eye

But is a-weary of thy common sight,
Save mine, which hath desired to see thee more;
Which now doth that I would not have it do, 90
Make blind itself with foolish tenderness.
PRINCE. I shall hereafter, my thrice gracious lord,
Be more myself.
KING. For all the world
As thou art to this hour was Richard then
When I from France set foot at Ravenspurgh, 95
And even as I was then is Percy now.
Now, by my sceptre and my soul to boot,
He hath more worthy interest to the state
Than thou the shadow of succession;
For of no right, nor colour like to right, 100
He doth fill fields with harness in the realm,
Turns head against the lion's armed jaws,
And, being no more in debt to years than thou,
Leads ancient lords and reverend bishops on
To bloody battles and to bruising arms. 105
What never-dying honour hath he got
Against renowned Douglas! whose high deeds,
Whose hot incursions and great name in arms
Holds from all soldiers chief majority
And military title capital 110
Through all the kingdoms that acknowledge Christ:
Thrice hath this Hotspur, Mars in swathling clothes,
This infant warrior, in his enterprizes
Discomfited great Douglas, ta'en him once,
Enlarged him and made a friend of him, 115
To fill the mouth of deep defiance up
And shake the peace and safety of our throne.
And what say you to this? Percy, Northumberland,
The Archbishop's grace of York, Douglas, Mortimer,
Capitulate against us and are up. 120
But wherefore do I tell these news to thee?
Why, Harry, do I tell thee of my foes,
Which art my near'st and dearest enemy?
Thou that art like enough, through vassal fear,
Base inclination and the start of spleen, 125

To fight against me under Percy's pay,
To dog his heels and curtsy at his frowns,
o show how much thou art degenerate.
PRINCE. Do not think so; you shall not find it so:
And God forgive them that so much have sway'd$_{130}$
Your majesty's good thoughts away from me!
I will redeem all this on Percy's head
And in the closing of some glorious day
Be bold to tell you that I am your son;
When I will wear a garment all of blood$_{135}$
And stain my favours in a bloody mask,
Which, wash'd away, shall scour my shame with it:
And that shall be the day, whene'er it lights,
That this same child of honour and renown,
This gallant Hotspur, this all-praised knight,$_{140}$
And your unthought-of Harry chance to meet.
For every honour sitting on his helm,
Would they were multitudes, and on my head
My shames redoubled! for the time will come,
That I shall make this northern youth exchange$_{145}$
His glorious deeds for my indignities.
Percy is but my factor, good my lord,
To engross up glorious deeds on my behalf;
And I will call him to so strict account,
That he shall render every glory up,$_{150}$
Yea, even the slightest worship of his time,
Or I will tear the reckoning from his heart.
This, in the name of God, I promise here:
The which if He be pleased I shall perform,
I do beseech your majesty may salve$_{155}$
The long-grown wounds of my intemperance:
If not, the end of life cancels all bands;
And I will die a hundred thousand deaths
Ere break the smallest parcel of this vow.
KING. A hundred thousand rebels die in this:$_{160}$
Thou shalt have charge and sovereign trust herein.
(Enter BLUNT.)
How now, good Blunt? thy looks are full of speed.
BLUNT. So hath the business that I come to speak of.

Lord Mortimer of Scotland hath sent word
That Douglas and the English rebels met$_{165}$
The eleventh of this month at Shrewsbury:
A mighty and a fearful head they are,
If promises be kept on every hand,
As ever offer'd foul play in a state.
KING. The Earl of Westmoreland set forth to-day;$_{170}$
With him my son, Lord John of Lancaster;
For this advertisement is five days old:
On Wednesday next, Harry, you shall set forward;
On Thursday we ourselves will march: our meeting
Is Bridgenorth: and, Harry, you shall march$_{175}$
Through Gloucestershire; by which account,
Our business valued, some twelve days hence
Our general forces at Bridgenorth shall meet.
Our hands are full of business: let's away;
Advantage feeds him fat, while men delay. *(Exeunt.)*$_{180}$

SCENE III. EASTCHEAP. THE BOAR'S-HEAD TAVERN

(ENTER FALSTAFF AND BARDOLPH.)

FAL. Bardolph, am I not fallen away vilely since this
last action? do I not bate? do I not dwindle? Why, my skin
hangs about me like an old lady's loose gown; I am withered
like an old apple-john. Well, I'll repent, and that suddenly,
while I am in some liking; I shall be out of heart$_5$
shortly, and then I shall have no strength to repent. An
I have not forgotten what the inside of a church is made of,
I am a peppercorn, a brewer's horse: the inside of a church!
Company, villanous company, hath been the spoil of me.
BARD. Sir John, you are so fretful, you cannot live long.$_{10}$
FAL. Why, there is it: come sing me a bawdy song;
make me merry. I was as virtuously given as a gentleman
need to be; virtuous enough; swore little; diced not above
seven times a week; went to a bawdy-house not above once
in a quarter—of an hour; paid money that I borrowed,$_{15}$
three or four times; lived well, and in good compass: and

now I live out of all order, out of all compass.

BARD. Why, you are so fat, Sir John, that you must
needs be out of all compass, out of all reasonable compass,
Sir John.$_{20}$

FAL. Do thou amend thy face, and I'll amend my life:
thou art our admiral, thou bearest the lantern in the poop,
but 'tis in the nose of thee; thou art the Knight of the
Burning Lamp.

BARD. Why, Sir John, my face does you no harm.$_{25}$

FAL. No, I'll be sworn; I make as good use of it as
many a man doth of a Death's-head or a memento mori:
I never see thy face but I think upon hell-fire, and Dives that
lived in purple; for there he is in his robes, burning,
burning. If thou wert any way given to virtue, I would swear$_{30}$
by thy face; my oath should be, 'By this fire, that's God's
angel:' but thou art altogether given over; and wert indeed,
but for the light in thy face, the son of utter darkness.
When thou rannest up Gadshill in the night to catch my
horse, if I did not think thou hadst been an ignis fatuus$_{35}$
or a ball of wildfire, there's no purchase in money. O, thou
art a perpetual triumph, an everlasting bonfire-light! Thou
hast saved me a thousand marks in links and torches,
walking with thee in the night betwixt tavern and tavern:
but the sack that thou hast drunk me would have bought me$_{40}$
lights as good cheap at the dearest chandler's in Europe.
I have maintained that salamander of yours with fire any
time this two and thirty years; God reward me for it!

BARD. 'Sblood, I would my face were in your belly!

FAL. God-a-mercy! so should I be sure to be heartburned.$_{45}$
(*ENTER HOSTESS.*)
How now, Dame Partlet the hen! have you inquired yet
who picked my pocket?

HOST. Why, Sir John, what do you think, Sir John? do
you think I keep thieves in my house? I have searched, I$_{50}$
have inquired, so has my husband, man by man, boy by
boy, servant by servant: the tithe of a hair was never lost
in my house before.

FAL. Ye lie, hostess: Bardolph was shaved, and lost
many a hair; and I'll be sworn my pocket was picked.$_{55}$

Go to, you are a woman, go.

Host. Who, I? no; I defy thee: God's light, I was
never called so in mine own house before.

Fal. Go to, I know you well enough.

Host. No, Sir John; you do not know me, Sir John. 60
I know you, Sir John: you owe me money, Sir John; and
now you pick a quarrel to beguile me of it: I bought you a
dozen of shirts to your back.

Fal. Dowlas, filthy dowlas: I have given them away to
bakers' wives, and they have made bolters of them. 65

Host. Now, as I am a true woman, holland of eight
shillings an ell. You owe money here besides, Sir John,
for your diet and by-drinkings, and money lent you, four
and twenty pound.

Fal. He had his part of it; let him pay. 70

Host. He? alas, he is poor; he hath nothing.

Fal. How! poor? look upon his face; what call you
rich? let them coin his nose, let them coin his cheeks: I'll
not pay a denier. What, will you make a younker of me?
shall I not take mine ease in mine inn but I shall have my 75
pocket picked? I have lost a seal-ring of my grandfather's
worth forty mark.

Host. O Jesu, I have heard the prince tell him, I know
not how oft, that that ring was copper!

Fal. How! the prince is a Jack, a sneak-cup: 'sblood, 80
an he were here, I would cudgel him like a dog, if he would
say so.

*(Enter the Prince and Peto, marching, and Falstaff meets them
    playing on his truncheon like a fife.)*

How now, lad! is the wind in that door, i' faith? must we
all march?

Bard. Yea, two and two, Newgate fashion. 85

Host. My lord, I pray you, hear me.

Prince. What sayest thou, Mistress Quickly? How
doth thy husband? I love him well; he is an honest man.

Host. Good my lord, hear me.

Fal. Prithee, let her alone, and list to me. 90

Prince. What sayest thou, Jack?

Fal. The other night I fell asleep here behind the

arras, and had my pocket picked: this house is turned
bawdy-house; they pick pockets.

PRINCE. What didst thou lose, Jack? 95

FAL. Wilt thou believe me, Hal? three or four bonds
of forty pound a-piece, and a seal-ring of my grandfather's.

PRINCE. A trifle, some eight-penny matter.

HOST. So I told him, my lord; and I said I heard
your grace say so: and, my lord, he speaks most vilely of 100
you, like a foul-mouthed man as he is; and said he would
cudgel you.

PRINCE. What! he did not?

HOST. There's neither faith, truth, nor womanhood in
me else. 105

FAL. There's no more faith in thee than in a stewed
prune; nor no more truth in thee than in a drawn fox; and
for womanhood, Maid Marian may be the deputy's wife of
the ward to thee. Go, you thing, go.

HOST. Say, what thing? what thing? 110

FAL. What thing! why, a thing to thank God on.

HOST. I am no thing to thank God on, I would thou
shouldst know it; I am an honest man's wife: and, setting
thy knighthood aside, thou art a knave to call me so.

FAL. Setting thy womanhood aside, thou art a beast 115
to say otherwise.

HOST. Say, what beast, thou knave, thou?

FAL. What beast! why, an otter.

PRINCE. An otter, Sir John! why an otter?

FAL. Why, she's neither fish nor flesh; a man knows 120
not where to have her.

HOST. Thou art an unjust man in saying so: thou or
any man knows where to have me, thou knave, thou!

PRINCE. Thou sayest true, hostess; and he slanders
thee most grossly. 125

HOST. So he doth you, my lord; and said this other
day you ought him a thousand pound.

PRINCE. Sirrah, do I owe you a thousand pound?

FAL. A thousand pound, Hal! a million: thy love is
worth a million: thou owest me thy love. 130

HOST. Nay, my lord, he called you Jack, and said he

would cudgel you.

FAL. Did I, Bardolph?

BARD. Indeed, Sir John, you said so.

FAL. Yea, if he said my ring was copper.$_{135}$

PRINCE. I say 'tis copper: darest thou be as good as
thy word now?

FAL. Why, Hal, thou knowest, as thou art but man, I
dare: but as thou art prince, I fear thee as I fear the roaring
of the lion's whelp.$_{140}$

PRINCE. And why not as the lion?

FAL. The king himself is to be feared as the lion: dost
thou think I'll fear thee as I fear thy father? nay, an I do,
I pray God my girdle break.

PRINCE. O, if it should, how would thy guts fall about$_{145}$
thy knees! But, sirrah, there's no room for faith, truth,
nor honesty in this bosom of thine; it is all filled up with
guts and midriff. Charge an honest woman with picking
thy pocket! why, thou whoreson, impudent, embossed
rascal, if there were anything in thy pocket but$_{150}$
tavern-reckonings, memorandums of bawdy-houses, and
one poor
penny-worth of sugar-candy to make thee long-winded, if
thy pocket were enriched with any other injuries but
these, I am a villain: and yet you will stand to it; you will
not pocket up wrong: art thou not ashamed?$_{155}$

FAL. Dost thou hear, Hal? thou knowest in the state
of innocency Adam fell; and what should poor Jack Falstaff
do in the days of villany? Thou seest I have more
flesh than another man; and therefore more frailty. You
confess then, you picked my pocket?$_{160}$

PRINCE. It appears so by the story.

FAL. Hostess, I forgive thee: go, make ready breakfast;
love thy husband, look to thy servants, cherish thy
guests: thou shalt find me tractable to any honest reason:
thou seest I am pacified still. Nay, prithee, be gone.$_{165}$
(Exit Hostess.) Now, Hal, to the news at court: for the
robbery, lad, how is that answered?

PRINCE. O, my sweet beef, I must still be good angel
to thee: the money is paid back again.

FAL. O, I do not like that paying back; 'tis a double _170_
labour.

PRINCE. I am good friends with my father, and may
do any thing.

FAL. Rob me the exchequer the first thing thou doest,
and do it with unwashed hands too. _175_

BARD. Do, my lord.

PRINCE. I have procured thee, Jack, a charge of foot.

FAL. I would it had been of horse. Where shall I find
one that can steal well? O for a fine thief, of the age of
two and twenty or thereabouts! I am heinously _180_
unprovided. Well, God be thanked for these rebels, they offend
none but the virtuous: I laud them, I praise them.

PRINCE. Bardolph!

BARD. My lord?

PRINCE. Go bear this letter to Lord John of Lancaster, _185_
to my brother John; this to my Lord of Westmoreland.
(Exit Bardolph.) Go, Peto, to horse, to horse; for thou and
I have thirty miles to ride yet ere dinner time. _(Exit Peto.)_
Jack, meet me to-morrow in the temple hall at two o'clock
in the afternoon. _190_
There shalt thou know thy charge; and there receive
Money and order for their furniture.
The land is burning; Percy stands on high;
And either we or they must lower lie. _(Exit.)_

FAL. Rare words! brave world! Hostess, my breakfast, come! _195_
O, I could wish this tavern were my drum! _(Exit.)_

ACT IV

SCENE I. THE REBEL CAMP NEAR SHREWSBURY.

(Enter Hotspur, Worcester, and Douglas.)

Hot. Well said, my noble Scot: if speaking truth
In this fine age were not thought flattery,
Such attribution should the Douglas have,
As not a soldier of this season's stamp
Should go so general current through the world. 5
By God, I cannot flatter; I do defy
The tongues of soothers; but a braver place
In my heart's love hath no man than yourself:
Nay, task me to my word; approve me, lord.
Doug. Thou art the king of honour: 10
No man so potent breathes upon the ground
But I will beard him.
Hot. Do so, and 'tis well.
(Enter a Messenger with letters.)
What letters hast thou there?—I can but thank you.
Mess. These letters come from your father.
Hot. Letters from him! why comes he not himself? 15
Mess. He cannot come, my lord; he is grievous sick.

HOT. 'Zounds! how has he the leisure to be sick
In such a justling time? Who leads his power?
Under whose government come they along?
MESS. His letters bear his mind, not I, my lord.$_{20}$
WOR. I prithee, tell me, doth he keep his bed?
MESS. He did, my lord, four days ere I set forth;
And at the time of my departure thence
He was much fear'd by his physicians.
WOR. I would the state of time had first been whole$_{25}$
Ere he by sickness had been visited:
His health was never better worth than now.
HOT. Sick now! droop now! this sickness doth infect
The very life-blood of our enterprise;
'Tis catching hither, even to our camp.$_{30}$
He writes me here, that inward sickness——
And that his friends by deputation could not
So soon be drawn, nor did he think it meet
To lay so dangerous and dear a trust
On any soul removed but on his own.$_{35}$
Yet doth he give us bold advertisement,
That with our small conjunction we should on,
To see how fortune is disposed to us;
For, as he writes, there is no quailing now,
Because the king is certainly possess'd$_{40}$
Of all our purposes. What say you to it?
WOR. Your father's sickness is a maim to us.
HOT. A perilous gash, a very limb lopp'd off:
And yet, in faith, it is not; his present want
Seems more than we shall find it: were it good$_{45}$
To set the exact wealth of all our states
All at one cast? to set so rich a main
On the nice hazard of one doubtful hour?
It were not good; for therein should we read
The very bottom and the soul of hope,$_{50}$
The very list, the very utmost bound
Of all our fortunes.
DOUG. Faith, and so we should;
Where now remains a sweet reversion:
We may boldly spend upon the hope of what

Is to come in:$_{55}$
A comfort of retirement lives in this.
HOT. A rendezvous, a home to fly unto,
If that the devil and mischance look big
Upon the maidenhead of our affairs.
WOR. But yet I would your father had been here.$_{60}$
The quality and hair of our attempt
Brooks no division: it will be thought
By some, that know not why he is away,
That wisdom, loyalty and mere dislike
Of our proceedings kept the earl from hence:$_{65}$
And think how such an apprehension
May turn the tide of fearful faction
And breed a kind of question in our cause;
For well you know we of the offering side
Must keep aloof from strict arbitrement,$_{70}$
And stop all sight-holes, every loop from whence
The eye of reason may pry in upon us:
This absence of your father's draws a curtain,
That shows the ignorant a kind of fear
Before not dreamt of.
HOT. You strain too far.$_{75}$
I rather of his absence make this use:
It lends a lustre and more great opinion,
A larger dare to our great enterprise,
Than if the earl were here; for men must think,
If we without his help can make a head$_{80}$
To push against a kingdom, with his help
We shall o'erturn it topsy-turvy down.
Yet all goes well, yet all our joints are whole.
DOUG. As heart can think: there is not such a word
Spoke of in Scotland as this term of fear.$_{85}$
(ENTER SIR RICHARD VERNON.)
HOT. My cousin Vernon! welcome, by my soul.
VER. Pray God my news be worth a welcome, lord.
The Earl of Westmoreland, seven thousand strong,
Is marching hitherwards; with him Prince John.
HOT. No harm: what more?
VER. And further, I have$_{90}$

The king himself in person is set forth,
Or hitherwards intended speedily,
With strong and mighty preparation.
Hot. He shall be welcome too. Where is his son,
The nimble-footed madcap Prince of Wales, 95
And his comrades, that daff'd the world aside,
And bid it pass?
Ver. All furnish'd, all in arms;
All plumed like estridges that with the wind
Baited like eagles having lately bathed;
Glittering in golden coats, like images; 100
As full of spirit as the month of May,
And gorgeous as the sun at midsummer;
Wanton as youthful goats, wild as young bulls.
I saw young Harry, with his beaver on,
His cuisses on his thighs, gallantly arm'd, 105
Rise from the ground like feather'd Mercury,
And vaulted with such ease into his seat,
As if an angel dropp'd down from the clouds,
To turn and wind a fiery Pegasus
And witch the world with noble horsemanship. 110
Hot. No more, no more: worse than the sun in March,
This praise doth nourish agues. Let them come;
They come like sacrifices in their trim,
And to the fire-eyed maid of smoky war
All hot and bleeding will we offer them: 115
The mailed Mars shall on his altar sit
Up to the ears in blood. I am on fire
To hear this rich reprisal is so nigh
And yet not ours. Come, let me taste my horse,
Who is to bear me like a thunderbolt 120
Against the bosom of the Prince of Wales:
Harry to Harry shall, hot horse to horse,
Meet and ne'er part till one drop down a corse.
O that Glendower were come!
Ver. There is more news:
I learn'd in Worcester, as I rode along, 125
He cannot draw his power this fourteen days.
Doug. That's the worst tidings that I hear of yet.

WOR. Ay, by my faith, that bears a frosty sound.

HOT. What may the king's whole battle reach unto?

VER. To thirty thousand.

HOT. Forty let it be:₁₃₀

My father and Glendower being both away,

The powers of us may serve so great a day.

Come, let us take a muster speedily:

Doomsday is near; die all, die merrily.

DOUG. Talk not of dying: I am out of fear₁₃₅

Of death or death's hand for this one half-year. *(Exeunt.)*

SCENE II. A PUBLIC ROAD NEAR COVENTRY

(ENTER FALSTAFF AND BARDOLPH.)

FAL. Bardolph, get thee before to Coventry; fill me a
bottle of sack: our soldiers shall march through; we'll to
Sutton Co'fil' to-night.

BARD. Will you give me money, captain?

FAL. Lay out, lay out.₅

BARD. This bottle makes an angel.

FAL. An if it do, take it for thy labour; and if it
make twenty, take them all; I'll answer the coinage. Bid
my lieutenant Peto meet me at town's end.

BARD. I will, captain: farewell. *(Exit.)*₁₀

FAL. If I be not ashamed of my soldiers, I am a soused
gurnet. I have misused the king's press damnably. I have
got, in exchange of a hundred and fifty soldiers, three hundred
and odd pounds. I press me none but good householders,
yeoman's sons; inquire me out contracted bachelors,₁₅
such as had been asked twice on the banns; such a
commodity of warm slaves, as had as lieve hear the devil
as a drum; such as fear the report of a caliver worse than a
struck fowl or a hurt wild-duck. I pressed me none but
such toasts-and-butter, with hearts in their bellies no bigger₂₀
than pins'-heads, and they have bought out their services;
and now my whole charge consists of ancients, corporals,
lieutenants, gentlemen of companies, slaves as ragged as

Lazarus in the painted cloth, where the glutton's dogs licked
his sores; and such as indeed were never soldiers, but$_{25}$
discarded unjust serving-men, younger sons to younger
brothers, revolted tapsters and ostlers trade-fallen, the cankers
of a calm world and a long peace, ten times more
dishonourable ragged than an old faced ancient: and such
    have I, to
fill up the rooms of them that have bought out their$_{30}$
services, that you would think that I had a hundred and fifty
tattered prodigals lately come from swine-keeping, from
eating draff and husks. A mad fellow met me on the way
and told me I had unloaded all the gibbets and pressed
the dead bodies. No eye hath seen such scarecrows. I'll$_{35}$
not march through Coventry with them, that's flat: nay,
and the villains march wide betwixt the legs, as if they had
gyves on; for indeed I had the most of them out of prison.
There's but a shirt and a half in all my company; and the
half shirt is two napkins tacked together and thrown over$_{40}$
the shoulders like an herald's coat without sleeves; and the

shirt, to say the truth, stolen from my host at Saint Alban's,
or the red-nose innkeeper of Daventry. But that's all one;
they'll find linen enough on every hedge.
(ENTER THE PRINCE AND WESTMORELAND.)
PRINCE. How now, blown Jack! how now, quilt!$_{45}$
FAL. What, Hal! how now, mad wag! what a devil
dost thou in Warwickshire? My good Lord of Westmoreland,
I cry you mercy: I thought your honour had already
been at Shrewsbury.
WEST. Faith, Sir John, 'tis more than time that I were$_{50}$
there, and you too; but my powers are there already. The
king, I can tell you, looks for us all: we must away all night.
FAL. Tut, never fear me: I am as vigilant as a cat to
steal cream.
PRINCE. I think, to steal cream indeed, for thy theft$_{55}$
hath already made thee butter. But tell me, Jack, whose
fellows are these that come after?
FAL. Mine, Hal, mine.
PRINCE. I did never see such pitiful rascals.

FAL. Tut, tut; good enough to toss; food for powder,$_{60}$
food for powder; they'll fill a pit as well as better: tush,
man, mortal men, mortal men.
WEST. Ay, but, Sir John, methinks they are exceeding
poor and bare, too beggarly.
FAL. Faith, for their poverty, I know not where they$_{65}$
had that; and for their bareness, I am sure they never
learned that of me.
PRINCE. No, I'll be sworn; unless you call three fingers
on the ribs bare. But, sirrah, make haste: Percy is already
in the field.$_{70}$
FAL. What, is the king encamped?
WEST. He is, Sir John: I fear we shall stay too long.
FAL. Well,
To the latter end of a fray and the beginning of a feast
Fits a dull fighter and a keen guest. *(Exeunt.)*$_{75}$

SCENE III. THE REBEL CAMP NEAR SHREWSBURY

(ENTER HOTSPUR, WORCESTER, DOUGLAS, AND VERNON.)

HOT. We'll fight with him to-night.
WOR. It may not be.
DOUG. You give him then advantage.
VER. Not a whit.
HOT. Why say you so? looks he not for supply?
VER. So do we.
HOT. His is certain, ours is doubtful.
WOR. Good cousin, be advised; stir not to-night.$_5$
VER. Do not, my lord.
DOUG. You do not counsel well:
You speak it out of fear and cold heart.
VER. Do me no slander, Douglas: by my life,
And I dare well maintain it with my life,
If well-respected honour bid me on,$_{10}$
I hold as little counsel with weak fear
As you, my lord, or any Scot that this day lives:
Let it be seen to-morrow in the battle

Which of us fears.

DOUG. Yea, or to-night.

VER. Content.

HOT. To-night, say I.$_{15}$

VER. Come, come, it may not be. I wonder much,
Being men of such great leading as you are,
That you foresee not what impediments
Drag back our expedition: certain horse
Of my cousin Vernon's are not yet come up:$_{20}$
Your uncle Worcester's horse came but to-day;
And now their pride and mettle is asleep,
Their courage with hard labour tame and dull,
That not a horse is half the half of himself.

HOT. So are the horses of the enemy$_{25}$
In general, journey-bated and brought low:
The better part of ours are full of rest.

WOR. The number of the king exceedeth ours:
For God's sake, cousin, stay till all come in.

(The trumpet sounds a parley.)

(ENTER SIR WALTER BLUNT.)

BLUNT. I come with gracious offers from the king,$_{30}$
If you vouchsafe me hearing and respect.

HOT. Welcome, Sir Walter Blunt; and would to God
You were of our determination!
Some of us love you well; and even those some
Envy your great deservings and good name,$_{35}$
Because you are not of our quality,
But stand against us like an enemy.

BLUNT. And God defend but still I should stand so,
So long as out of limit and true rule
You stand against anointed majesty.$_{40}$
But to my charge. The king hath sent to know
The nature of your griefs, and whereupon
You conjure from the breast of civil peace
Such bold hostility, teaching his duteous land
Audacious cruelty. If that the king$_{45}$
Have any way your good deserts forgot,
Which he confesseth to be manifold,
He bids you name your griefs; and with all speed

You shall have your desires with interest
And pardon absolute for yourself and these [50]
Herein misled by your suggestion.
Hot. The king is kind; and well we know the king
Knows at what time to promise, when to pay.
My father and my uncle and myself
Did give him that same royalty he wears; [55]
And when he was not six and twenty strong,
Sick in the world's regard, wretched and low,
A poor unminded outlaw sneaking home,
My father gave him welcome to the shore;
And when he heard him swear and vow to God [60]
He came but to be Duke of Lancaster,
To sue his livery and beg his peace,
With tears of innocency and terms of zeal,
My father, in kind heart and pity moved,
Swore him assistance and perform'd it too. [65]
Now when the lords and barons of the realm
Perceived Northumberland did lean to him,
The more and less came in with cap and knee;
Met him in boroughs, cities, villages,
Attended him on bridges, stood in lanes, [70]
Laid gifts before him, proffer'd him their oaths,
Gave him their heirs, as pages follow'd him
Even at the heels in golden multitudes.
He presently, as greatness knows itself,
Steps me a little higher than his vow [75]
Made to my father, while his blood was poor,
Upon the naked shore at Ravenspurgh;
And now, forsooth, takes on him to reform
Some certain edicts and some strait decrees
That lie too heavy on the commonwealth, [80]
Cries out upon abuses, seems to weep
Over his country's wrongs; and by this face,
This seeming brow of justice, did he win
The hearts of all that he did angle for;
Proceeded further; cut me off the heads [85]
Of all the favourites that the absent king
In deputation left behind him here,

When he was personal in the Irish war.
BLUNT. Tut, I came not to hear this.
HOT. Then to the point.
In short time after, he deposed the king;90
Soon after that, deprived him of his life;
And in the neck of that, task'd the whole state;
To make that worse, suffer'd his kinsman March,
Who is, if every owner were well placed,
Indeed his king, to be engaged in Wales,95
There without ransom to lie forfeited;
Disgraced me in my happy victories,
Sought to entrap me by intelligence;
Rated mine uncle from the council-board;
In rage dismiss'd my father from the court;100
Broke oath on oath, committed wrong on wrong,
And in conclusion drove us to seek out
This head of safety; and withal to pry
Into his title, the which we find
Too indirect for long continuance.105
BLUNT. Shall I return this answer to the king?
HOT. Not so, Sir Walter: we'll withdraw awhile.
Go to the king; and let there be impawn'd
Some surety for a safe return again,
And in the morning early shall my uncle110
Bring him our purposes: and so farewell.
BLUNT. I would you would accept of grace and love.
HOT. And may be so we shall.
BLUNT. Pray God you do. *(Exeunt.)*

SCENE IV. YORK. THE ARCHBISHOP'S PALACE

(ENTER THE ARCHBISHOP OF YORK AND SIR MICHAEL.)

ARCH. Hie, good Sir Michael; bear this sealed brief
With winged haste to the lord marshal;
This to my cousin Scroop, and all the rest
To whom they are directed. If you knew
How much they do import, you would make haste.5

SIR M. My good lord,
I guess their tenour.
ARCH. Like enough you do.
To-morrow, good Sir Michael, is a day
Wherein the fortune of ten thousand men
Must bide the touch; for, sir, at Shrewsbury,$_{10}$
As I am truly given to understand,
The king with mighty and quick-raised power
Meets with Lord Harry: and, I fear, Sir Michael,
What with the sickness of Northumberland,
Whose power was in the first proportion,$_{15}$
And what with Owen Glendower's absence thence,
Who with them was a rated sinew too
And comes not in, o'er-ruled by prophecies,
I fear the power of Percy is too weak
To wage an instant trial with the king.$_{20}$
SIR M. Why, my good lord, you need not fear;
There is Douglas and Lord Mortimer.
ARCH. No, Mortimer is not there.
SIR M. But there is Mordake, Vernon, Lord Harry Percy,
And there is my Lord of Worcester and a head$_{25}$
Of gallant warriors, noble gentlemen.
ARCH. And so there is: but yet the king hath drawn
The special head of all the land together:
The Prince of Wales, Lord John of Lancaster,
The noble Westmoreland and warlike Blunt;$_{30}$
And many moe corrivals and dear men
Of estimation and command in arms.
SIR M. Doubt not, my lord, they shall be well opposed.
ARCH. I hope no less, yet needful 'tis to fear;
And, to prevent the worst, Sir Michael, speed:$_{35}$
For if Lord Percy thrive not, ere the king
Dismiss his power, he means to visit us,
For he hath heard of our confederacy,
And 'tis but wisdom to make strong against him:
Therefore make haste. I must go write again$_{40}$
To other friends; and so farewell, Sir Michael. *(Exeunt.)*

ACT V

SCENE I. THE KING'S CAMP NEAR SHREWSBURY.

(Enter the King, Prince of Wales, Lord John of Lancaster, Earl of Westmoreland, Sir Walter Blunt, and Falstaff.)

KING. How bloodily the sun begins to peer
Above yon busky hill! the day looks pale
At his distemperature.
PRINCE. The southern wind
Doth play the trumpet to his purposes,
And by his hollow whistling in the leaves 5
Foretells a tempest and a blustering day.
KING. Then with the losers let it sympathise,
For nothing can seem foul to those that win.
(The trumpet sounds.)
(Enter Worcester and Vernon.)
How now, my Lord of Worcester! 'tis not well
That you and I should meet upon such terms 10
As now we meet. You have deceived our trust,
And made us doff our easy robes of peace,
To crush our old limbs in ungentle steel:
This is not well, my lord, this is not well.

What say you to it? will you again unknit$_{15}$
This churlish knot of all-abhorred war?
And move in that obedient orb again
Where you did give a fair and natural light,
And be no more an exhaled meteor,
A prodigy of fear and a portent$_{20}$
Of broached mischief to the unborn times?
WOR. Hear me, my liege:
For mine own part, I could be well content
To entertain the lag-end of my life
With quiet hours; for, I do protest,$_{25}$
I have not sought the day of this dislike.
KING. You have not sought it! how comes it, then?
FAL. Rebellion lay in his way, and he found it.
PRINCE. Peace, chewet, peace!
WOR. It pleased your majesty to turn your looks$_{30}$
Of favour from myself and all our house;
And yet I must remember you, my lord,
We were the first and dearest of your friends.
For you my staff of office did I break
In Richard's time; and posted day and night$_{35}$
To meet you on the way, and kiss your hand,
When yet you were in place and in account
Nothing so strong and fortunate as I.
It was myself, my brother, and his son,
That brought you home, and boldly did outdare$_{40}$
The dangers of the time. You swore to us,
And you did swear that oath at Doncaster,
That you did nothing purpose 'gainst the state;
Nor claim no further than your new-fall'n right,
The seat of Gaunt, dukedom of Lancaster:$_{45}$
To this we swore our aid. But in short space
It rain'd down fortune showering on your head;
And such a flood of greatness fell on you,
What with our help, what with the absent king,
What with the injuries of a wanton time,$_{50}$
The seeming sufferances that you had borne,
And the contrarious winds that held the king
So long in his unlucky Irish wars

That all in England did repute him dead:
And from this swarm of fair advantages$_{55}$
You took occasion to be quickly woo'd
To gripe the general sway into your hand;
Forgot your oath to us at Doncaster;
And being fed by us you used us so
As that ungentle gull, the cuckoo's bird,$_{60}$
Useth the sparrow; did oppress our nest;
Grew by our feeding to so great a bulk
That even our love durst not come near your sight
For fear of swallowing; but with nimble wing
We were enforced, for safety sake, to fly$_{65}$
Out of your sight and raise this present head;
Whereby we stand opposed by such means
As you yourself have forged against yourself
By unkind usage, dangerous countenance,
And violation of all faith and troth$_{70}$
Sworn to us in your younger enterprise.
KING. These things indeed you have articulate,
Proclaim'd at market-crosses, read in churches,
To face the garment of rebellion
With some fine colour that may please the eye$_{75}$
Of fickle changelings and poor discontents,
Which gape and rub the elbow at the news
Of hurlyburly innovation:
And never yet did insurrection want
Such water-colours to impaint his cause;$_{80}$
Nor moody beggars, starving for a time
Of pellmell havoc and confusion.
PRINCE. In both your armies there is many a soul
Shall pay full dearly for this encounter,
If once they join in trial. Tell your nephew,$_{85}$
The Prince of Wales doth join with all the world
In praise of Henry Percy: by my hopes,
This present enterprise set off his head,
I do not think a braver gentleman,
More active-valiant or more valiant-young,$_{90}$
More daring or more bold, is now alive
To grace this latter age with noble deeds.

For my part, I may speak it to my shame,
I have a truant been to chivalry;
And so I hear he doth account me too; 95
Yet this before my father's majesty—
I am content that he shall take the odds
Of his great name and estimation,
And will, to save the blood on either side,
Try fortune with him in a single fight. 100
KING. And, Prince of Wales, so dare we venture thee,
Albeit considerations infinite
Do make against it. No, good Worcester, no,
We love our people well; even those we love
That are misled upon your cousin's part; 105
And, will they take the offer of our grace,
Both he and they and you, yea, every man
Shall be my friend again and I'll be his:
So tell your cousin, and bring me word
What he will do: but if he will not yield, 110
Rebuke and dread correction wait on us
And they shall do their office. So, be gone;
We will not now be troubled with reply:
We offer fair; take it advisedly.
(Exeunt Worcester and Vernon.)
PRINCE. It will not be accepted, on my life: 115
The Douglas and the Hotspur both together
Are confident against the world in arms.
KING. Hence, therefore, every leader to his charge;
For, on their answer, will we set on them:
And God befriend us, as our cause is just! 120
(Exeunt all but the Prince of Wales and Falstaff.)
FAL. Hal, if thou see me down in the battle, and
bestride me, so; 'tis a point of friendship.
PRINCE. Nothing but a colossus can do thee that
friendship. Say thy prayers, and farewell.
FAL. I would 'twere bed-time, Hal, and all well. 125
PRINCE. Why, thou owest God a death. *(Exit.)*
FAL. 'Tis not due yet; I would be loath to pay him
before his day. What need I be so forward with him that
calls not on me? Well, 'tis no matter; honour pricks me

on. Yea, but how if honour prick me off when I come on?₍₁₃₀₎
how then? Can honour set to a leg? no: or an arm? no:
or take away the grief of a wound? no. Honour hath no
skill in surgery, then? no. What is honour? a word. What
is in that word honour? what is that honour? air. A trim
reckoning! Who hath it? he that died o' Wednesday.₍₁₃₅₎
Doth he feel it? no. Doth he hear it? no. 'Tis insensible,
then. Yea, to the dead. But will it not live with the living?
no. Why? detraction will not suffer it. Therefore I'll none
of it. Honour is a mere scutcheon: and so ends my
catechism. *(Exit.)*₍₁₄₀₎

SCENE II. THE REBEL CAMP

(ENTER WORCESTER AND VERNON.)

WOR. O, no, my nephew must not know, Sir Richard,
The liberal and kind offer of the king.
VER. 'Twere best he did.
WOR. Then are we all undone.
It is not possible, it cannot be,
The king should keep his word in loving us;₍₅₎
He will suspect us still, and find a time
To punish this offence in other faults:
Suspicion all our lives shall be stuck full of eyes;
For treason is but trusted like the fox,
Who, ne'er so tame, so cherish'd and lock'd up,₍₁₀₎
Will have a wild trick of his ancestors.
Look how we can, or sad or merrily,
Interpretation will misquote our looks,
And we shall feed like oxen at a stall,
The better cherish'd, still the nearer death.₍₁₅₎
My nephew's trespass may be well forgot;
It hath the excuse of youth and heat of blood;
And an adopted name of privilege,
A hare-brain'd Hotspur, govern'd by a spleen:
All his offences live upon my head₍₂₀₎
And on his father's; we did train him on,

And, his corruption being ta'en from us,
We, as the spring of all, shall pay for all.
Therefore, good cousin, let not Harry know,
In any case, the offer of the king.$_{25}$
VER. Deliver what you will; I'll say 'tis so.
Here comes your cousin.
(ENTER HOTSPUR AND DOUGLAS.)
HOT. My uncle is return'd:
Deliver up my Lord of Westmoreland.
Uncle, what news?$_{30}$
WOR. The king will bid you battle presently.
DOUG. Defy him by the Lord of Westmoreland.
HOT. Lord Douglas, go you and tell him so.
DOUG. Marry, and shall, and very willingly. *(Exit.)*
WOR. There is no seeming mercy in the king.$_{35}$
HOT. Did you beg any? God forbid!
WOR. I told him gently of our grievances,
Of his oath-breaking; which he mended thus,
By now forswearing that he is forsworn:
He calls us rebels, traitors; and will scourge$_{40}$
With haughty arms this hateful name in us.
(Re-enter DOUGLAS.)
DOUG. Arm, gentlemen; to arms! for I have thrown
A brave defiance in King Henry's teeth,
And Westmoreland, that was engaged, did bear it;
Which cannot choose but bring him quickly on.$_{45}$
WOR. The Prince of Wales stepp'd forth before the king,
And, nephew, challenged you to single fight.
HOT. O, would the quarrel lay upon our heads,
And that no man might draw short breath to-day
But I and Harry Monmouth! Tell me, tell me,$_{50}$
How show'd his tasking? seem'd it in contempt?
VER. No, by my soul; I never in my life
Did hear a challenge urged more modestly,
Unless a brother should a brother dare
To gentle exercise and proof of arms.$_{55}$
He gave you all the duties of a man;
Trimm'd up your praises with a princely tongue,
Spoke your deservings like a chronicle,

Making you ever better than his praise
By still dispraising praise valued with you: $_{60}$
And, which became him like a prince indeed,
He made a blushing cital of himself;
And chid his truant youth with such a grace
As if he master'd there a double spirit
Of teaching and of learning instantly. $_{65}$
There did he pause: but let me tell the world,
If he outlive the envy of this day,
England did never owe so sweet a hope,
So much misconstrued in his wantonness.
Hot. Cousin, I think thou art enamoured $_{70}$
On his follies: never did I hear
Of any prince so wild a libertine.
But be he as he will, yet once ere night
I will embrace him with a soldier's arm,
That he shall shrink under my courtesy. $_{75}$
Arm, arm with speed: and, fellows, soldiers, friends,
Better consider what you have to do
Than I, that have not well the gift of tongue,
Can lift your blood up with persuasion.
(Enter a Messenger.)
Mess. My lord, here are letters for you. $_{80}$
Hot. I cannot read them now.
O gentlemen, the time of life is short!
To spend that shortness basely were too long,
If life did ride upon a dial's point,
Still ending at the arrival of an hour. $_{85}$
An if we live, we live to tread on kings;
If die, brave death, when princes die with us!
Now, for our consciences, the arms are fair,
When the intent of bearing them is just.
(Enter another Messenger.)
Mess. My Lord, prepare; the king comes on apace. $_{90}$
Hot. I thank him, that he cuts me from my tale,
For I profess not talking; only this—
Let each man do his best: and here draw I
A sword, whose temper I intend to stain
With the best blood that I can meet withal $_{95}$

In the adventure of this perilous day.
Now, Esperance! Percy! and set on.
Sound all the lofty instruments of war,
And by that music let us all embrace;
For, heaven to earth, some of us never shall$_{100}$
A second time do such a courtesy.
(The trumpets sound. They embrace, and exeunt.)

SCENE III. PLAIN BETWEEN THE CAMPS

(The King enters with his power. Alarum to the battle. Then enter Douglas and Sir Walter Blunt.)

BLUNT. What is thy name, that in the battle thus
Thou crossest me? what honour dost thou seek
Upon my head?
DOUG. Know then, my name is Douglas;
And I do haunt thee in the battle thus
Because some tell me that thou art a king.$_5$
BLUNT. They tell thee true.
DOUG. The Lord of Stafford dear to-day hath bought
Thy likeness, for instead of thee, King Harry,
This sword hath ended him: so shall it thee,
Unless thou yield thee as my prisoner.$_{10}$
BLUNT. I was not born a yielder, thou proud Scot;
And thou shalt find a king that will revenge
Lord Stafford's death. (They fight. Douglas kills Blunt.)
(Enter Hotspur.)
HOT. O Douglas, hadst thou fought at Holmedon thus,
I never had triumph'd upon a Scot.$_{15}$
DOUG. All's done, all's won; here breathless lies the king.
HOT. Where?
DOUG. Here.
HOT. This, Douglas? no: I know this face full well:
A gallant knight he was, his name was Blunt;$_{20}$
Semblably furnish'd like the king himself.
DOUG. A fool go with thy soul, whither it goes!
A borrowed title hast thou bought too dear:

Why didst thou tell me that thou wert a king?

HOT. The king hath many marching in his coats.$_{25}$

DOUG. Now, by my sword, I will kill all his coats;
I'll murder all his wardrobe, piece by piece,
Until I meet the king.

HOT. Up, and away!
Our soldiers stand full fairly for the day. *(Exeunt.)*

(Alarum. Enter FALSTAFF, solus.)

FAL. Though I could 'scape shot-free at London, I fear$_{30}$
the shot here; here's no scoring but upon the pate. Soft!
who are you? Sir Walter Blunt: there's honour for you!
here's no vanity! I am as hot as molten lead, and as
heavy too: God keep lead out of me! I need no more
weight than mine own bowels. I have led my ragamuffins$_{35}$
where they are peppered: there's not three of my hundred
and fifty left alive; and they are for the town's end, to beg
during life. But who comes here?

(Enter the PRINCE.)

PRINCE. What, stand'st thou idle here? lend me thy sword:
Many a nobleman lies stark and stiff$_{40}$
Under the hoofs of vaunting enemies,
Whose deaths are yet unrevenged: I prithee, lend me thy
    sword.

FAL. O Hal, I prithee, give me leave to breathe awhile.
Turk Gregory never did such deeds in arms as I have done
this day. I have paid Percy, I have made him sure.$_{45}$

PRINCE. He is, indeed; and living to kill thee. I
prithee, lend me thy sword.

FAL. Nay, before God, Hal, if Percy be alive, thou
get'st not my sword; but take my pistol, if thou wilt.

PRINCE. Give it me: what, is it in the case?$_{50}$

FAL. Ay, Hal; 'tis hot, 'tis hot; there's that will sack a
city.

(The Prince draws it out, and finds it to be a bottle of sack.)

PRINCE. What, is it a time to jest and dally now?

(He throws the bottle at him. Exit.)

FAL. Well, if Percy be alive, I'll pierce him. If he do
come in my way, so: if he do not, if I come in his willingly,$_{55}$
let him make a carbonado of me. I like not such grinning

honour as Sir Walter hath: give me life: which if I can save, so; if not, honour comes unlooked for, and there's an end. *(Exit.)*

SCENE IV. ANOTHER PART OF THE FIELD

(ALARUM. EXCURSIONS. ENTER THE KING, THE PRINCE, LORD JOHN OF LANCASTER, AND EARL OF WESTMORELAND.)

KING. I prithee,
Harry, withdraw thyself; thou bleed'st too much.
Lord John of Lancaster, go you with him.
LAN. Not I, my lord, unless I did bleed too.
PRINCE. I beseech your majesty, make up, 5
Lest your retirement do amaze your friends.
KING. I will do so.
My Lord of Westmoreland, lead him to his tent.
WEST. Come, my lord, I'll lead you to your tent.
PRINCE. Lead me, my lord? I do not need your help: 10
And God forbid a shallow scratch should drive
The Prince of Wales from such a field as this,
Where stain'd nobility lies trodden on,
And rebels' arms triumph in massacres!
LAN. We breathe too long: come, cousin Westmoreland, 15
Our duty this way lies; for God's sake, come.
(Exeunt Prince John and Westmoreland.)
PRINCE. By God, thou hast deceived me, Lancaster;
I did not think thee lord of such a spirit:
Before, I loved thee as a brother, John;
But now, I do respect thee as my soul. 20
KING. I saw him hold Lord Percy at the point
With lustier maintenance than I did look for
Of such an ungrown warrior.
PRINCE. O, this boy
Lends mettle to us all! *(Exit.)*
(ENTER DOUGLAS.)
DOUG. Another king! they grow like Hydra's heads: 25
I am the Douglas, fatal to all those

That wear those colours on them: what art thou,
That counterfeit'st the person of a king?

K. HEN. The king himself; who, Douglas, grieves at heart
So many of his shadows thou hast met$_{30}$
And not the very king. I have two boys
Seek Percy and thyself about the field:
But, seeing thou fall'st on me so luckily,
I will assay thee: so, defend thyself.

DOUG. I fear thou art another counterfeit;$_{35}$
And yet, in faith, thou bear'st thee like a king:
But mine I am sure thou art, whoe'er thou be,
And thus I win thee.

(They fight; the King being in danger, re-enter Prince of Wales.)

PRINCE. Hold up thy head, vile Scot, or thou art like
Never to hold it up again! the spirits$_{40}$
Of valiant Shirley, Stafford, Blunt, are in my arms:
It is the Prince of Wales that threatens thee;
Who never promiseth but he means to pay.

(They fight: Douglas flies.)

Cheerly, my lord: how fares your grace?
Sir Nicholas Gawsey hath for succour sent,$_{45}$
And so hath Clifton: I'll to Clifton straight.

KING. Stay, and breathe awhile:
Thou hast redeem'd thy lost opinion,
And show'd thou makest some tender of my life,
In this fair rescue thou hast brought to me.$_{50}$

PRINCE. O God! they did me too much injury
That ever said I hearken'd for your death.
If it were so, I might have let alone
The insulting hand of Douglas over you,
Which would have been as speedy in your end$_{55}$
As all the poisonous potions in the world,
And saved the treacherous labour of your son.

KING. Make up to Clifton: I'll to Sir Nicholas Gawsey. *(Exit.)*

(ENTER HOTSPUR.)

HOT. If I mistake not, thou art Harry Monmouth.

PRINCE. Thou speak'st as if I would deny my name.$_{60}$

HOT. My name is Harry Percy.

PRINCE. Why, then I see

A very valiant rebel of the name.
I am the Prince of Wales; and think not, Percy,
To share with me in glory any more:
Two stars keep not their motion in one sphere;$_{65}$
Nor can one England brook a double reign,
Of Harry Percy and the Prince of Wales.
HOT. Nor shall it, Harry; for the hour is come
To end the one of us; and would to God
Thy name in arms were now as great as mine!$_{70}$
PRINCE. I'll make it greater ere I part from thee;
And all the budding honours on thy crest
I'll crop, to make a garland for my head.
HOT. I can no longer brook thy vanities. *(They fight).*
(ENTER FALSTAFF.)
FAL. Well said, Hal! to it, Hal! Nay, you shall find$_{75}$
no boy's play here, I can tell you.
(Re-enter DOUGLAS; he fights with FALSTAFF, who falls down as if he
*   were dead, and exit DOUGLAS. HOTSPUR is wounded, and falls.)*
HOT. O, Harry, thou hast robb'd me of my youth!
I better brook the loss of brittle life
Than those proud titles thou hast won of me;
They wound my thoughts worse than thy sword my flesh:$_{80}$
But thought's the slave of life, and life time's fool;
And time, that takes survey of all the world,
Must have a stop. O, I could prophesy,
But that the earthy and cold hand of death
Lies on my tongue: no, Percy, thou art dust,$_{85}$
And food for— *(Dies.)*
PRINCE. For worms, brave Percy: fare thee well, great heart!
Ill-weaved ambition, how much art thou shrunk!
When that this body did contain a spirit,
A kingdom for it was too small a bound;$_{90}$
But now two paces of the vilest earth
Is room enough: this earth that bears thee dead
Bears not alive so stout a gentleman.
If thou wert sensible of courtesy,
I should not make so dear a show of zeal:$_{95}$
But let my favours hide thy mangled face;
And, even in thy behalf, I'll thank myself

For doing these fair rites of tenderness.
Adieu, and take thy praise with thee to heaven!
Thy ignominy sleep with thee in the grave,$_{100}$
But not remember'd in thy epitaph!
(He spieth Falstaff on the ground.)
What, old acquaintance! could not all this flesh
Keep in a little life? Poor Jack, farewell!
I could have better spared a better man:
O, I should have a heavy miss of thee,$_{105}$
If I were much in love with vanity!
Death hath not struck so fat a deer to-day,
Though many dearer, in this bloody fray.
Embowell'd will I see thee by and by:
Till then in blood by noble Percy lie. *(Exit.)*$_{110}$
FAL. *(Rising up)* Embowelled! if thou embowel me
to-day, I'll give you leave to powder me and eat me too
to-morrow. 'Sblood, 'twas time to counterfeit, or that hot
termagant Scot had paid me scot and lot too. Counterfeit? I
lie, I am no counterfeit: to die, is to be a counterfeit; for$_{115}$
he is but the counterfeit of a man who hath not the life of
a man: but to counterfeit dying, when a man thereby liveth,
is to be no counterfeit, but the true and perfect image of
life indeed. The better part of valour is discretion; in the
which better part I have saved my life. 'Zounds, I am$_{120}$
afraid of this gunpowder Percy, though he be dead: how, if
he should counterfeit too, and rise? by my faith, I am
afraid he would prove the better counterfeit. Therefore
I'll make him sure; yea, and I'll swear I killed him. Why
may not he rise as well as I? Nothing confutes me but$_{125}$
eyes, and nobody sees me. Therefore, sirrah *(stabbing
him)*, with a new wound in your thigh, come you along
with me. (Takes up Hotspur on his back.)
*(RE-ENTER THE PRINCE OF WALES AND LORD JOHN OF
LANCASTER.)*
PRINCE. Come, brother John; full bravely hast thou flesh'd
Thy maiden sword.
LAN. But, soft! whom have we here?$_{130}$
Did you not tell me this fat man was dead?
PRINCE. I did; I saw him dead,

Breathless and bleeding on the ground. Art thou alive?
Or is it fantasy that plays upon our eyesight?
I prithee, speak; we will not trust our eyes$_{135}$
Without our ears: thou art not what thou seem'st.
FAL. No, that's certain; I am not a double man: but if
I be not Jack Falstaff, then am I a Jack. There is Percy
(throwing the body down): if your father will do me any
honour, so; if not, let him kill the next Percy himself. I$_{140}$
look to be either earl or duke, I can assure you.
PRINCE. Why, Percy I killed myself, and saw thee dead.
FAL. Didst thou? Lord, Lord, how this world is given
to lying! I grant you I was down and out of breath; and
so was he: but we rose both at an instant, and fought a long$_{145}$
hour by Shrewsbury clock. If I may be believed, so; if not,
let them that should reward valour bear the sin upon their
own heads. I'll take it upon my death, I gave him this
wound in the thigh: if the man were alive, and would deny
it, 'zounds, I would make him eat a piece of my sword.$_{150}$
LAN. This is the strangest tale that ever I heard.
PRINCE. This is the strangest fellow, brother John.
Come, bring your luggage nobly on your back:
For my part, if a lie may do thee grace,
I'll gild it with the happiest terms I have.$_{155}$
(A retreat is sounded.)
The trumpet sounds retreat; the day is ours.
Come, brother, let us to the highest of the field,
To see what friends are living, who are dead.
(Exeunt Prince of Wales and Lancaster.)
FAL. I'll follow, as they say, for reward. He that rewards
me, God reward him! If I do grow great, I'll grow$_{160}$
less; for I'll purge, and leave sack, and live cleanly as a
nobleman should do. *(Exit.)*

SCENE V. ANOTHER PART OF THE FIELD

*(THE TRUMPETS SOUND. ENTER THE KING, PRINCE OF WALES, LORD
JOHN OF LANCASTER, EARL OF WESTMORELAND, WITH WORCESTER AND
VERNON PRISONERS.)*

KING. Thus ever did rebellion find rebuke.
Ill-spirited Worcester! did not we send grace,
Pardon and terms of love to all of you?
And wouldst thou turn our offers contrary?
Misuse the tenour of thy kinsman's trust?$_5$
Three knights upon our party slain to-day,
A noble earl and many a creature else
Had been alive this hour,
If like a Christian thou hadst truly borne
Betwixt our armies true intelligence.$_{10}$
WOR. What I have done my safety urged me to;
And I embrace this fortune patiently,
Since not to be avoided it falls on me.
KING. Bear Worcester to the death, and Vernon too:
Other offenders we will pause upon.$_{15}$
(Exeunt Worcester and Vernon, guarded.)
How goes the field?
PRINCE. The noble Scot, Lord Douglas, when he saw
The fortune of the day quite turn'd from him,
The noble Percy slain, and all his men
Upon the foot of fear, fled with the rest;$_{20}$
And falling from a hill, he was so bruised
That the pursuers took him. At my tent
The Douglas is; and I beseech your grace
I may dispose of him.
KING. With all my heart.
PRINCE. Then, brother John of Lancaster, to you$_{25}$
This honourable bounty shall belong:
Go to the Douglas, and deliver him
Up to his pleasure, ransomless and free:
His valour shown upon our crests to-day
Hath taught us how to cherish such high deeds$_{30}$
Even in the bosom of our adversaries.
LAN. I thank your grace for this high courtesy,
Which I shall give away immediately.
KING. Then this remains, that we divide our power.
You, son John, and my cousin Westmoreland$_{35}$
Towards York shall bend you with your dearest speed,
To meet Northumberland and the prelate Scroop,

Who, as we hear, are busily in arms:
Myself and you, son Harry, will towards Wales,
To fight with Glendower and the Earl of March. 40
Rebellion in this land shall lose his sway,
Meeting the check of such another day:
And since this business so fair is done,
Let us not leave till all our own be won. *(Exeunt.)*

HENRY IV, PART 2

DRAMATIS PERSONÆ

RUMOUR, the Presenter.
KING HENRY the Fourth.
HENRY, PRINCE of WALES, afterwards King Henry V.,
THOMAS, DUKE OF CLARENCE,
PRINCE JOHN OF LANCASTER,
PRINCE HUMPHREY OF GLOUCESTER,
EARL OF WARWICK.
EARL OF WESTMORELAND.
EARL OF SURREY.
GOWER.
HARCOURT.
BLUNT.
Lord Chief-Justice of the King's Bench.
A Servant of the Chief-Justice.
EARL OF NORTHUMBERLAND.
SCROOP, Archbishop of York.
LORD MOWBRAY.
LORD HASTINGS.
LORD BARDOLPH.
SIR JOHN COLVILLE..
TRAVERS *and* MORTON, retainers of Northumberland.
SIR JOHN FALSTAFF.
His Page.

Bardolph.
Pistol.
Poins.
Peto.
Shallow,
Silence,
Davy, Servant to Shallow.
Mouldy, Shadow, Wart, Feeble, *and* Bullcalf, recruits.
Fang *and* Snare, sheriff's officers.
Lady Northumberland.
Lady Percy.
Mistress Quickly, hostess of a tavern in Eastcheap.
Doll Tearsheet.
Lords and Attendants; Porter, Drawers, Beadles, Grooms, &c.
A Dancer, speaker of the epilogue.

Scene: England.

INDUCTION

WARKWORTH. BEFORE THE CASTLE.

(Enter Rumour, painted full of tongues.)

RUM. Open your ears; for which of you will stop
The vent of hearing when loud Rumour speaks?
I, from the orient to the drooping west,
Making the wind my post-horse, still unfold
The acts commenced on this ball of earth: 5
Upon my tongues continual slanders ride,
The which in every language I pronounce,
Stuffing the ears of men with false reports.
I speak of peace, while covert enmity
Under the smile of safety wounds the world: 10
And who but Rumour, who but only I,
Make fearful musters and prepared defence,
Whiles the big year, swoln with some other grief,
Is thought with child by the stern tyrant war,
And no such matter? Rumour is a pipe 15
Blown by surmises, jealousies, conjectures,
And of so easy and so plain a stop
That the blunt monster with uncounted heads,
The still-discordant wavering multitude,
Can play upon it. But what need I thus 20
My well-known body to anatomize

Among my household? Why is Rumour here?
I run before King Harry's victory;
Who in a bloody field by Shrewsbury
Hath beaten down young Hotspur and his troops,[25]
Quenching the flame of bold rebellion
Even with the rebels' blood. But what mean I
To speak so true at first? my office is
To noise abroad that Harry Monmouth fell
Under the wrath of noble Hotspur's sword,[30]
And that the king before the Douglas' rage
Stoop'd his anointed head as low as death.
This have I rumour'd through the peasant towns
Between that royal field of Shrewsbury
And this worm-eaten hold of ragged stone,[35]
Where Hotspur's father, old Northumberland,
Lies crafty-sick: the posts come tiring on,
And not a man of them brings other news
Than they have learn'd of me: from Rumour's tongues
They bring smooth comforts false, worse than true wrongs.[40]

(Exit.)

ACT I

SCENE I. THE SAME

(Enter Lord Bardolph.)

L. BARD. Who keeps the gate here, ho?
(The Porter opens the gate.)
Where is the earl?
PORT. What shall I say you are?
L. BARD. Tell thou the earl
That the Lord Bardolph doth attend him here.
PORT. His lordship is walk'd forth into the orchard:
Please it your honour, knock but at the gate,$_5$
And he himself will answer.
(Enter Northumberland.)
L. BARD. Here comes the earl.
(Exit Porter.)
NORTH. What news, Lord Bardolph? every minute now
Should be the father of some stratagem:
The times are wild; contention, like a horse
Full of high feeding, madly hath broke loose$_{10}$
And bears down all before him.
L. BARD. Noble earl,

I bring you certain news from Shrewsbury.
NORTH. Good, an God will!
L. BARD. As good as heart can wish:
The king is almost wounded to the death;
And, in the fortune of my lord your son,$_{15}$
Prince Harry slain outright; and both the Blunts
Kill'd by the hand of Douglas; young Prince John
And Westmoreland and Stafford fled the field;
And Harry Monmouth's brawn, the hulk Sir John,
Is prisoner to your son: O, such a day,$_{20}$
So fought, so follow'd and so fairly won.
Came not till now to dignify the times,
Since Cæsar's fortunes!
NORTH. How is this derived?
Saw you the field? came you from Shrewsbury?
L. BARD. I spake with one, my lord, that came from thence,$_{25}$
A gentleman well bred and of good name,
That freely render'd me these news for true.
NORTH. Here comes my servant Travers, whom I sent
On Tuesday last to listen after news.
(ENTER TRAVERS.)
L. BARD. My lord, I over-rode him on the way;$_{30}$
And he is furnish'd with no certainties
More than he haply may retail from me.
NORTH. Now, Travers, what good tidings comes with you?
TRA. My lord, Sir John Umfrevile turn'd me back
With joyful tidings; and, being better horsed,$_{35}$
Out-rode me. After him came spurring hard
A gentleman, almost forspent with speed,
That stopp'd by me to breathe his bloodied horse.
He ask'd the way to Chester; and of him
I did demand what news from Shrewsbury:$_{40}$
He told me that rebellion had bad luck
And that young Harry Percy's spur was cold.
With that, he gave his able horse the head,
And bending forward struck his armed heels
Against the panting sides of his poor jade$_{45}$
Up to the rowel-head, and starting so
He seem'd in running to devour the way,

Staying no longer question.
NORTH. Ha! Again:
Said he young Harry Percy's spur was cold?
Of Hotspur Coldspur? that rebellion [50]
Had met ill luck?
L. BARD. My lord, I'll tell you what;
If my young lord your son have not the day,
Upon mine honour, for a silken point
I'll give my barony: never talk of it.
NORTH. Why should that gentleman that rode by Travers [55]
Give then such instances of loss?
L. BARD. Who, he?
He was some hilding fellow that had stolen
The horse he rode on, and, upon my life,
Spoke at a venture. Look, here comes more news.
(ENTER MORTON.)
NORTH. Yea, this man's brow, like to a title-leaf, [60]
Foretells the nature of a tragic volume:
So looks the strond whereon the imperious flood
Hath left a witness'd usurpation.
Say, Morton, didst thou come from Shrewsbury?
MOR. I ran from Shrewsbury, my noble lord; [65]
Where hateful death put on his ugliest mask
To fright our party.
NORTH. How doth my son and brother?
Thou tremblest; and the whiteness in thy cheek
Is apter than thy tongue to tell thy errand.
Even such a man, so faint, so spiritless, [70]
So dull, so dead in look, so woe-begone,
Drew Priam's curtain in the dead of night,
And would have told him half his Troy was burnt;
But Priam found the fire ere he his tongue,
And I my Percy's death ere thou report'st it. [75]
This thou wouldst say, 'Your son did thus and thus;
Your brother thus: so fought the noble Douglas:'
Stopping my greedy ear with their bold deeds:
But in the end, to stop my ear indeed,
Thou hast a sigh to blow away this praise, [80]
Ending with 'Brother, son, and all are dead.'

MOR. Douglas is living, and your brother, yet;
But, for my lord your son,—
NORTH. Why, he is dead.
See what a ready tongue suspicion hath!
He that but fears the thing he would not know$_{85}$
Hath by instinct knowledge from others' eyes
That what he fear'd is chanced. Yet speak, Morton;
Tell thou an earl his divination lies,
And I will take it as a sweet disgrace,
And make thee rich for doing me such wrong.$_{90}$
MOR. You are too great to be by me gainsaid:
Your spirit is too true, your fears too certain.
NORTH. Yet, for all this, say not that Percy's dead.
I see a strange confession in thine eye:
Thou shakest thy head, and hold'st it fear or sin$_{95}$
To speak a truth. If he be slain, say so;
The tongue offends not that reports his death:
And he doth sin that doth belie the dead;
Not he which says the dead is not alive.
Yet the first bringer of unwelcome news$_{100}$
Hath but a losing office, and his tongue
Sounds ever after as a sullen bell,
Remember'd tolling a departing friend.
L. BARD. I cannot think, my lord, your son is dead.
MOR. I am sorry I should force you to believe$_{105}$
That which I would to God I had not seen;
But these mine eyes saw him in bloody state,
Rendering faint quittance, wearied and outbreathed,
To Harry Monmouth; whose swift wrath beat down
The never-daunted Percy to the earth,$_{110}$
From whence with life he never more sprung up.
In few, his death, whose spirit lent a fire
Even to the dullest peasant in his camp,
Being bruited once, took fire and heat away
From the best-temper'd courage in his troops;$_{115}$
For from his metal was his party steel'd;
Which once in him abated, all the rest
Turn'd on themselves, like dull and heavy lead:
And as the thing that's heavy in itself,

Upon enforcement flies with greatest speed,$_{120}$
So did our men, heavy in Hotspur's loss,
Lend to this weight such lightness with their fear
That arrows fled not swifter toward their aim
Than did our soldiers, aiming at their safety,
Fly from the field. Then was that noble Worcester$_{125}$
Too soon ta'en prisoner; and that furious Scot,
The bloody Douglas, whose well-labouring sword
Had three times slain the appearance of the king,
'Gan vail his stomach and did grace the shame
Of those that turn'd their backs, and in his flight,$_{130}$
Stumbling in fear, was took. The sum of all
Is that the king hath won, and hath sent out
A speedy power to encounter you, my lord,
Under the conduct of young Lancaster
And Westmoreland. This is the news at full.$_{135}$
NORTH. For this I shall have time enough to mourn.
In poison there is physic; and these news,
Having been well, that would have made me sick,
Being sick, have in some measure made me well:
And as the wretch, whose fever-weaken'd joints,$_{140}$
Like strengthless hinges, buckle under life,
Impatient of his fit, breaks like a fire
Out of his keeper's arms, even so my limbs,
Weaken'd with grief, being now enraged with grief,
Are thrice themselves. Hence, therefore, thou nice crutch!$_{145}$
A scaly gauntlet now with joints of steel
Must glove this hand: and hence, thou sickly quoif!
Thou art a guard too wanton for the head
Which princes, flesh'd with conquest, aim to hit.
Now bind my brows with iron; and approach$_{150}$
The ragged'st hour that time and spite dare bring
To frown upon the enraged Northumberland!
Let heaven kiss earth! now let not Nature's hand
Keep the wild flood confined! let order die!
And let this world no longer be a stage$_{155}$
To feed contention in a lingering act;
But let one spirit of the first-born Cain
Reign in all bosoms, that, each heart being set

On bloody courses, the rude scene may end,
And darkness be the burier of the dead!$_{160}$
TRA. This strained passion doth you wrong, my lord.
L. BARD. Sweet earl, divorce not wisdom from your honour.
MOR. The lives of all your loving complices
Lean on your health; the which, if you give o'er
To stormy passion, must perforce decay.$_{165}$
You cast the event of war, my noble lord,
And summ'd the account of chance, before you said
'Let us make head.' It was your presurmise,
That, in the dole of blows, your son might drop:
You knew he walk'd o'er perils, on an edge,$_{170}$
More likely to fall in than to get o'er;
You were advised his flesh was capable
Of wounds and scars and that his forward spirit
Would lift him where most trade of danger ranged:
Yet did you say 'Go forth;' and none of this,$_{175}$
Though strongly apprehended, could restrain
The stiff-borne action: what hath then befallen,
Or what hath this bold enterprise brought forth,
More than that being which was like to be?
L. BARD. We all that are engaged to this loss$_{180}$
Knew that we ventured on such dangerous seas
That if we wrought out life 'twas ten to one;
And yet we ventured, for the gain proposed
Choked the respect of likely peril fear'd;
And since we are o'erset, venture again.$_{185}$
Come, we will all put forth, body and goods.
MOR. 'Tis more than time: and, my most noble lord,
I hear for certain, and do speak the truth,
The gentle Archbishop of York is up
With well-appointed powers: he is a man$_{190}$
Who with a double surety binds his followers.
My lord your son had only but the corpse,
But shadows and the shows of men, to fight;
For that same word, rebellion, did divide
The action of their bodies from their souls;$_{195}$
And they did fight with queasiness, constrain'd,
As men drink potions, that their weapons only

Seem'd on our side; but, for their spirits and souls,
This word, rebellion, it had froze them up,
As fish are in a pond. But now the bishop$_{200}$
Turns insurrection to religion:
Supposed sincere and holy in his thoughts,
He's followed both with body and with mind;
And doth enlarge his rising with the blood
Of fair King Richard, scraped from Pomfret stones;$_{205}$
Derives from heaven his quarrel and his cause;
Tells them he doth bestride a bleeding land,
Gasping for life under great Bolingbroke;
And more and less do flock to follow him.
NORTH. I knew of this before; but, to speak truth,$_{210}$
This present grief had wiped it from my mind.
Go in with me; and counsel every man
The aptest way for safety and revenge:
Get posts and letters, and make friends with speed:
Never so few, and never yet more need. *(Exeunt.)*$_{215}$

SCENE II. LONDON. A STREET

(Enter FALSTAFF, with his Page bearing his sword and buckler.)

FAL. Sirrah, you giant, what says the doctor to my
water?
PAGE. He said, sir, the water itself was a good healthy
water; but, for the party that owed it, he might have more
diseases than he knew for.$_5$
FAL. Men of all sorts take a pride to gird at me: the
brain of this foolish-compounded clay, man, is not able to
invent any thing that tends to laughter, more than I invent
or is invented on me: I am not only witty in myself, but
the cause that wit is in other men. I do here walk before$_{10}$
thee like a sow that hath overwhelmed all her litter but one.
If the prince put thee into my service for any other reason
than to set me off, why then I have no judgement. Thou
whoreson mandrake, thou art fitter to be worn in my cap
than to wait at my heels. I was never manned with an$_{15}$

agate till now: but I will inset you neither in gold nor silver,
but in vile apparel, and send you back again to your master,
for a jewel,—the juvenal, the prince your master, whose chin
is not yet fledged. I will sooner have a beard grow in the
palm of my hand than he shall get one on his cheek; and$_{20}$
yet he will not stick to say his face is a face-royal: God
may finish it when he will, 'tis not a hair amiss yet: he may
keep it still at a face-royal, for a barber shall never earn
sixpence out of it; and yet he'll be crowing as if he had
writ man ever since his father was a bachelor. He may$_{25}$
keep his own grace, but he's almost out of mine, I can
assure him. What said Master Dombledon about the satin
for my short cloak and my slops?

PAGE. He said, sir, you should procure him better
assurance than Bardolph: he would not take his band$_{30}$
and yours; he liked not the security.

FAL. Let him be damned, like the glutton! pray God
his tongue be hotter! A whoreson Achitophel! a rascally
yea-forsooth knave! to bear a gentleman in hand, and then
stand upon security! The whoreson smooth-pates do now$_{35}$
wear nothing but high shoes, and bunches of keys at their
girdles; and if a man is through with them in honest taking
up, then they must stand upon security. I had as lief they
would put ratsbane in my mouth as offer to stop it with
security. I looked a' should have sent me two and twenty$_{40}$
yards of satin, as I am a true knight, and he sends me
security. Well, he may sleep in security; for he hath the
horn of abundance, and the lightness of his wife shines
through it: and yet cannot he see, though he have his own
lanthorn to light him. Where's Bardolph?$_{45}$

PAGE. He's gone into Smithfield to buy your worship
a horse.

FAL. I bought him in Paul's, and he'll buy me a horse
in Smithfield: an I could get me but a wife in the stews, I
were manned, horsed, and wived.$_{50}$

(Enter the Lord Chief Justice and Servant.)

PAGE. Sir, here comes the nobleman that committed
the prince for striking him about Bardolph.

FAL. Wait close; I will not see him.

CH. JUST. What's he that goes there?

SERV. Falstaff, an't please your lordship.[55]

CH. JUST. He that was in question for the robbery?

SERV. He, my lord: but he hath since done good service
at Shrewsbury; and, as I hear, is now going with some
charge to the Lord John of Lancaster.

CH. JUST. What, to York? Call him back again.[60]

SERV. Sir John Falstaff!

FAL. Boy, tell him I am deaf.

PAGE. You must speak louder; my master is deaf.

CH. JUST. I am sure he is, to the hearing of any thing
good. Go, pluck him by the elbow; I must speak with him.[65]

SERV. Sir John!

FAL. What! a young knave, and begging! Is there not
wars? is there not employment? doth not the king lack
subjects? do not the rebels need soldiers? Though it be a
shame to be on any side but one, it is worse shame to beg[70]
than to be on the worst side, were it worse than the name
of rebellion can tell how to make it.

SERV. You mistake me, sir.

FAL. Why, sir, did I say you were an honest man?
setting my knighthood and my soldiership aside, I had lied in[75]
my throat, if I had said so.

SERV. I pray you, sir, then set your knighthood and
your soldiership aside; and give me leave to tell you, you
lie in your throat, if you say I am any other than an
honest man.[80]

FAL. I give thee leave to tell me so! I lay aside that
which grows to me! If thou gettest any leave of me, hang
me; if thou takest leave, thou wert better be hanged. You
hunt counter: hence! avaunt!

SERV. Sir, my lord would speak with you.[85]

CH. JUST. Sir John Falstaff, a word with you.

FAL. My good lord! God give your lordship good time
of day. I am glad to see your lordship abroad: I heard say
your lordship was sick: I hope your lordship goes abroad
by advice. Your lordship, though not clean past your[90]
youth, hath yet some smack of age in you, some relish of
the saltness of time; and I most humbly beseech your

lordship to have a reverend care of your health.

CH. JUST. Sir John, I sent for you before your expedition to Shrewsbury.95

FAL. An't please your lordship, I hear his majesty is returned with some discomfort from Wales.

CH. JUST. I talk not of his majesty: you would not come when I sent for you.

FAL. And I hear, moreover, his highness is fallen into100 this same whoreson apoplexy.

CH. JUST. Well, God mend him! I pray you, let me speak with you.

FAL. This apoplexy is, as I take it, a kind of lethargy, an't please your lordship; a kind of sleeping in the blood,105 a whoreson tingling.

CH. JUST. What tell you me of it? be it as it is.

FAL. It hath its original from much grief, from study and perturbation of the brain: I have read the cause of his effects in Galen: it is a kind of deafness.110

CH. JUST. I think you are fallen into the disease; for you hear not what I say to you.

FAL. Very well, my lord, very well: rather, an't please you, it is the disease of not listening, the malady of not marking, that I am troubled withal.115

CH. JUST. To punish you by the heels would amend the attention of your ears; and I care not if I do become your physician.

FAL. I am as poor as Job, my lord, but not so patient: your lordship may minister the potion of imprisonment to120 me in respect of poverty; but how I should be your patient to follow your prescriptions, the wise may make some dram of a scruple, or indeed a scruple itself.

CH. JUST. I sent for you, when there were matters against you for your life, to come speak with me.125

FAL. As I was then advised by my learned counsel in the laws of this land-service, I did not come.

CH. JUST. Well, the truth is, Sir John, you live in great infamy.

FAL. He that buckles him in my belt cannot live in less.130

CH. JUST. Your means are very slender, and your waste

is great.

FAL. I would it were otherwise; I would my means
were greater, and my waist slenderer.

CH. JUST. You have misled the youthful prince.135

FAL. The young prince hath misled me: I am the fellow
with the great belly, and he my dog.

CH. JUST. Well, I am loath to gall a new-healed wound:
your day's service at Shrewsbury hath a little gilded over
your night's exploit on Gads-hill: you may thank the unquiet140
time for your quiet o'er-posting that action.

FAL. My lord?

CH. JUST. But since all is well, keep it so: wake not a
sleeping wolf.

FAL. To wake a wolf is as bad as to smell a fox.145

CH. JUST. What! you are as a candle, the better part
burnt out.

FAL. A wassail candle, my lord, all tallow: if I did say
of wax, my growth would approve the truth.

CH. JUST. There is not a white hair on your face but150
should have his effect of gravity.

FAL. His effect of gravy, gravy, gravy.

CH. JUST. You follow the young prince up and down,
like his ill angel.

FAL. Not so, my lord; your ill angel is light; but I155
hope he that looks upon me will take me without
weighing: and yet, in some respects, I grant, I cannot go: I
cannot tell. Virtue is of so little regard in these
costermonger times that true valour is turned bear-herd:
pregnancy
is made a tapster, and hath his quick wit wasted in giving160
reckonings: all the other gifts appertinent to man, as the
malice of this age shapes them, are not worth a gooseberry.
You that are old consider not the capacities of us that are
young; you do measure the heat of our livers with the
bitterness of your galls: and we that are in the vaward of
our165
youth, I must confess, are wags too.

CH. JUST. Do you set down your name in the scroll of
youth, that are written down old with all the characters of

age? Have you not a moist eye? a dry hand? a yellow
cheek? a white beard? a decreasing leg? an increasing$_{170}$
belly? is not your voice broken? your wind short? your
chin double? your wit single? and every part about you
blasted with antiquity? and will you yet call yourself
young? Fie, fie, fie, Sir John!

FAL. My lord, I was born about three of the clock in the$_{175}$
afternoon, with a white head and something a round belly.
For my voice, I have lost it with halloing and singing of
anthems. To approve my youth further, I will not: the
truth is, I am only old in judgement and understanding;
and he that will caper with me for a thousand marks, let$_{180}$
him lend me the money, and have at him. For the box of
the ear that the prince gave you, he gave it like a rude
prince, and you took it like a sensible lord. I have checked
him for it; and the young lion repents; marry, not in
ashes and sackcloth, but in new silk and old sack.$_{185}$

CH. JUST. Well, God send the prince a better
companion!

FAL. God send the companion a better prince! I cannot
rid my hands of him.

CH. JUST. Well, the king hath severed you and Prince$_{190}$
Harry: I hear you are going with Lord John of Lancaster
against the Archbishop and the Earl of Northumberland.

FAL. Yea; I thank your pretty sweet wit for it. But
look you pray, all you that kiss my lady Peace at home,
that our armies join not in a hot day; for, by the Lord, I$_{195}$
take but two shirts out with me, and I mean not to sweat
extraordinarily: if it be a hot day, and I brandish any
thing but a bottle, I would I might never spit white again.
There is not a dangerous action can peep out his head, but
I am thrust upon it: well, I cannot last ever: but it was$_{200}$
alway yet the trick of our English nation, if they have a
good thing, to make it too common. If ye will needs say
I am an old man, you should give me rest. I would to
God my name were not so terrible to the enemy as it is:
I were better to be eaten to death with a rust than to be$_{205}$
scoured to nothing with perpetual motion.

CH. JUST. Well, be honest, be honest; and God bless

your expedition!

FAL. Will your lordship lend me a thousand pound to
furnish me forth?$_{210}$

CH. JUST. Not a penny, not a penny; you are too impatient
to bear crosses. Fare you well: commend me to
my cousin Westmoreland.

(Exeunt Chief-Justice and Servant.)

FAL. If I do, fillip me with a three-man beetle. A man
can no more separate age and covetousness than a' can$_{215}$
part young limbs and lechery: but the gout galls the one,
and the pox pinches the other; and so both the degrees
prevent my curses. Boy!

PAGE. *Sir?*

FAL. What money is in my purse?$_{220}$

PAGE. Seven groats and two pence.

FAL. I can get no remedy against this consumption of
the purse: borrowing only lingers and lingers it out, but
the disease is incurable. Go bear this letter to my Lord of
Lancaster; this to the prince; this to the Earl of$_{225}$
Westmoreland; and this to old Mistress Ursula, whom I have
weekly sworn to marry since I perceived the first white
hair on my chin. About it: you know where to find me.
(Exit Page.) A pox of this gout! or, a gout of this pox!
for the one or the other plays the rogue with my great toe.$_{230}$
'Tis no matter if I do halt; I have the wars for my colour,
and my pension shall seem the more reasonable. A good
wit will make use of any thing: I will turn diseases to
commodity. *(Exit.)*

SCENE III. YORK. THE ARCHBISHOP'S PALACE

*(ENTER THE ARCHBISHOP, THE LORDS HASTINGS, MOWBRAY, AND
BARDOLPH.)*

ARCH. Thus have you heard our cause and known our means;
And, my most noble friends, I pray you all,
Speak plainly your opinions of our hopes:
And first, lord marshal, what say you to it?

Mowb. I well allow the occasion of our arms;$_5$
But gladly would be better satisfied
How in our means we should advance ourselves
To look with forehead bold and big enough
Upon the power and puissance of the king.
Hast. Our present musters grow upon the file$_{10}$
To five and twenty thousand men of choice;
And our supplies live largely in the hope
Of great Northumberland, whose bosom burns
With an incensed fire of injuries.
L. Bard. The question then. Lord Hastings, standeth thus;$_{15}$
Whether our present five and twenty thousand
May hold up head without Northumberland?
Hast. With him, we may.
L. Bard. Yea, marry, there's the point:
But if without him we be thought too feeble,
My judgement is, we should not step too far$_{20}$
Till we had his assistance by the hand;
For in a theme so bloody-faced as this
Conjecture, expectation, and surmise
Of aids incertain should not be admitted.
Arch. 'Tis very true, Lord Bardolph; for indeed$_{25}$
It was young Hotspur's case at Shrewsbury.
L. Bard. It was, my lord; who lined himself with hope,
Eating the air on promise of supply,
Flattering himself in project of a power
Much smaller than the smallest of his thoughts:$_{30}$
And so, with great imagination
Proper to madmen, led his powers to death
And winking leap'd into destruction.
Hast. But, by your leave, it never yet did hurt
To lay down likelihoods and forms of hope.$_{35}$
L. Bard. Yes, if this present quality of war,
Indeed the instant action: a cause on foot,
Lives so in hope, as in an early spring
We see the appearing buds; which to prove fruit,
Hope gives not so much warrant as despair$_{40}$
That frosts will bite them. When we mean to build,
We first survey the plot, then draw the model;

And when we see the figure of the house,
Then must we rate the cost of the erection;
Which if we find outweighs ability,$_{45}$
What do we then but draw anew the model;
In fewer offices, or at least desist
To build at all? Much more, in this great work,
Which is almost to pluck a kingdom down
And set another up, should we survey$_{50}$
The plot of situation and the model,
Consent upon a sure foundation,
Question surveyors, know our own estate,
How able such a work to undergo,
To weigh against his opposite; or else$_{55}$
We fortify in paper and in figures,
Using the names of men instead of men:
Like one that draws the model of a house
Beyond his power to build it; who, half through,
Gives o'er and leaves his part-created cost$_{60}$
A naked subject to the weeping clouds,
And waste for churlish winter's tyranny.
HAST. Grant that our hopes, yet likely of fair birth,
Should be still-born, and that we now possess'd
The utmost man of expectation,$_{65}$
I think we are a body strong enough,
Even as we are, to equal with the king.
L. BARD. What, is the king but five and twenty thousand?
HAST. To us no more; nay, not so much, Lord Bardolph.
For his divisions, as the times do brawl,$_{70}$
Are in three heads: one power against the French,
And one against Glendower; perforce a third
Must take up us: so is the unfirm king
In three divided; and his coffers sound
With hollow poverty and emptiness.$_{75}$
ARCH. That he should draw his several strengths together
And come against us in full puissance,
Need not be dreaded.
HAST. If he should do so,
He leaves his back unarm'd, the French and Welsh
Baying him at the heels: never fear that.$_{80}$

L. Bard. Who is it like should lead his forces hither?
Hast. The Duke of Lancaster and Westmoreland;
Against the Welsh, himself and Harry Monmouth:
But who is substituted 'gainst the French,
I have no certain notice.
Arch. Let us $_{85}$
And publish the occasion of our arms.
The commonwealth is sick of their own choice;
Their over-greedy love hath surfeited:
An habitation giddy and unsure
Hath he that buildeth on the vulgar heart. $_{90}$
O thou fond many, with what loud applause
Didst thou beat heaven with blessing Bolingbroke,
Before he was what thou wouldst have him be!
And being now trimm'd in thine own desires,
Thou, beastly feeder, art so full of him, $_{95}$
That thou provokest thyself to cast him up.
So, so, thou common dog, didst thou disgorge
Thy glutton bosom of the royal Richard;
And now thou wouldst eat thy dead vomit up,
And howl'st to find it. What trust is in these times? $_{100}$
They that, when Richard lived, would have him die,
Are now become enamour'd on his grave:
Thou, that threw'st dust upon his goodly head
When through proud London he came sighing on
After the admired heels of Bolingbroke, $_{105}$
Criest now 'O earth, yield us that king again,
And take thou this!' O thoughts of men accursed!
Past and to come seems best; things present, worst.
Mowb. Shall we go draw our numbers, and set on?
Hast. We are time's subjects, and time bids be gone. $_{110}$
(Exeunt.)

ACT II

SCENE I. LONDON. A STREET

(Enter Hostess, Fang and his Boy with her, and Snare following.)

Host. Master Fang, have you entered the action?
Fang. It is entered.
Host. Where's your yeoman? Is't a lusty yeoman?
will a' stand to't?
Fang. Sirrah, where's Snare? 5
Host. O Lord, ay! good Master Snare.
Snare. Here, here.
Fang. Snare, we must arrest Sir John Falstaff.
Host. Yea, good Master Snare; I have entered him
and all. 10
Snare. It may chance cost some of us our lives, for he
will stab.
Host. Alas the day! take heed of him; he stabbed me
in mine own house, and that most beastly: in good faith,
he cares not what mischief he does, if his weapon be out: 15
he will foin like any devil; he will spare neither man,
woman, nor child.
Fang. If I can close with him, I care not for his thrust.

HOST. No, nor I neither: I'll be at your elbow.

FANG. An I but fist him once; an a' come but within$_{20}$ my vice,—

HOST. I am undone by his going; I warrant you, he's an infinitive thing upon my score. Good Master Fang, hold him sure: good Master Snare, let him not 'scape. A' comes continuantly to Pie-corner—saving your manhoods—to buy$_{25}$ a saddle; and he is indited to dinner to the Lubber's-head in Lumbert street, to Master Smooth's the silkman: I pray ye, since my exion is entered and my case so openly known to the world, let him be brought in to his answer. A hundred mark is a long one for a poor lone woman to$_{30}$ bear: and I have borne, and borne, and borne; and have been fubbed off, and fubbed off, and fubbed off, from this day to that day, that it is a shame to be thought on. There is no honesty in such dealing; unless a woman should be made an ass and a beast, to bear every knave's wrong.$_{35}$ Yonder he comes; and that arrant malmsey-nose knave, Bardolph, with him. Do your offices, do your offices: Master Fang and Master Snare, do me, do me, do me your offices.

(ENTER FALSTAFF, PAGE, AND BARDOLPH.)

FAL. How now! whose mare's dead? what's the matter?

FANG. Sir John, I arrest you at the suit of Mistress$_{40}$ Quickly.

FAL. Away, varlets! Draw, Bardolph: cut me off the villain's head: throw the quean in the channel.

HOST. Throw me in the channel! I'll throw thee in the channel. Wilt thou? wilt thou? thou bastardly rogue!$_{45}$ Murder, murder! Ah, thou honey-suckle villain! wilt thou kill God's officers and the king's? Ah, thou honey-seed rogue! thou art a honey-seed, a man-queller, and a woman-queller.

FAL. Keep them off, Bardolph.$_{50}$

FANG. A rescue! a rescue!

HOST. Good people, bring a rescue or two. Thou wo't, wo't thou? thou wo't, wo't ta? do, do, thou rogue! do, thou hemp-seed!

FAL. Away, you scullion! you rampallian! you fustilarian!$_{55}$ I'll tickle your catastrophe.

(Enter the Lord Chief-Justice, *and his men.)*

Ch. Just. What is the matter? keep the peace here, ho!

Host. Good my lord, be good to me. I beseech you,
stand to me.

Ch. Just. How now, Sir John! what are you brawling here?$_{60}$
Doth this become your place, your time and business?
You should have been well on your way to York.
Stand from him, fellow: wherefore hang'st upon him?

Host. O my most worshipful lord, an't please your
grace, I am a poor widow of Eastcheap, and he is arrested$_{65}$
at my suit.

Ch. Just. For what sum?

Host. It is more than for some, my lord; it is for all,
all I have. He hath eaten me out of house and home; he
hath put all my substance into that fat belly of his: but I$_{70}$
will have some of it out again, or I will ride thee o'nights
like the mare.

Fal. I think I am as like to ride the mare, if I have
any vantage of ground to get up.

Ch. Just. How comes this, Sir John? Fie! what man$_{75}$
of good temper would endure this tempest of exclamation?
Are you not ashamed to enforce a poor widow to so rough
a course to come by her own?

Fal. What is the gross sum that I owe thee?

Host. Marry, if thou wert an honest man, thyself and the$_{80}$
money too. Thou didst swear to me upon a parcel-gilt
goblet, sitting in my Dolphin-chamber, at the round table, by
a sea-coal fire, upon Wednesday in Wheeson week, when
the prince broke thy head for liking his father to a singing-man
of Windsor, thou didst swear to me then, as I was$_{85}$
washing thy wound, to marry me and make me my lady thy
wife. Canst thou deny it? Did not goodwife Keech, the
butcher's wife, come in then and call me gossip Quickly?
coming in to borrow a mess of vinegar; telling us she had
a good dish of prawns; whereby thou didst desire to eat$_{90}$
some; whereby I told thee they were ill for a green wound?
And didst thou not, when she was gone down stairs, desire
me to be no more so familiarity with such poor people;
saying that ere long they should call me madam? And didst

thou not kiss me and bid me fetch thee thirty shillings? I$_{95}$
put thee now to thy book-oath: deny it, if thou canst.

FAL. My lord, this is a poor mad soul; and she says
up and down the town that her eldest son is like you: she
hath been in good case, and the truth is, poverty hath
distracted
her. But for these foolish officers, I beseech you I$_{100}$
may have redress against them.

CH. JUST. Sir John, Sir John, I am well acquainted
with your manner of wrenching the true cause the false
way. It is not a confident brow, nor the throng of words
that come with such more than impudent sauciness from$_{105}$
you, can thrust me from a level consideration: you have,
as it appears to me, practised upon the easy-yielding spirit
of this woman, and made her serve your uses both in purse
and in person.

HOST. Yea, in truth, my lord.$_{110}$

CH. JUST. Pray thee, peace. Pay her the debt you owe
her, and unpay the villany you have done her: the one
you may do with sterling money, and the other with current
repentance.

FAL. My lord, I will not undergo this sneap without$_{115}$
reply. You call honourable boldness impudent sauciness:
if a man will make courtesy and say nothing, he is virtuous:
no, my lord, my humble duty remembered, I will
not be your suitor. I say to you, I do desire deliverance
from these officers, being upon hasty employment in the$_{120}$
king's affairs.

CH. JUST. You speak as having power to do wrong:
but answer in the effect of your reputation, and satisfy the
poor woman.

FAL. Come hither, hostess.$_{125}$

(Enter GOWER.)

CH. JUST. Now, Master Gower, what news?

GOW. The king, my lord, and Harry Prince of Wales
Are near at hand: the rest the paper tells.

FAL. As I am a gentleman.

HOST. Faith, you said so before.$_{130}$

FAL. As I am a gentleman. Come, no more words

of it.

Host. By this heavenly ground I tread on, I must be
fain to pawn both my plate and the tapestry of my
dining-chambers.$_{135}$

Fal. Glasses, glasses, is the only drinking: and for thy
walls, a pretty slight drollery, or the story of the Prodigal,
or the German hunting in water-work, is worth a thousand
of these bed-hangings and these fly-bitten tapestries. Let
it be ten pound, if thou canst. Come, an 'twere not for$_{140}$
thy humours, there's not a better wench in England. Go,
wash thy face, and draw the action. Come, thou must not
be in this humour with me; dost not know me? come,
come, I know thou wast set on to this.

Host. Pray thee, Sir John, let it be but twenty nobles:$_{145}$
i' faith, I am loath to pawn my plate, so God save me, la!

Fal. Let it alone; I'll make other shift: you'll be a
fool still.

Host. Well, you shall have it, though I pawn my
gown. I hope you'll come to supper. You'll pay me$_{150}$
all together?

Fal. Will I live? *(To Bardolph)* Go, with her, with
her; hook on, hook on.

Host. Will you have Doll Tearsheet meet you at
supper?$_{155}$

Fal. No more words; let's have her.
(Exeunt Hostess, Bardolph, Officers, and Boy.)

Ch. Just. I have heard better news.

Fal. What's the news, my lord?

Ch. Just. Where lay the king last night?

Gow. At Basingstoke, my lord.$_{160}$

Fal. I hope, my lord, all's well: what is the news, my
lord?

Ch. Just. Come all his forces back?

Gow. No; fifteen hundred foot, five hundred horse,
Are march'd up to my lord of Lancaster,$_{165}$
Against Northumberland and the Archbishop.

Fal. Comes the king back from Wales, my noble lord?

Ch. Just. You shall have letters of me presently:
Come, go along with me, good Master Gower.

FAL. My lord!$_{170}$
CH. JUST. What's the matter?
FAL. Master Gower, shall I entreat you with me to
dinner?
GOW. I must wait upon my good lord here; I thank
you, good Sir John.$_{175}$
CH. JUST. Sir John, you loiter here too long, being you
are to take soldiers up in counties as you go.
FAL. Will you sup with me, Master Gower?
CH. JUST. What foolish master taught you these
manners, Sir John?$_{180}$
FAL. Master Gower, if they become me not, he was a
fool that taught them me. This is the right fencing grace,
my lord; tap for tap, and so part fair.
CH. JUST. Now the Lord lighten thee! thou art a great
fool. *(Exeunt.)*$_{185}$

SCENE II. LONDON. ANOTHER STREET

(Enter PRINCE HENRY and POINS.)

PRINCE. Before God, I am exceeding weary.
POINS. Is't come to that? I had thought weariness
durst not have attached one of so high blood.
PRINCE. Faith, it does me; though it discolours the
complexion of my greatness to acknowledge it. Doth it$_5$
not show vilely in me to desire small beer?
POINS. Why, a prince should not be so loosely studied
as to remember so weak a composition.
PRINCE. Belike then my appetite was not princely got;
for, by my troth, I do now remember the poor creature,$_{10}$
small beer. But, indeed, these humble considerations make
me out of love with my greatness. What a disgrace is it
to me to remember thy name! or to know thy face
tomorrow! or to take note how many pair of silk stockings
thou hast, viz. these, and those that were thy peach-coloured$_{15}$
ones! or to bear the inventory of thy shirts, as, one for
superfluity, and another for use! But that the

tennis-court-keeper knows better than I; for it is a low ebb of
    linen with
thee when thou keepest not racket there; as thou hast not
done a great while, because the rest of thy low countries[20]
have made a shift to eat up thy holland: and God knows
whether those that bawl out the ruins of thy linen shall
inherit his kingdom: but the midwives say the children
are not in the fault; whereupon the world increases, and
kindreds are mightily strengthened.[25]

POINS. How ill it follows, after you have laboured so
hard, you should talk so idly! Tell me, how many good
young princes would do so, their fathers being so sick as
yours at this time is?

PRINCE. Shall I tell thee one thing, Poins?[30]

POINS. Yes, faith; and let it be an excellent good thing.

PRINCE. It shall serve among wits of no higher breeding
than thine.

POINS. Go to; I stand the push of your one thing that
you will tell.[35]

PRINCE. Marry, I tell thee, it is not meet that I should
be sad, now my father is sick: albeit I could tell to thee, as
to one it pleases me, for fault of a better, to call my friend,
I could be sad, and sad indeed too.

POINS. Very hardly upon such a subject.[40]

PRINCE. By this hand, thou thinkest me as far in the
devil's book as thou and Falstaff for obduracy and persistency:
let the end try the man. But I tell thee, my heart
bleeds inwardly that my father is so sick: and keeping such
vile company as thou art hath in reason taken from me all[45]
ostentation of sorrow.

POINS. The reason?

PRINCE. What wouldst thou think of me, if I should
weep?

POINS. I would think thee a most princely hypocrite.[50]

PRINCE. It would be every man's thought; and thou art
a blessed fellow to think as every man thinks: never a man's
thought in the world keeps the road-way better than thine:
every man would think me an hypocrite indeed. And what
accites your most worshipful thought to think so?[55]

POINS. Why, because you have been so lewd, and so
much engraffed to Falstaff.

PRINCE. And to thee.

POINS. By this light, I am well spoke on; I can hear it
with mine own ears: the worst that they can say of me is$_{60}$
that I am a second brother, and that I am a proper fellow
of my hands; and those two things, I confess, I cannot
help. By the mass, here comes Bardolph.

(Enter BARDOLPH and Page.)

PRINCE. And the boy that I gave Falstaff: a' had him
from me Christian; and look, if the fat villain have not$_{65}$
transformed him ape.

BARD. God save your grace!

PRINCE. And yours, most noble Bardolph!

BARD. Come, you virtuous ass, you bashful fool, must
you be blushing? wherefore blush you now? What a$_{70}$
maidenly man-at-arms are you become! Is't such a
matter to get a pottle-pot's maidenhead?

PAGE. A' calls me e'en now, my lord, through a red
lattice, and I could discern no part of his face from the
window: at last I spied his eyes; and methought he had$_{75}$
made two holes in the ale-wife's new petticoat and so
peeped through.

PRINCE. Has not the boy profited?

BARD. Away, you whoreson upright rabbit, away!

PAGE. Away, you rascally Althæa's dream, away!$_{80}$

PRINCE. Instruct us, boy; what dream, boy?

PAGE. Marry, my lord, Althæa dreamed she was
delivered of a fire-brand; and therefore I call him her dream.

PRINCE. A crown's worth of good interpretation: there
'tis, boy.$_{85}$

POINS. O, that this good blossom could be kept from
cankers! Well, there is sixpence to preserve thee.

BARD. An you do not make him hanged among you,
the gallows shall have wrong.

PRINCE. And how doth thy master, Bardolph?$_{90}$

BARD. Well, my lord. He heard of your grace's coming
to town: there's a letter for you.

POINS. Delivered with good respect. And how doth

the martlemas, your master?

BARD. In bodily health, sir.₉₅

POINS. Marry, the immortal part needs a physician; but
that moves not him: though that be sick, it dies not.

PRINCE. I do allow this wen to be as familiar with me
as my dog; and he holds his place; for look you how he
writes.₁₀₀

POINS. *(Reads)* 'John Falstaff, knight,'—every man must
know that, as oft as he has occasion to name himself: even
like those that are kin to the king; for they never prick
their finger but they say, 'There's some of the king's blood
spilt.' 'How comes that?' says he, that takes upon him₁₀₅
not to conceive. The answer is as ready as a borrower's
cap, 'I am the king's poor cousin, sir.'

PRINCE. Nay, they will be kin to us, or they will fetch
it from Japhet. But to the letter:

POINS. *(Reads)* 'Sir John Falstaff, knight, to the son of the₁₁₀
king, nearest his father, Harry Prince of Wales, greeting.' Why,
this is a certificate.

PRINCE. *Peace!*

POINS. *(Reads)* 'I will imitate the honourable Romans in
brevity:' he sure means brevity in breath, short-winded. 'I₁₅
commend me to thee, I commend thee, and I leave thee.

Be not
too familiar with Poins; for he misuses thy favours so much,
that he
swears thou art to marry his sister Nell. Repent at idle times
as thou
mayest; and so, farewell.
'Thine, by yea and no, which is as much as to say, as₁₂₀
thou usest him, Jack Falstaff with my
familiars, John with my brothers and sisters, and Sir
John with all Europe.'
My lord, I'll steep this letter in sack, and make him eat it.

PRINCE. That's to make him eat twenty of his words.₁₂₅
But do you use me thus, Ned? must I marry your sister?

POINS. God send the wench no worse fortune! But I
never said so.

PRINCE. Well, thus we play the fools with the time;

and the spirits of the wise sit in the clouds and mock us. 130
Is your master here in London?

BARD. Yea, my lord.

PRINCE. Where sups he? doth the old boar feed in the
old frank?

BARD. At the old place, my lord, in Eastcheap. 135

PRINCE. What company?

PAGE. Ephesians, my lord, of the old church.

PRINCE. Sup any women with him?

PAGE. None, my lord, but old Mistress Quickly and
Mistress Doll Tearsheet. 140

PRINCE. What pagan may that be?

PAGE. A proper gentlewoman, sir, and a kinswoman of
my master's.

PRINCE. Even such kin as the parish heifers are to the
town bull. Shall we steal upon them, Ned, at supper? 145

POINS. I am your shadow, my lord; I'll follow you.

PRINCE. Sirrah, you boy, and Bardolph, no word to
your master that I am yet come to town: there's for your
silence.

BARD. I have no tongue, sir. 150

PAGE. And for mine, sir, I will govern it.

PRINCE. *Fare you well; go. (Exeunt Bardolph and Page.)*
This Doll Tearsheet should be some road.

POINS. I warrant you, as common as the way between
Saint Alban's and London. 155

PRINCE. How might we see Falstaff bestow himself to-night
in his true colours, and not ourselves be seen?

POINS. Put on two leathern jerkins and aprons, and
wait upon him at his table as drawers.

PRINCE. From a God to a bull? a heavy descension! it 160
was Jove's case. From a prince to a prentice? a low
transformation! that shall be mine; for in every thing the
purpose must weigh with the folly. Follow me, Ned.
(Exeunt.)

SCENE III. WARKWORTH. BEFORE THE CASTLE

(Enter NORTHUMBERLAND, LADY NORTHUMBERLAND, and LADY PERCY.)

NORTH. I pray thee, loving wife, and gentle daughter,
Give even way unto my rough affairs:
Put not you on the visage of the times,
And be like them to Percy troublesome.
LADY N. I have given over, I will speak no more: 5
Do what you will; your wisdom be your guide.
NORTH. Alas, sweet wife, my honour is at pawn;
And, but my going, nothing can redeem it.
LADY P. O yet, for God's sake, go not to these wars!
The time was, father, that you broke your word, 10
When you were more endear'd to it than now;
When your own Percy, when my heart's dear Harry,
Threw many a northward look to see his father
Bring up his powers; but he did long in vain.
Who then persuaded you to stay at home? 15
There were two honours lost, yours and your son's.
For yours, the God of heaven brighten it!
For his, it stuck upon him as the sun
In the grey vault of heaven, and by his light
Did all the chivalry of England move 20
To do brave acts: he was indeed the glass
Wherein the noble youth did dress themselves:
He had no legs that practised not his gait;
And speaking thick, which nature made his blemish,
Became the accents of the valiant; 25
For those that could speak low and tardily
Would turn their own perfection to abuse,
To seem like him: so that in speech, in gait,
In diet, in affections of delight,
In military rules, humours of blood, 30
He was the mark and glass, copy and book,
That fashion'd others. And him, O wondrous him!
O miracle of men! him did you leave,
Second to none, unseconded by you,

To look upon the hideous god of war$_{35}$
In disadvantage; to abide a field
Where nothing but the sound of Hotspur's name
Did seem defensible: so you left him.
Never, O never, do his ghost the wrong
To hold your honour more precise and nice$_{40}$
With others than with him! let them alone:
The marshal and the archbishop are strong:
Had my sweet Harry had but half their numbers,
To-day might I, hanging on Hotspur's neck,
Have talk'd of Monmouth's grave.
NORTH. Beshrew your heart,$_{45}$
Fair daughter, you do draw my spirits from me
With new lamenting ancient oversights.
But I must go and meet with danger there,
Or it will seek me in another place
And find me worse provided.
LADY N. O, fly to Scotland,$_{50}$
Till that the nobles and the armed commons
Have of their puissance made a little taste.
LADY P. If they get ground and vantage of the king,
Then join you with them, like a rib of steel,
To make strength stronger; but, for all our loves,$_{55}$
First let them try themselves. So did your son;
He was so suffer'd: so came I a widow;
And never shall have length of life enough
To rain upon remembrance with mine eyes,
That it may grow and sprout as high as heaven,$_{60}$
For recordation to my noble husband.
NORTH. Come, come, go in with me. 'Tis with my mind
As with the tide swell'd up unto his height,
That makes a still-stand, running neither way:
Fain would I go to meet the archbishop,$_{65}$
But many thousand reasons hold me back.
I will resolve for Scotland: there am I,
Till time and vantage crave my company. *(Exeunt.)*

SCENE IV. LONDON. THE BOAR'S-HEAD TAVERN IN EASTCHEAP.

(Enter two Drawers.)

FIRST DRAW. What the devil hast thou brought there?
apple-johns? thou knowest Sir John cannot endure an
apple-john.
SEC. DRAW. Mass, thou sayest true. The prince once
set a dish of apple-johns before him, and told him there 5
were five more Sir Johns; and, putting off his hat, said 'I
will now take my leave of these six dry, round, old, withered
knights.' It angered him to the heart: but he hath forgot
that.
FIRST DRAW. Why, then, cover, and set them down: and 10
see if thou canst find out Sneak's noise; Mistress Tearsheet
would fain hear some music. Dispatch: the room where
they supped is too hot; they'll come in straight.
SEC. DRAW. Sirrah, here will be the prince and Master
Poins anon; and they will put on two of our jerkins and 15
aprons; and Sir John must not know of it: Bardolph hath
brought word.
FIRST DRAW. By the mass, here will be old utis: it will
be an excellent stratagem.
SEC. DRAW. I'll see if I can find out Sneak. *(Exit.)* 20
(ENTER HOSTESS AND DOLL TEARSHEET.)
HOST. I'faith, sweetheart, methinks now you are in an
excellent good temperality: your pulsidge beats as extraor-
      dinarily
as heart would desire; and your colour, I warrant
you, is as red as any rose, in good truth, la! But, i'
faith, you have drunk too much canaries; and that's a 25
marvellous searching wine, and it perfumes the blood ere
one can say 'What's this?' How do you now?
DOL. Better than I was: hem!
HOST. Why, that's well said; a good heart's worth
gold. Lo, here comes Sir John. 30
(ENTER FALSTAFF.)

FAL. *(Singing)* 'When Arthur first in court'——Empty *the jordan. (Exit First Drawer).*——*(Singing) 'And was a worthy king.'* How now, Mistress Doll!

HOST. Sick of a calm; yea, good faith.

FAL. So is all her sect; an they be once in a calm, they are sick.

DOL. You muddy rascal, is that all the comfort you give me?

FAL. You make fat rascals, Mistress Doll.

DOL. I make them! gluttony and diseases make them; I make them not.

FAL. If the cook help to make the gluttony, you help to make the diseases, Doll: we catch of you, Doll, we catch of you; grant that, my poor virtue, grant that.

DOL. Yea, joy, our chains and our jewels.

FAL. 'Your brooches, pearls, and ouches:' for to serve bravely is to come halting off, you know: to come off the breach with his pike bent bravely, and to surgery bravely; to venture upon the charged chambers bravely,——

DOL. Hang yourself, you muddy conger, hang yourself!

HOST. By my troth, this is the old fashion; you two never meet but you fall to some discord: you are both, i' good truth, as rheumatic as two dry toasts; you cannot one bear with another's confirmities. What the good-year! one must bear, and that must be you: you are the weaker vessel, as they say, the emptier vessel.

DOL. Can a weak empty vessel bear such a huge full hogshead? there's a whole merchant's venture of Bourdeaux stuff in him; you have not seen a hulk better stuffed in the hold. Come, I'll be friends with thee, Jack: thou art going to the wars; and whether I shall ever see thee again or no, there is nobody cares.

(Re-enter First Drawer.)

FIRST DRAW. Sir, Ancient Pistol's below, and would speak with you.

DOL. Hang him, swaggering rascal! let him not come hither: it is the foul-mouthedst rogue in England.

HOST. If he swagger, let him not come here: no, by my faith; I must live among my neighbours; I'll no swaggerers:

I am in good name and fame with the very best:
shut the door; there comes no swaggerers here: I have[70]
not lived all this while, to have swaggering now: shut the
door, I pray you.

FAL. Dost thou hear, hostess?

HOST. Pray ye, pacify yourself, Sir John: there comes
no swaggerers here.[75]

FAL. Dost thou hear? it is mine ancient.

HOST. Tilly-fally, Sir John, ne'er tell me: your ancient
swaggerer comes not in my doors. I was before Master
Tisick, the debuty, t'other day; and, as he said to me, 'twas
no longer ago than Wednesday last, 'I' good faith,[80]
neighbour Quickly,' says he; Master Dumbe, our minister, was
by then; 'neighbour Quickly,' says he, 'receive those that
are civil; for,' said he, 'you are in an ill name:' now a' said
so, I can tell whereupon; 'for,' says he, 'you are an honest
woman, and well thought on; therefore take heed what[85]
guests you receive: receive,' says he, 'no swaggering
companions.' There comes none here: you would bless you to
hear what he said: no, I'll no swaggerers.

FAL. He's no swaggerer, hostess; a tame cheater, i'
faith; you may stroke him as gently as a puppy greyhound:[90]
he'll not swagger with a Barbary hen, if her
feathers turn back in any show of resistance. Call him
up, drawer. *(Exit First Drawer.)*

HOST. Cheater, call you him? I will bar no honest man
my house, nor no cheater: but I do not love swaggering,[95]
by my troth; I am the worse, when one says swagger: feel,
masters, how I shake; look you, I warrant you.

DOL. So you do, hostess.

HOST. Do I? yea, in very truth, do I, an 'twere an
aspen leaf: I cannot abide swaggerers.[100]

(ENTER PISTOL, BARDOLPH, AND PAGE.)

PIST. God save you, Sir John!

FAL. Welcome, Ancient Pistol. Here, Pistol, I charge
you with a cup of sack: do you discharge upon mine
hostess.

PIST. I will discharge upon her, Sir John, with two[105]
bullets.

FAL. She is pistol-proof, sir; you shall hardly offend her.

HOST. Come, I'll drink no proofs nor no bullets: I'll drink no more than will do me good, for no man's pleasure, I.₁₁₀

PIST. Then to you, Mistress Dorothy; I will charge you.

DOL. Charge me! I scorn you, scurvy companion. What! you poor, base, rascally, cheating, lack-linen mate! Away, you mouldy rogue, away! I am meat for your master.

PIST. I know you, Mistress Dorothy.₁₁₅

DOL. Away, you cut-purse rascal! you filthy bung, away! by this wine, I'll thrust my knife in your mouldy chaps, an you play the saucy cuttle with me. Away, you bottle-ale rascal! you basket-hilt stale juggler, you! Since when, I pray you, sir? God's light, with two points on₁₂₀ your shoulder? much!

PIST. God let me not live, but I will murder your ruff for this.

FAL. No more, Pistol; I would not have you go off here: discharge yourself of our company, Pistol.₁₂₅

HOST. No, good Captain Pistol; not here, sweet captain.

DOL. Captain! thou abominable damned cheater, art thou not ashamed to be called captain? An captains were of my mind, they would truncheon you out, for taking their names upon you before you have earned them. You₁₃₀ a captain! you slave, for what? for tearing a poor whore's ruff in a bawdy-house? He a captain! hang him, rogue! he lives upon mouldy stewed prunes and dried cakes. A captain! God's light, these villains will make the word as odious as the word 'occupy;' which was an excellent good₁₃₅ word before it was ill sorted: therefore captains had need look to't.

BARD. Pray thee, go down, good ancient.

FAL. Hark thee hither, Mistress Doll.

PIST. Not I: I tell thee what, Corporal Bardolph, I₁₄₀ could tear her: I'll be revenged of her.

PAGE. Pray thee, go down.

PIST. I'll see her damned first; to Pluto's damned lake, by this hand, to the infernal deep, with Erebus and tortures vile also. Hold hook and line, say I. Down,₁₄₅

down, dogs! down, faitors! Have we not Hiren here?
HOST. Good Captain Peesel, be quiet; 'tis very late,
i' faith: I beseek you now, aggravate your choler.
PIST. These be good humours, indeed! Shall pack-horses,
And hollow pamper'd jades of Asia, 150
Which cannot go but thirty mile a-day,
Compare with Cæsars, and with Cannibals,
And Trojan Greeks? nay, rather damn them with
King Cerberus; and let the welkin roar.
Shall we fall foul for toys? 155
HOST. By my troth, captain, these are very bitter words.
BARD. Be gone, good ancient: this will grow to a brawl
anon.
PIST. Die men like dogs! give crowns like pins! Have
we not Hiren here? 160
HOST. O' my word, captain, there's none such here.
What the good-year! do you think I would deny her? For
God's sake, be quiet.
PIST. Then feed, and be fat, my fair Calipolis. Come,
give's some sack. 165
'Si fortune me tormente, sperato me contento.'
Fear we broadsides? no, let the fiend give fire:
Give me some sack: and, sweetheart, lie thou there.
(Laying down his sword.)
Come we to full points here; and are etceteras nothing?
FAL. Pistol, I would be quiet. 170
PIST. Sweet knight, I kiss thy neif: what! we have
seen the seven stars.
DOL. For God's sake, thrust him down stairs: I cannot
endure such a fustian rascal.
PIST. Thrust him down stairs! know we not Galloway 175
nags?
FAL. Quoit him down, Bardolph, like a shove-groat
shilling: nay, an a' do nothing but speak nothing, a' shall
be nothing here.
BARD. Come, get you down stairs. 180
PIST. What! shall we have incision? shall we imbrue?
(Snatching up his sword.)
Then death rock me asleep, abridge my doleful days!

Why, then, let grievous, ghastly, gaping wounds
Untwine the Sisters Three! Come, Atropos, I say!
Host. Here's goodly stuff toward!$_{185}$
Fal. Give me my rapier, boy.
Dol. I pray thee, Jack, I pray thee, do not draw.
Fal. Get you down stairs.
(Drawing, and driving Pistol out.)
Host. Here's a goodly tumult! I'll forswear keeping
house, afore I'll be in these tirrits and frights. So; murder,$_{190}$
I warrant now. Alas, alas! put up your naked weapons, put
up your naked weapons. (Exeunt Pistol and Bardolph.)
Dol. I pray thee, Jack, be quiet; the rascal's gone.
Ah, you whoreson little valiant villain, you!
Host. Are you not hurt i' the groin? methought a'$_{195}$
made a shrewd thrust at your belly.
(Re-enter Bardolph.)
Fal. Have you turned him out o' doors?
Bard. Yea, sir. The rascal's drunk: you have hurt
him, sir, i' the shoulder.
Fal. A rascal! to brave me!$_{200}$
Dol. Ah, you sweet little rogue, you! Alas, poor ape,
how thou sweatest! come, let me wipe thy face; come on,
you whoreson chops: ah, rogue! i' faith, I love thee:
thou art as valorous as Hector of Troy, worth five of
    Agamemnon,
and ten times better than the Nine Worthies: ah,$_{205}$
villain!
Fal. A rascally slave! I will toss the rogue in a blanket.
Dol. Do, an thou darest for thy heart: an thou dost, I'll
canvass thee between a pair of sheets.
(Enter Music.)
Page. The music is come, sir.$_{210}$
Fal. Let them play. Play, sirs. Sit on my knee,
Doll. A rascal bragging slave! the rogue fled from me
like quicksilver.
Dol. I' faith, and thou followedst him like a church.
Thou whoreson little tidy Bartholomew boar-pig, when$_{215}$
wilt thou leave fighting o' days and foining o' nights, and
begin to patch up thine old body for heaven?

(Enter, behind, PRINCE HENRY and POINS, disguised.)

FAL. Peace, good Doll! do not speak like a death's-head;
do not bid me remember mine end.

DOL. Sirrah, what humour's the prince of? $_{220}$

FAL. A good shallow young fellow: a' would have
made a good pantler, a' would ha' chipped bread well.

DOL. They say Poins has a good wit.

FAL. He a good wit? hang him, baboon! his wit's as
thick as Tewksbury mustard; there's no more conceit in $_{225}$
him than is in a mallet.

DOL. Why does the prince love him so, then?

FAL. Because their legs are both of a bigness; and a'
plays at quoits well; and eats conger and fennel; and
drinks off candles' ends for flap-dragons; and rides the $_{230}$
wild-mare with the boys; and jumps upon joined-stools;
and swears with a good grace; and wears his boots very
smooth, like unto the sign of the leg; and breeds no bate
with telling of discreet stories; and such other gambol
faculties a' has, that show a weak mind and an able body, $_{235}$
for the which the prince admits him: for the prince himself
is such another; the weight of a hair will turn the scales
between their avoirdupois.

PRINCE. Would not this nave of a wheel have his ears
cut off? $_{240}$

POINS. Let's beat him before his whore.

PRINCE. Look, whether the withered elder hath not
his poll clawed like a parrot.

POINS. Is it not strange that desire should so many
years outlive performance? $_{245}$

FAL. Kiss me, Doll.

PRINCE. Saturn and Venus this year in conjunction!
what says the almanac to that?

POINS. And, look, whether the fiery Trigon, his man,
be not lisping to his master's old tables, his note-book, $_{250}$
his counsel-keeper.

FAL. Thou dost give me flattering busses.

DOL. By my troth, I kiss thee with a most constant heart.

FAL. I am old, I am old.

DOL. I love thee better than I love e'er a scurvy young $_{255}$

boy of them all.

FAL. What stuff wilt have a kirtle of? I shall receive money o' Thursday: shalt have a cap to-morrow. A merry song, come: it grows late; we'll to bed. Thou'lt forget me when I am gone.$_{260}$

DOL. By my troth, thou'lt set me a-weeping, an thou sayest so: prove that ever I dress myself handsome till thy return: well, hearken at the end.

FAL. Some sack, Francis.

PRINCE. } Anon, anon, sir. *(Coming forward.)*$_{265}$
POINS. }

FAL. Ha! a bastard son of the king's? And art not thou Poins his brother?

PRINCE. Why, thou globe of sinful continents, what a life dost thou lead!

FAL. A better than thou: I am a gentleman; thou$_{270}$ art a drawer.

PRINCE. Very true, sir; and I come to draw you out by the ears.

HOST. O, the Lord preserve thy good grace! by my troth, welcome to London. Now, the Lord bless that$_{275}$ sweet face of thine! O Jesu, are you come from Wales?

FAL. Thou whoreson mad compound of majesty, by this light flesh and corrupt blood, thou art welcome.

DOL. How, you fat fool! I scorn you.

POINS. My lord, he will drive you out of your revenge$_{280}$ and turn all to a merriment, if you take not the heat.

PRINCE. You whoreson candle-mine, you, how vilely did you speak of me even now before this honest, virtuous, civil gentlewoman!

HOST. God's blessing of your good heart! and so she$_{285}$ is, by my troth.

FAL. Didst thou hear me?

PRINCE. Yea, and you knew me, as you did when you ran away by Gad's-hill: you knew I was at your back, and spoke it on purpose to try my patience.$_{290}$

FAL. No, no, no; not so; I did not think thou wast within hearing.

PRINCE. I shall drive you then to confess the wilful

abuse; and then I know how to handle you.

FAL. No abuse, Hal, o' mine honour; no abuse.₂₉₅

PRINCE. Not to dispraise me, and call me pantler and
bread-chipper and I know not what?

FAL. No abuse, Hal.

POINS. No abuse?

FAL. No abuse, Ned, i' the world; honest Ned, none.₃₀₀
I dispraised him before the wicked, that the wicked might
not fall in love with him; in which doing, I have done the
part of a careful friend and a true subject, and thy father is
to give me thanks for it. No abuse, Hal: none, Ned, none:
no, faith, boys, none.₃₀₅

PRINCE. See now, whether pure fear and entire cowardice
doth not make thee wrong this virtuous gentlewoman to close
with us? is she of the wicked? is thine hostess here of the
wicked? or is thy boy of the wicked? or honest Bardolph,
whose zeal burns in his nose, of the wicked?₃₁₀

POINS. Answer, thou dead elm, answer.

FAL. The fiend hath pricked down Bardolph irrecoverable;
and his face is Lucifer's privy-kitchen, where he doth
nothing but roast malt-worms. For the boy, there is a
good angel about him; but the devil outbids him too.₃₁₅

PRINCE. For the women?

FAL. For one of them, she is in hell already, and burns
poor souls. For the other, I owe her money; and whether
she be damned for that, I know not.

HOST. No, I warrant you.₃₂₀

FAL. No, I think thou art not; I think thou art quit
for that. Marry, there is another indictment upon thee, for
suffering flesh to be eaten in thy house, contrary to the
law; for the which I think thou wilt howl.

HOST. All victuallers do so: what's a joint of mutton₃₂₅
or two in a whole Lent?

PRINCE. You, gentlewoman,—

DOL. What says your grace?

FAL. His grace says that which his flesh rebels against.
(Knocking within.)

HOST. Who knocks so loud at door? Look to the₃₃₀
door there, Francis.

(Enter PETO.)

PRINCE. Peto, how now! what news?

PETO. The king your father is at Westminster;
And there are twenty weak and wearied posts
Come from the north: and, as I came along,_335_
I met and overtook a dozen captains,
Bare-headed, sweating, knocking at the taverns,
And asking every one for Sir John Falstaff.

PRINCE. By heaven, Poins, I feel me much to blame,
So idly to profane the precious time;_340_
When tempest of commotion, like the south
Borne with black vapour, doth begin to melt,
And drop upon our bare unarmed heads.
Give me my sword and cloak. Falstaff, good night.

(Exeunt Prince Henry, Poins, Peto, and Bardolph.)

FAL. Now comes in the sweetest morsel of the night, and_345_
we must hence, and leave it unpicked. *(Knocking within.)*
More knocking at the door!

(Re-enter BARDOLPH.)

How now! what's the matter?

BARD. You must away to court, sir, presently;
A dozen captains stay at door for you._350_

FAL. *(To the Page)* Pay the musicians, sirrah. Farewell,
hostess; farewell, Doll. You see, my good wenches, how
men of merit are sought after: the undeserver may sleep,
when the man of action is called on. Farewell, good wenches:
if I be not sent away post, I will see you again ere I go._355_

DOL. I cannot speak; if my heart be not ready to burst,—well,
sweet Jack, have a care of thyself.

FAL. Farewell, farewell. *(Exeunt Falstaff and Bardolph.)*

HOST. Well, fare thee well: I have known thee these
twenty nine years, come peascod-time; but an honester and_360_
truer-hearted man,—well, fare thee well.

BARD. *(Within)* Mistress Tearsheet!

HOST. What's the matter?

BARD. *(Within)* Bid Mistress Tearsheet come to my
master._365_

HOST. O, run, Doll, run; run, good Doll: come. *(She comes blubbered.)* Yea, will you come, Doll? *(Exeunt.)*

ACT III

SCENE I. WESTMINSTER. THE PALACE

(ENTER THE KING IN HIS NIGHTGOWN, WITH A PAGE.)

KING. Go call the Earls of Surrey and of Warwick;
But, ere they come, bid them o'er-read these letters,
And well consider of them: make good speed. *(Exit Page.)*
How many thousand of my poorest subjects
Are at this hour asleep! O sleep, O gentle sleep, 5
Nature's soft nurse, how have I frighted thee,
That thou no more wilt weigh my eyelids down,
And steep my senses in forgetfulness?
Why rather, sleep, liest thou in smoky cribs,
Upon uneasy pallets stretching thee, 10
And hush'd with buzzing night-flies to thy slumber,
Than in the perfumed chambers of the great,
Under the canopies of costly state,
And lull'd with sound of sweetest melody?
O thou dull god, why liest thou with the vile 15
In loathsome beds, and leavest the kingly couch
A watch-case or a common 'larum-bell?
Wilt thou upon the high and giddy mast

Seal up the ship-boy's eyes, and rock his brains
In cradle of the rude imperious surge, 20
And in the visitation of the winds,
Who take the ruffian billows by the top,
Curling their monstrous heads and hanging them
With deafening clamour in the slippery clouds,
That, with the hurly, death itself awakes? 25
Canst thou, O partial sleep, give thy repose
To the wet sea-boy in an hour so rude;
And in the calmest and most stillest night,
With all appliances and means to boot,
Deny it to a king? Then happy low, lie down! 30
Uneasy lies the head that wears a crown.
(ENTER WARWICK AND SURREY.)
WAR. Many good morrows to your majesty!
KING. Is it good morrow, lords?
WAR. 'Tis one o'clock, and past.
KING. Why, then, good morrow to you all, my lords. 35
Have you read o'er the letters that I sent you?
WAR. We have, my liege.
KING. Then you perceive the body of our kingdom
How foul it is; what rank diseases grow,
And with what danger, near the heart of it. 40
WAR. It is but as a body yet distemper'd;
Which to his former strength may be restored
With good advice and little medicine:
My Lord Northumberland will soon be cool'd.
KING. O God! that one might read the book of fate, 45
And see the revolution of the times
Make mountains level, and the continent,
Weary of solid firmness, melt itself
Into the sea! and, other times, to see
The beachy girdle of the ocean 50
Too wide for Neptune's hips; how chances mock,
And changes fill the cup of alteration
With divers liquors! O, if this were seen,
The happiest youth, viewing his progress through,
What perils past, what crosses to ensue, 55
Would shut the book, and sit him down and die.

'Tis not ten years gone
Since Richard and Northumberland, great friends,
Did feast together, and in two years after
Were they at wars: it is but eight years since$_{60}$
This Percy was the man nearest my soul;
Who like a brother toil'd in my affairs,
And laid his love and life under my foot;
Yea, for my sake, even to the eyes of Richard
Gave him defiance. But which of you was by— $_{65}$
You, cousin Nevil, as I may remember— *(To Warwick.)*
When Richard, with his eye brimful of tears,
Then check'd and rated by Northumberland,
Did speak these words, now proved a prophecy?
'Northumberland, thou ladder by the which$_{70}$
My cousin Bolingbroke ascends my throne;'
Though then, God knows, I had no such intent,
But that necessity so bow'd the state,
That I and greatness were compell'd to kiss:
'The time shall come,' thus did he follow it,$_{75}$
'The time will come, that foul sin, gathering head,
Shall break into corruption:' so went on,
Foretelling this same time's condition,
And the division of our amity.
WAR. There is a history in all men's lives,$_{80}$
Figuring the nature of the times deceased;
The which observed, a man may prophesy,
With a near aim, of the main chance of things
As yet not come to life, which in their seeds
And weak beginnings lie intreasured.$_{85}$
Such things become the hatch and brood of time;
And by the necessary form of this
King Richard might create a perfect guess
That great Northumberland, then false to him,
Would of that seed grow to a greater falseness;$_{90}$
Which should not find a ground to root upon,
Unless on you.
KING. Are these things then necessities?
Then let us meet them like necessities:
And that same word even now cries out on us:

They say the bishop and Northumberland$_{95}$
Are fifty thousand strong.
WAR. It cannot be, my lord;
Rumour doth double, like the voice and echo,
The numbers of the fear'd. Please it your grace
To go to bed. Upon my soul, my lord,
The powers that you already have sent forth$_{100}$
Shall bring this prize in very easily.
To comfort you the more, I have received
A certain instance that Glendower is dead.
Your majesty hath been this fortnight ill;
And these unseason'd hours perforce must add$_{105}$
Unto your sickness.
K. HEN. I will take your counsel:
And were these inward wars once out of hand,
We would, dear lords, unto the Holy Land. *(Exeunt.)*

SCENE II. GLOUCESTERSHIRE. BEFORE JUSTICE SHALLOW'S HOUSE

(ENTER SHALLOW AND SILENCE, MEETING; MOULDY, SHADOW, WART, FEEBLE, BULLCALF, A SERVANT OR TWO WITH THEM.)

SHAL. Come on, come on, come on, sir; give me your
hand, sir, give me your hand, sir: an early stirrer, by the
rood! And how doth my good cousin Silence?
SIL. Good morrow, good cousin Shallow.
SHAL. And how doth my cousin, your bedfellow? and$_5$
your fairest daughter and mine, my god-daughter Ellen?
SIL. Alas, a black ousel, cousin Shallow!
SHAL. By yea and nay, sir, I dare say my cousin William
is become a good scholar: he is at Oxford still, is he not?
SIL. Indeed, sir, to my cost.$_{10}$
SHAL. A' must, then, to the inns o'court shortly: I was
once of Clement's Inn, where I think they will talk of mad
Shallow yet.
SIL. You were called 'lusty Shallow' then, cousin.
SHAL. By the mass, I was called any thing; and I would$_{15}$

have done any thing indeed too, and roundly too. There
was I, and little John Doit of Staffordshire, and black George
Barnes, and Francis Pickbone, and Will Squele, a Cotswold
man; you had not four such swinge-bucklers in all the inns
o'court again: and I may say to you, we knew where the
bona-robas were and had the best of them all at
commandment. Then was Jack Falstaff, now Sir John, a
 boy, and
page to Thomas Mowbray, Duke of Norfolk.

SIL. This Sir John, cousin, that comes hither anon about
soldiers?

SHAL. The same Sir John, the very same. I see him
break Skogan's head at the court-gate, when a' was a crack
not thus high: and the very same day did I fight with one
Sampson Stockfish, a fruiterer, behind Gray's Inn. Jesu,
Jesu, the mad days that I have spent! and to see how many
of my old acquaintance are dead!

SIL. We shall all follow, cousin.

SHAL. Certain, 'tis certain; very sure, very sure: death,
as the Psalmist saith, is certain to all; all shall die. How
a good yoke of bullocks at Stamford fair?

SIL. By my troth, I was not there.

SHAL. Death is certain. Is old Double of your town
living yet?

SIL. Dead, sir.

SHAL. Jesu, Jesu, dead! a' drew a good bow; and
dead! a' shot a fine shoot: John a Gaunt loved him well,
and betted much money on his head. Dead! a' would have
clapped i' the clout at twelve score; and carried you a
 fore-hand
shaft a fourteen and fourteen and a half, that it would
have done a man's heart good to see. How a score of ewes
now?

SIL. Thereafter as they be: a score of good ewes may
be worth ten pounds.

SHAL. And is old Double dead?

SIL. Here come two of Sir John Falstaff's men, as I think.
(Enter BARDOLPH and one with him.)

BARD. Good morrow, honest gentlemen: I beseech you,

which is Justice Shallow?

SHAL. I am Robert Shallow, sir; a poor esquire of this
county, and one of the king's justices of the peace: what is
your good pleasure with me? 55

BARD. My captain, sir, commends him to you; my
captain, Sir John Falstaff, a tall gentleman, by heaven, and a
most gallant leader.

SHAL. He greets me well, sir. I knew him a good backsword
man. How doth the good knight? may I ask how 60
my lady his wife doth?

BARD. Sir, pardon; a soldier is better accommodated
than with a wife.

SHAL. It is well said, in faith, sir; and it is well said
indeed too. Better accommodated! it is good; yea, indeed, 65
is it: good phrases are surely, and ever were, very
  commendable.
Accommodated! it comes of 'accommodo:'
very good; a good phrase.

BARD. Pardon me, sir; I have heard the word. Phrase
call you it? by this good day, I know not the phrase; but 70
I will maintain the word with my sword to be a soldier-like
word, and a word of exceeding good command, by heaven.
Accommodated; that is, when a man is, as they say, accommodated;
or when a man is, being, whereby a' may be
thought to be accommodated; which is an excellent thing. 75

SHAL. It is very just.

(ENTER FALSTAFF.)

Look, here comes good Sir John. Give me your good hand,
give me your worship's good hand: by my troth, you like
well and bear your years very well: welcome, good Sir
John. 80

FAL. I am glad to see you well, good Master Robert
Shallow: Master Surecard, as I think?

SHAL. No, Sir John; it is my cousin Silence, in commission
with me.

FAL. Good Master Silence, it well befits you should be 85
of the peace.

SIL. Your good worship is welcome.

FAL. Fie! this is hot weather, gentlemen. Have you
provided me here half a dozen sufficient men?

SHAL. Marry, have we, sir. Will you sit? $_{90}$

FAL. Let me see them, I beseech you.

SHAL. Where's the roll? where's the roll? where's the
roll? Let me see, let me see, let me see. So, so, so, so, so,
so, so: yea, marry, sir: Ralph Mouldy! Let them appear as
I call; let them do so, let them do so. Let me see; where $_{95}$
is Mouldy?

MOUL. Here, an't please you.

SHAL. What think you, Sir John? a good-limbed fellow;
young, strong, and of good friends.

FAL. Is thy name Mouldy? $_{100}$

MOUL. Yea, an't please you.

FAL. 'Tis the more time thou wert used.

SHAL. Ha, ha, ha! most excellent, i' faith! things that
are mouldy lack use: very singular good! in faith, well
said, Sir John; very well said. $_{105}$

FAL. Prick him.

MOUL. I was pricked well enough before, an you could
have let me alone: my old dame will be undone now, for
one to do her husbandry and her drudgery: you need not
to have pricked me; there are other men fitter to go out $_{110}$
than I.

FAL. Go to: peace, Mouldy; you shall go. Mouldy, it
is time you were spent.

MOUL. Spent!

SHAL. Peace, fellow, peace; stand aside: know you $_{115}$
where you are? For the other, Sir John: let me see:
Simon Shadow!

FAL. Yea, marry, let me have him to sit under: he's
like to be a cold soldier.

SHAL. Where's Shadow? $_{120}$

Shad. Here, sir.

FAL. Shadow, whose son art thou?

Shad. My mother's son, sir.

FAL. Thy mother's son! like enough, and thy father's
shadow: so the son of the female is the shadow of the male: $_{125}$
it is often so, indeed; but much of the father's substance!

SHAL. Do you like him, Sir John?
FAL. Shadow will serve for summer; prick him, for we
have a number of shadows to fill up the muster-book.
SHAL. Thomas Wart!$_{130}$
FAL. Where's he?
Wart. Here, sir.
FAL. Is thy name Wart?
Wart. Yea, sir.
FAL. Thou art a very ragged wart.$_{135}$
SHAL. Shall I prick him down, Sir John?
FAL. It were superfluous; for his apparel is built upon
his back, and the whole frame stands upon pins: prick him
no more.
SHAL. Ha, ha, ha! you can do it, sir; you can do it: I$_{140}$
commend you well. Francis Feeble!
FEE. Here, sir.
FAL. What trade art thou, Feeble?
FEE. A woman's tailor, sir.
SHAL. Shall I prick him, sir?$_{145}$
FAL. You may: but if he had been a man's tailor,
he'ld ha' pricked you. Wilt thou make as many holes in an
enemy's battle as thou hast done in a woman's petticoat?
FEE. I will do my good will, sir: you can have no more.
FAL. Well said, good woman's tailor! well said,$_{150}$
courageous Feeble! thou wilt be as valiant as the wrathful
dove or most magnanimous mouse. Prick the woman's
tailor: well, Master Shallow; deep, Master Shallow.
FEE. I would Wart might have gone, sir.
FAL. I would thou wert a man's tailor, that thou mightst$_{155}$
mend him and make him fit to go. I cannot put him to a
private soldier, that is the leader of so many thousands: let
that suffice, most forcible Feeble.
FEE. It shall suffice, sir.
FAL. I am bound to thee, reverend Feeble. Who is$_{160}$
next?
SHAL. Peter Bullcalf o' the green!
FAL. Yea, marry, let's see Bullcalf.
BULL. Here, sir.
FAL. 'Fore God, a likely fellow! Come, prick me$_{165}$

Bullcalf till he roar again.

BULL. O Lord! good my lord captain,—

FAL. What, dost thou roar before thou art pricked?

BULL. O Lord, sir! I am a diseased man.

FAL. What disease hast thou?$_{170}$

BULL. A whoreson cold, sir, a cough, sir, which I caught with ringing in the king's affairs upon his coronation-day, sir.

FAL. Come, thou shalt go to the wars in a gown; we will have away thy cold; and I will take such order that$_{175}$ thy friends shall ring for thee. Is here all?

SHAL. Here is two more called than your number; you must have but four here, sir: and so, I pray you, go in with me to dinner.

FAL. Come, I will go drink with you, but I cannot$_{180}$ tarry dinner. I am glad to see you, by my troth, Master Shallow.

SHAL. O, Sir John, do you remember since we lay all night in the windmill in Saint George's field?

FAL. No more of that, good Master Shallow, no more$_{185}$ of that.

SHAL. Ha! 'twas a merry night. And is Jane Nightwork alive?

FAL. She lives, Master Shallow.

SHAL. She never could away with me.$_{190}$

FAL. Never, never; she would always say she could not abide Master Shallow.

SHAL. By the mass, I could anger her to the heart. She was then a bona-roba. Doth she hold her own well?

FAL. Old, old, Master Shallow.$_{195}$

SHAL. Nay, she must be old; she cannot choose but be old; certain she's old; and had Robin Nightwork by old Nightwork before I came to Clement's Inn.

SIL. That's fifty five year ago.

SHAL. Ha, cousin Silence, that thou hadst seen that$_{200}$ that this knight and I have seen! Ha, Sir John, said I well?

FAL. We have heard the chimes at midnight, Master Shallow.

SHAL. That we have, that we have, that we have; in$_{205}$
faith, Sir John, we have: our watch-word was 'Hem boys!'
Come, let's to dinner; come, let's to dinner: Jesus, the
days that we have seen! Come, come.
(Exeunt Falstaff and the Justices.)
BULL. Good Master Corporate Bardolph, stand my
friend; and here's four Harry ten shillings in French$_{210}$
crowns for you. In very truth, sir, I had as lief be hanged,
sir, as go: and yet, for mine own part, sir, I do not care;
but rather, because I am unwilling, and, for mine own part,
have a desire to stay with my friends; else, sir, I did not
care, for mine own part, so much.$_{215}$
BARD. Go to; stand aside.
MOUL. And, good master corporal captain, for my old
dame's sake, stand my friend: she has nobody to do any
thing about her when I am gone; and she is old, and cannot
help herself: you shall have forty, sir.$_{220}$
BARD. Go to; stand aside.
FEE. By my troth, I care not; a man can die but once:
we owe God a death: I'll ne'er bear a base mind: an't
be my destiny, so; an't be not, so: no man is too good to
serve's prince; and let it go which way it will, he that dies$_{225}$
this year is quit for the next.
BARD. Well said; thou'rt a good fellow.
FEE. Faith, I'll bear no base mind.
(Re-enter FALSTAFF and the Justices.)
FAL. Come, sir, which men shall I have?
SHAL. Four of which you please.$_{230}$
BARD. Sir, a word with you: I have three pound to
free Mouldy and Bullcalf.
FAL. Go to; well.
SHAL. Come, Sir John, which four will you have?
FAL. Do you choose for me.$_{235}$
SHAL. Marry, then, Mouldy, Bullcalf, Feeble and
Shadow.
FAL. Mouldy and Bullcalf: for you, Mouldy, stay at
home till you are past service: and for your part, Bullcalf,
grow till you come unto it: I will none of you.$_{240}$
SHAL. Sir John, Sir John, do not yourself wrong: they

are your likeliest men, and I would have you served with
the best.

FAL. Will you tell me, Master Shallow, how to choose
a man? Care I for the limb, the thewes, the stature, bulk,$_{245}$
and big assemblance of a man! Give me the spirit, Master
Shallow. Here's Wart; you see what a ragged appearance
it is: a' shall charge you and discharge you with the
motion of a pewterer's hammer, come off and on swifter than
he that gibbets on the brewer's bucket. And this same$_{250}$
half-faced fellow, Shadow; give me this man: he presents no
mark to the enemy; the foeman may with as great aim
level at the edge of a penknife. And for a retreat; how
swiftly will this Feeble the woman's tailor run off! O, give
me the spare men, and spare me the great ones. Put me a$_{255}$
caliver into Wart's hand, Bardolph.

BARD. Hold, Wart, traverse; thus, thus, thus.

FAL. Come, manage me your caliver. So: very well:
go to: very good, exceeding good. O, give me always a
little, lean, old, chapt, bald shot. Well said, i' faith, Wart;$_{260}$
thou'rt a good scab: hold, there's a tester for thee.

SHAL. He is not his craft's-master; he doth not do it
right. I remember at Mile-end Green, when I lay at Clement's
Inn,—I was then Sir Dagonet in Arthur's
show,—there was a little quiver fellow, and a' would manage
    you$_{265}$
his piece thus; and a' would about and about, and come
you in and come you in: 'rah, tah, tah,' would a' say;
'bounce' would a' say; and away again would a' go, and
again would a' come: I shall ne'er see such a fellow.

FAL. These fellows will do well, Master Shallow. God$_{270}$
keep you, Master Silence: I will not use many words with
you. Fare you well, gentlemen both: I thank you: I must
a dozen mile to-night. Bardolph, give the soldiers coats.

SHAL. Sir John, the Lord bless you! God prosper your
affairs! God send us peace! At your return visit our$_{275}$
house; let our old acquaintance be renewed: peradventure
I will with ye to the court.

FAL. 'Fore God, I would you would, Master Shallow.

SHAL. Go to; I have spoke at a word. God keep you.

FAL. Fare you well, gentle gentlemen. *(Exeunt)* [280]
Justices. On, Bardolph; lead the men away.
(Exeunt Bardolph, Recruits, &c.)
As I return, I will fetch off these
justices: I do see the bottom of Justice Shallow. Lord,
Lord, how subject we old men are to this vice of lying!
This same starved justice hath done nothing but prate to [285]
me of the wildness of his youth, and the feats he hath done
about Turnbull Street; and every third word a lie, duer
paid to the hearer than the Turk's tribute. I do remember
him at Clement's Inn like a man made after supper of a
cheese-paring: when a' was naked, he was, for all the [290]
world, like a forked radish, with a head fantastically carved
upon it with a knife: a' was so forlorn, that his dimensions
to any thick sight were invincible: a' was the very genius
of famine; yet lecherous as a monkey, and the whores
called him mandrake: a' came ever in the rearward of the [295]
fashion, and sung those tunes to the overscutched huswives
that he heard the carmen whistle, and sware they were his
fancies or his good-nights. And now is this Vice's dagger
become a squire, and talks as familiarly of John a Gaunt
as if he had been sworn brother to him; and I'll be sworn [300]
a' ne'er saw him but once in the Tilt-yard; and then he
burst his head for crowding among the marshal's men.
I saw it, and told John a Gaunt he beat his own name;
for you might have thrust him and all his apparel into an
eel-skin; the case of a treble hautboy was a mansion for [305]
him, a court: and now has he land and beefs. Well, I'll
be acquainted with him, if I return; and it shall go hard
but I will make him a philosopher's two stones to me:
if the young dace be a bait for the old pike, I see no
reason in the law of nature but I may snap at him. Let [310]
time shape, and there an end. *(Exit.)*

ACT IV

SCENE I. YORKSHIRE. GAULTREE FOREST

(Enter the Archbishop of York, Mowbray, Hastings, and others.)

Arch. What is this forest call'd?
Hast. 'Tis Gaultree Forest, an't shall please your grace.
Arch. Here stand, my lords; and send discoverers forth
To know the numbers of our enemies.
Hast. We have sent forth already.
Arch. 'Tis well done. 5
My friends and brethren in these great affairs,
I must acquaint you that I have received
New-dated letters from Northumberland;
Their cold intent, tenour and substance, thus:
Here doth he wish his person, with such powers 10
As might hold sortance with his quality,
The which he could not levy; whereupon
He is retired, to ripe his growing fortunes,
To Scotland: and concludes in hearty prayers
That your attempts may overlive the hazard 15
And fearful meeting of their opposite.
Mowb. Thus do the hopes we have in him touch ground

And dash themselves to pieces.
(Enter a Messenger.)
HAST. Now, what news?
Mess. West of this forest, scarcely off a mile,
In goodly form comes on the enemy;$_{20}$
And, by the ground they hide, I judge their number
Upon or near the rate of thirty thousand.
MOWB. The just proportion that we gave them out.
Let us sway on and face them in the field.
ARCH. What well-appointed leader fronts us here?$_{25}$
(ENTER WESTMORELAND.)
MOWB. I think it is my Lord of Westmoreland.
WEST. Health and fair greeting from our general,
The prince, Lord John and Duke of Lancaster.
ARCH. Say on, my Lord of Westmoreland, in peace:
What doth concern your coming?
WEST. Then, my$_{30}$
Unto your grace do I in chief address
The substance of my speech. If that rebellion
Came like itself, in base and abject routs,
Led on by bloody youth, guarded with rags,
And countenanced by boys and beggary,$_{35}$
I say, if damn'd commotion so appear'd,
In his true, native and most proper shape,
You, reverend father, and these noble lords
Had not been here, to dress the ugly form
Of base and bloody insurrection$_{40}$
With your fair honours. You, lord archbishop,
Whose see is by a civil peace maintain'd,
Whose beard the silver hand of peace hath touch'd,
Whose learning and good letters peace hath tutor'd,
Whose white investments figure innocence,$_{45}$
The dove and very blessed spirit of peace,
Wherefore do you so ill translate yourself
Out of the speech of peace that bears such grace,
Into the harsh and boisterous tongue of war;
Turning your books to graves, your ink to blood,$_{50}$
Your pens to lances and your tongue divine
To a loud trumpet and a point of war?

ARCH. Wherefore do I this? so the question stands.
Briefly to this end: we are all diseased,
And with our surfeiting and wanton hours$_{55}$
Have brought ourselves into a burning fever,
And we must bleed for it; of which disease
Our late king, Richard, being infected, died.
But, my most noble Lord of Westmoreland,
I take not on me here as a physician,$_{60}$
Nor do I as an enemy to peace
Troop in the throngs of military men;
But rather show awhile like fearful war,
To diet rank minds sick of happiness
And purge the obstructions which begin to stop$_{65}$
Our very veins of life. Hear me more plainly.
I have in equal balance justly weigh'd
What wrongs our arms may do, what wrongs we suffer.
And find our griefs heavier than our offences.
We see which way the stream of time doth run,$_{70}$
And are enforced from our most quiet there
By the rough torrent of occasion;
And have the summary of all our griefs,
When time shall serve, to show in articles;
Which long ere this we offer'd to the king,$_{75}$
And might by no suit gain our audience:
When we are wrong'd and would unfold our griefs,
We are denied access unto his person
Even by those men that most have done us wrong.
The dangers of the days but newly gone,$_{80}$
Whose memory is written on the earth
With yet appearing blood, and the examples
Of every minute's instance, present now,
Hath put us in these ill-beseeming arms,
Not to break peace or any branch of it,$_{85}$
But to establish here a peace indeed,
Concurring both in name and quality.
WEST. When ever yet was your appeal denied?
Wherein have you been galled by the king?
What peer hath been suborn'd to grate on you,$_{90}$
That you should seal this lawless bloody book

Of forged rebellion with a seal divine
And consecrate commotion's bitter edge?
ARCH. My brother general, the commonwealth,
To brother born an household cruelty;₉₅
I make my quarrel in particular.
WEST. There is no need of any such redress;
Or if there were, it not belongs to you.
MOWB. Why not to him in part, and to us all
That feel the bruises of the days before,₁₀₀
And suffer the condition of these times
To lay a heavy and unequal hand
Upon our honours?
WEST. O, my good Lord Mowbray,
Construe the times to their necessities,
And you shall say indeed, it is the time,₁₀₅
And not the king, that doth you injuries.
Yet for your part, it not appears to me
Either from the king or in the present time
That you should have an inch of any ground
To build a grief on: were you not restored₁₁₀
To all the Duke of Norfolk's signories,
Your noble and right well remember'd father's?
MOWB. What thing, in honour, had my father lost,
That need to be revived and breathed in me?
The king that loved him, as the state stood then,₁₁₅
Was force perforce compell'd to banish him:
And then that Henry Bolingbroke and he,
Being mounted and both roused in their seats,
Their neighing coursers daring of the spur,
Their armed staves in charge, their beavers down,₁₂₀
Their eyes of fire sparkling through sights of steel
And the loud trumpet blowing them together,
Then, then, when there was nothing could have stay'd
My father from the breast of Bolingbroke,
O, when the king did throw his warder down,₁₂₅
His own life hung upon the staff he threw;
Then threw he down himself and all their lives
That by indictment and by dint of sword
Have since miscarried under Bolingbroke.

WEST. You speak, Lord Mowbray, now you know not what.[130]
The Earl of Hereford was reputed then
In England the most valiant gentleman:
Who knows on whom fortune would then have smiled?
But if your father had been victor there,
He ne'er had borne it out of Coventry:[135]
For all the country in a general voice
Cried hate upon him; and all their prayers and love
Were set on Hereford, whom they doted on
And bless'd and graced indeed, more than the king.
But this is mere digression from my purpose.[140]
Here come I from our princely general
To know your griefs; to tell you from his grace
That he will give you audience; and wherein
It shall appear that your demands are just,
You shall enjoy them, every thing set off[145]
That might so much as think you enemies.
MOWB. But he hath forced us to compel this offer;
And it proceeds from policy, not love.
WEST. Mowbray, you overween to take it so;
This offer comes from mercy, not from fear:[150]
For, lo! within a ken our army lies,
Upon mine honour, all too confident
To give admittance to a thought of fear.
Our battle is more full of names than yours,
Our men more perfect in the use of arms,[155]
Our armour all as strong, our cause the best;
Then reason will our hearts should be as good:
Say you not then our offer is compell'd.
MOWB. Well, by my will we shall admit no parley.
WEST. That argues but the shame of your offence:[160]
A rotten case abides no handling.
HAST. Hath the Prince John a full commission,
In very ample virtue of his father,
To hear and absolutely to determine
Of what conditions we shall stand upon?[165]
WEST. That is intended in the general's name:
I muse you make so slight a question.
ARCH. Then take, my Lord of Westmoreland, this schedule,

For this contains our general grievances:
Each several article herein redress'd, [170]
All members of our cause, both here and hence,
That are insinewed to this action,
Acquitted by a true substantial form,
And present execution of our wills
To us and to our purposes confined, [175]
We come within our awful banks again,
And knit our powers to the arm of peace.
WEST. This will I show the general. Please you, lords,
In sight of both our battles we may meet;
And either end in peace, which God so frame! [180]
Or to the place of difference call the swords
Which must decide it.
Which must decide it.
ARCH. My lord, we will do so. *(Exit West.)*
MOWB. There is a thing within my bosom tells me
That no conditions of our peace can stand.
HAST. Fear you not that: if we can make our peace [185]
Upon such large terms and so absolute
As our conditions shall consist upon,
Our peace shall stand as firm as rocky mountains.
MOWB. Yea, but our valuation shall be such
That every slight and false-derived cause, [190]
Yea, every idle, nice and wanton reason
Shall to the king taste of this action;
That, were our royal faiths martyrs in love,
We shall be winnow'd with so rough a wind
That even our corn shall seem as light as chaff [195]
And good from bad find no partition.
ARCH. No, no, my lord. Note this; the king is weary
Of dainty and such picking grievances:
For he hath found to end one doubt by death
Revives two greater in the heirs of life, [200]
And therefore will he wipe his tables clean
And keep no tell-tale to his memory
That may repeat and history his loss
To new remembrance; for full well he knows
He cannot so precisely weed this land [205]

As his misdoubts present occasion:
His foes are so enrooted with his friends
That, plucking to unfix an enemy,
He doth unfasten so and shake a friend.
So that this land, like an offensive wife$_{210}$
That hath enraged him on to offer strokes,
As he is striking, holds his infant up
And hangs resolved correction in the arm
That was uprear'd to execution.
HAST. Besides, the king hath wasted all his rods$_{215}$
On late offenders, that he now doth lack
The very instruments of chastisement:
So that his power, like to a fangless lion,
May offer, but not hold.
ARCH. 'Tis very true:
And therefore be assured, my good lord marshal,$_{220}$
If we do now make our atonement well,
Our peace will, like a broken limb united,
Grow stronger for the breaking.
MOWB. Be it so.
Here is return'd my Lord of Westmoreland.
(RE-ENTER WESTMORELAND.)
WEST. The prince is here at hand: pleaseth your lordship$_{225}$
To meet his grace just distance 'tween our armies.
MOWB. Your grace of York, in God's name, then, set forward.
ARCH. Before, and greet his grace: my lord, we come. *(Exeunt.)*

SCENE II. ANOTHER PART OF THE FOREST

(Enter, from one side, MOWBRAY, attended; afterwards the ARCHBISHOP, HASTINGS, and others: from the other side, PRINCE JOHN of LANCASTER, and WESTMORELAND; Officers, and others with them.)

LAN. You are well encounter'd here, my cousin Mowbray:
Good day to you, gentle lord archbishop;
And so to you, Lord Hastings, and to all.
My Lord of York, it better show'd with you
When that your flock, assembled by the bell,$_5$

Encircled you to hear with reverence
Your exposition on the holy text
Than now to see you here an iron man,
Cheering a rout of rebels with your drum,
Turning the word to sword and life to death. $_{10}$
That man that sits within a monarch's heart,
And ripens in the sunshine of his favour,
Would he abuse the countenance of the king,
Alack, what mischiefs might he set abroach
In shadow of such greatness! With you, lord bishop, $_{15}$
It is even so. Who hath not heard it spoken
How deep you were within the books of God?
To us the speaker in his parliament;
To us the imagined voice of God himself;
The very opener and intelligencer $_{20}$
Between the grace, the sanctities of heaven
And our dull workings. O, who shall believe
But you misuse the reverence of your place,
Employ the countenance and grace of heaven,
As a false favourite doth his prince's name, $_{25}$
In deeds dishonourable? You have ta'en up,
Under the counterfeited zeal of God,
The subjects of his substitute, my father,
And both against the peace of heaven and him
Have here up-swarm'd them.
ARCH. Good my Lord of Lancaster, $_{30}$
I am not here against your father's peace;
But, as I told my Lord of Westmoreland,
The time misorder'd doth, in common sense,
Crowd us and crush us to this monstrous form,
To hold our safety up. I sent your grace $_{35}$
The parcels and particulars of our grief,
The which hath been with scorn shoved from the court,
Whereon this Hydra son of war is born;
Whose dangerous eyes may well be charm'd asleep
With grant of our most just and right desires, $_{40}$
And true obedience, of this madness cured,
Stoop tamely to the foot of majesty.
MOWB. If not, we ready are to try our fortunes

To the last man.

HAST. And though we here fall down,
We have supplies to second our attempt:$_{45}$
If they miscarry, theirs shall second them;
And so success of mischief shall be born
And heir from heir shall hold this quarrel up
Whiles England shall have generation.

LAN. You are too shallow, Hastings, much too shallow,$_{50}$
To sound the bottom of the after-times.

WEST. Pleaseth your grace to answer them directly
How far forth you do like their articles.

LAN. I like them all, and do allow them well;
And swear here, by the honour of my blood,$_{55}$
My father's purposes have been mistook;
And some about him have too lavishly
Wrested his meaning and authority.
My lord, these griefs shall be with speed redress'd;
Upon my soul, they shall. If this may please you,$_{60}$
Discharge your powers unto their several counties,
As we will ours: and here between the armies
Let's drink together friendly and embrace,
That all their eyes may bear those tokens home
Of our restored love and amity.$_{65}$

ARCH. I take your princely word for these redresses.

LAN. I give it you, and will maintain my word:
And thereupon I drink unto your grace.

HAST. Go, captain, and deliver to the army
This news of peace: let them have pay, and part:$_{70}$
I know it will well please them. Hie thee, captain.
(Exit Officer.)

ARCH. To you, my noble Lord of Westmoreland.

WEST. I pledge your grace; and, if you knew what pains
I have bestow'd to breed this present peace,
You would drink freely: but my love to ye$_{75}$
Shall show itself more openly hereafter.

ARCH. I do not doubt you.

WEST. I am glad of it.
Health to my lord and gentle cousin, Mowbray.

MOWB. You wish me health in very happy season;

For I am, on the sudden, something ill.$_{80}$
Arch. Against ill chances men are ever merry;
But heaviness foreruns the good event.
West. Therefore be merry, coz; since sudden sorrow
Serves to say thus, 'some good thing comes to-morrow.'
Arch. Believe me, I am passing light in spirit.$_{85}$
Mowb. So much the worse, if your own rule be true.
(Shouts within.)
Lan. The word of peace is render'd: hark, how they shout!
Mowb. This had been cheerful after victory.
Arch. A peace is of the nature of a conquest;
For then both parties nobly are subdued,$_{90}$
And neither party loser.
Lan. Go, my lord,
And let our army be discharged too. *(Exit Westmoreland.)*
And, good my lord, so please you, let our trains
March by us, that we may peruse the men
We should have coped withal.
Arch. Go, good Lord Hastings,$_{95}$
And, ere they be dismiss'd, let them march by. *(Exit Hastings.)*
Lan. I trust, lords, we shall lie to-night together.
(Re-enter Westmoreland.)
Now, cousin, wherefore stands our army still?
West. The leaders, having charge from you to stand,
Will not go off until they hear you speak.$_{100}$
Lan. They know their duties.
(Re-enter Hastings.)
Hast. My lord, our army is dispersed already:
Like youthful steers unyoked, they take their courses
East, west, north, south; or, like a school broke up,
Each hurries toward his home and sporting-place.$_{105}$
West. Good tidings, my Lord Hastings; for the which
I do arrest thee, traitor, of high treason:
And you, lord archbishop, and you, lord Mowbray,
Of capital treason I attach you both.
Mowb. Is this proceeding just and honourable?$_{110}$
West. Is your assembly so?
Arch. Will you thus break your faith?
Lan. I pawn'd thee none:

I promised you redress of these same grievances
Whereof you did complain; which, by mine honour,
I will perform with a most Christian care.$_{115}$
But for you, rebels, look to taste the due
Meet for rebellion and such acts as yours.
Most shallowly did you these arms commence,
Fondly brought here and foolishly sent hence.
Strike up our drums, pursue the scatter'd stray:$_{120}$
God, and not we, hath safely fought to-day.
Some guard these traitors to the block of death,
Treason's true bed and yielder up of breath. *(Exeunt.)*

SCENE III. ANOTHER PART OF THE FOREST

(ALARUM. EXCURSIONS. ENTER FALSTAFF AND COLEVILE, MEETING.)

FAL. What's your name, sir? of what condition are you,
and of what place, I pray?
COLE. I am a knight, sir; and my name is Colevile of
the dale.
FAL. Well, then, Colevile is your name, a knight is your$_5$
degree, and your place the dale: Colevile shall be still your
name, a traitor your degree, and the dungeon your place,
a place deep enough; so shall you be still Colevile of the
dale.
COLE. Are not you Sir John Falstaff?$_{10}$
FAL. As good a man as he, sir, whoe'er I am. Do ye
yield, sir? or shall I sweat for you? If I do sweat, they are
the drops of thy lovers, and they weep for thy death: therefore
rouse up fear and trembling, and do observance to my
mercy.$_{15}$
COLE. I think you are Sir John Falstaff, and in that
thought yield me.
FAL. I have a whole school of tongues in this belly of
mine, and not a tongue of them all speaks any other word
but my name. An I had but a belly of any indifferency, I$_{20}$
were simply the most active fellow in Europe: my womb,
my womb, my womb, undoes me. Here comes our general.

(Enter Prince John of Lancaster, Westmoreland, Blunt, and others.)

Lan. The heat is past; follow no further now:
Call in the powers, good cousin Westmoreland. *(Exit West-
moreland.)*
Now, Falstaff, where have you been all this while?$_{25}$
When every thing is ended, then you come:
These tardy tricks of yours will, on my life,
One time or other break some gallows' back.
Fal. I would be sorry, my lord, but it should be thus:
I never knew yet but rebuke and check was the reward of$_{30}$
valour. Do you think me a swallow, an arrow, or a bullet?
have I, in my poor and old motion, the expedition of
thought? I have speeded hither with the very extremest
inch of possibility; I have foundered nine score and odd
posts: and here, travel-tainted as I am, have, in my pure$_{35}$
and immaculate valour, taken Sir John Colevile of the
dale, a most furious knight and valorous enemy. But
what of that? he saw me, and yielded; that I may justly
say, with the hook-nosed fellow of Rome, 'I came, saw, and
overcame.'$_{40}$
Lan. It was more of his courtesy than your deserving.
Fal. I know not: here he is, and here I yield him: and
I beseech your grace, let it be booked with the rest of this
day's deeds; or, by the Lord, I will have it in a particular$_{45}$
ballad else, with mine own picture on the top on't, Colevile
kissing my foot: to the which course if I be enforced, if you
do not all show like gilt two-pences to me, and I in the
clear sky of fame o'ershine you as much as the full moon
doth the cinders of the element, which show like pins' heads$_{50}$
to her, believe not the word of the noble: therefore let me
have right, and let desert mount.
Lan. Thine's too heavy to mount.
Fal. Let it shine, then.
Lan. Thine's too thick to shine.$_{55}$
Fal. Let it do something, my good lord, that may do
me good, and call it what you will.
Lan. Is thy name Colevile?
Cole. It is, my lord.

LAN. A famous rebel art thou, Colevile.$_{60}$

FAL. And a famous true subject took him.

COLE. I am, my lord, but as my betters are

That led me hither: had they been ruled by me,

You should have won them dearer than you have.

FAL. I know not how they sold themselves: but thou,$_{65}$

like a kind fellow, gavest thyself away gratis; and I thank

thee for thee.

(RE-ENTER WESTMORELAND.)

LAN. Now, have you left pursuit?

WEST. Retreat is made and execution stay'd.

LAN. Send Colevile with his confederates$_{70}$

To York, to present execution:

Blunt, lead him hence; and see you guard him sure.

(Exeunt Blunt and others with Colevile.)

And now dispatch we toward the court, my lords:

I hear the king my father is sore sick:

Our news shall go before us to his majesty,$_{75}$

Which, cousin, you shall bear to comfort him;

And we with sober speed will follow you.

FAL. My lord, I beseech you, give me leave to go

Through Gloucestershire: and, when you come to court,

Stand my good lord, pray, in your good report.$_{80}$

LAN. Fare you well, Falstaff: I, in my condition,

Shall better speak of you than you deserve.

(Exeunt all except Falstaff.)

FAL. I would you had but the wit: 'twere better than

your dukedom. Good faith, this same young sober-blooded

boy doth not love me; nor a man cannot make him laugh;$_{85}$

but that's no marvel, he drinks no wine. There's never none

of these demure boys come to any proof; for thin drink doth

so over-cool their blood, and making many fish-meals, that

they fall into a kind of male green-sickness; and then, when

they marry, they get wenches: they are generally fools and$_{90}$

cowards; which some of us should be too, but for

    inflammation.

A good sherris-sack hath a two-fold operation in it. It

ascends me into the brain; dries me there all the

    foolish and

dull and crudy vapours which environ it; makes it appre-
hensive,
quick, forgetive, full of nimble fiery and delectable$_{95}$
shapes; which, delivered o'er to the voice, the tongue, which
is the birth, becomes excellent wit. The second property of
your excellent sherris is, the warming of the blood; which,
before cold and settled, left the liver white and pale, which
is the badge of pusillanimity and cowardice; but the sherris$_{100}$
warms it and makes it course from the inwards to the parts
extreme: it illumineth the face, which as a beacon gives
warning to all the rest of this little kingdom, man, to arm;
and then the vital commoners and inland petty spirits muster
me all to their captain, the heart, who, great and puffed$_{105}$
up with this retinue, doth any deed of courage; and this
valour comes of sherris. So that skill in the weapon is
nothing without sack, for that sets it a-work; and learning
a mere hoard of gold kept by a devil, till sack commences
it and sets it in act and use. Hereof comes it that Prince$_{110}$
Harry is valiant; for the cold blood he did naturally inherit
of his father, he hath, like lean sterile and bare land,
manured, husbanded and tilled with excellent endeavour
of drinking good and good store of fertile sherris, that he
is become very hot and valiant. If I had a thousand sons,$_{115}$
the first humane principle I would teach them should be, to
forswear thin potations, and to addict themselves to sack.
(*ENTER BARDOLPH.*)
How now, Bardolph?
BARD. The army is discharged all and gone.
FAL. Let them go. I'll through Gloucestershire; and$_{120}$
there will I visit Master Robert Shallow, esquire: I have him
already tempering between my finger and my thumb, and
shortly will I seal with him. Come away. (*Exeunt.*)

SCENE IV. WESTMINSTER. THE JERUSALEM CHAMBER

(*ENTER THE KING, THE PRINCES THOMAS OF CLARENCE AND HUMPHREY OF GLOUCESTER, WARWICK, AND OTHERS.*)

KING. Now, lords, if God doth give successful end
To this debate that bleedeth at our doors,
We will our youth lead on to higher fields
And draw no swords but what are sanctified.
Our navy is address'd, our power collected,$_5$
Our substitutes in absence well invested,
And every thing lies level to our wish:
Only, we want a little personal strength;
And pause us, till these rebels, now afoot,
Come underneath the yoke of government.$_{10}$
WAR. Both which we doubt not but your majesty
Shall soon enjoy.
KING. Humphrey, my son of Gloucester,
Where is the prince your brother?
GLOU. I think he's gone to hunt, my lord, at Windsor.
KING. And how accompanied?
GLOU. I do not know, my lord.$_{15}$
KING. Is not his brother, Thomas of Clarence, with him?
GLOU. No, my good lord; he is in presence here.
CLAR. What would my lord and father?
KING. Nothing but well to thee, Thomas of Clarence.
How chance thou art not with the prince thy brother?$_{20}$
He loves thee, and thou dost neglect him, Thomas;
Thou hast a better place in his affection
Than all thy brothers: cherish it, my boy,
And noble offices thou mayst effect
Of mediation, after I am dead,$_{25}$
Between his greatness and thy other brethren:
Therefore omit him not; blunt not his love,
Nor lose the good advantage of his grace
By seeming cold or careless of his will;
For he is gracious, if he be observed:$_{30}$
He hath a tear for pity and a hand
Open as day for melting charity:
Yet notwithstanding, being incensed, he's flint,
As humorous as winter and as sudden
As flaws congealed in the spring of day.$_{35}$
His temper, therefore, must be well observed:
Chide him for faults, and do it reverently,

When you perceive his blood inclined to mirth;
But, being moody, give him line and scope,
Till that his passions, like a whale on ground,$_{40}$
Confound themselves with working. Learn this, Thomas,
And thou shalt prove a shelter to thy friends,
A hoop of gold to bind thy brothers in,
That the united vessel of their blood,
Mingled with venom of suggestion—$_{45}$
As, force perforce, the age will pour it in—
Shall never leak, though it do work as strong
As aconitum or rash gunpowder.
CLAR. I shall observe him with all care and love.
KING. Why art thou not at Windsor with him, Thomas?$_{50}$
CLAR. He is not there to-day; he dines in London.
KING. And how accompanied? canst thou tell that?
CLAR. With Poins, and other his continual followers.
KING. Most subject is the fattest soil to weeds;
And he, the noble image of my youth,$_{55}$
Is overspread with them: therefore my grief
Stretches itself beyond the hour of death:
The blood weeps from my heart when I do shape
In forms imaginary the unguided days
And rotten times that you shall look upon$_{60}$
When I am sleeping with my ancestors.
For when his headstrong riot hath no curb,
When rage and hot blood are his counsellors,
When means and lavish manners meet together,
O, with what wings shall his affections fly$_{65}$
Towards fronting peril and opposed decay!
WAR. My gracious lord, you look beyond him quite:
The prince but studies his companions
Like a strange tongue, wherein, to gain the language,
'Tis needful that the most immodest word$_{70}$
Be look'd upon and learn'd; which once attain'd,
Your highness knows, comes to no further use
But to be known and hated. So, like gross terms,
The prince will in the perfectness of time
Cast off his followers; and their memory$_{75}$
Shall as a pattern or a measure live,

By which his grace must mete the lives of others,
Turning past evils to advantages.
KING. 'Tis seldom when the bee doth leave her comb
In the dead carrion.
(ENTER WESTMORELAND.)
Who's here? Westmoreland?$_{80}$
WEST. Health to my sovereign, and new happiness
Added to that that I am to deliver!
Prince John your son doth kiss your grace's hand:
Mowbray, the Bishop Scroop, Hastings and all
Are brought to the correction of your law;$_{85}$
There is not now a rebel's sword unsheath'd,
But Peace puts forth her olive every where.
The manner how this action hath been borne
Here at more leisure may your highness read,
With every course in his particular.$_{90}$
KING. O Westmoreland, thou art a summer bird,
Which ever in the haunch of winter sings
The lifting up of day.
(ENTER HARCOURT.)
Look, here's more news.
HAR. From enemies heaven keep your majesty;
And, when they stand against you, may they fall$_{95}$
As those that I am come to tell you of!
The Earl Northumberland and the Lord Bardolph,
With a great power of English and of Scots,
Are by the sheriff of Yorkshire overthrown:
The manner and true order of the fight,$_{100}$
This packet, please it you, contains at large.
KING. And wherefore should these good news make me sick?
Will Fortune never come with both hands full,
But write her fair words still in foulest letters?
She either gives a stomach and no food;$_{105}$
Such are the poor, in health; or else a feast
And takes away the stomach; such are the rich,
That have abundance and enjoy it not.
I should rejoice now at this happy news;
And now my sight fails, and my brain is giddy:$_{110}$
O me! come near me; now I am much ill.

GLOU. Comfort, your majesty!

CLAR. O my royal father!

WEST. My sovereign lord, cheer up yourself, look up.

WAR. Be patient, princes; you do know, these fits
Are with his highness very ordinary.$_{115}$
Stand from him, give him air; he'll straight be well.

CLAR. No, no, he cannot long hold out these pangs:
The incessant care and labour of his mind
Hath wrought the mure, that should confine it in,
So thin that life looks through and will break out.$_{120}$

GLOU. The people fear me; for they do observe
Unfather'd heirs and loathly births of nature:
The seasons change their manners, as the year
Had found some months asleep and leap'd them over.

CLAR. The river hath thrice flow'd, no ebb between;$_{125}$
And the old folk, time's doting chronicles,
Say it did so a little time before
That our great-grandsire, Edward, sick'd and died.

WAR. Speak lower, princes, for the king recovers.

GLOU. This apoplexy will ceitain be his end.$_{130}$

KING. I pray you, take me up, and bear me hence
Into some other chamber: softly, pray.

SCENE V. ANOTHER CHAMBER

*(THE KING LYING ON A BED: CLARENCE, GLOUCESTER, WARWICK, AND
OTHERS IN ATTENDANCE.)*

KING. Let there be no noise made, my gentle friends;
Unless some dull and favourable hand
Will whisper music to my weary spirit.

WAR. Call for the music in the other room.

KING. Set me the crown upon my pillow here.$_5$

CLAR. His eye is hollow, and he changes much.

WAR. Less noise, less noise!

(ENTER PRINCE HENRY.)

PRINCE. Who saw the Duke of Clarence?

CLAR. I am here, brother, full of heaviness.

PRINCE. How now! rain within doors, and none abroad!
How doth the king?$_{10}$
GLOU. Exceeding ill.
PRINCE. Heard he the good news yet?
Tell it him.
GLOU. He alter'd much upon the hearing it.
PRINCE. If he be sick with joy, he'll recover without
physic.$_{15}$
WAR. Not so much noise, my lords: sweet prince, speak low;
The king your father is disposed to sleep.
CLAR. Let us withdraw into the other room.
WAR. Will't please your grace to go along with us?
PRINCE. No; I will sit and watch here by the king.$_{20}$
(Exeunt all except the Prince.)
Why doth the crown lie there upon his pillow,
Being so troublesome a bedfellow?
O polish'd perturbation! golden care!
That keep'st the ports of slumber open wide
To many a watchful night! sleep with it now!$_{25}$
Yet not so sound and half so deeply sweet
As he whose brow with homely biggen bound
Snores out the watch of night. O majesty!
When thou dost pinch thy bearer, thou dost sit
Like a rich armour worn in heat of day,$_{30}$
That scalds with safety. By his gates of breath
There lies a downy feather which stirs not:
Did he suspire, that light and weightless down
Perforce must move. My gracious lord! my father!
This sleep is sound indeed; this is a sleep,$_{35}$
That from this golden rigol hath divorced
So many English kings. Thy due from me
Is tears and heavy sorrows of the blood,
Which nature, love, and filial tenderness,
Shall, O dear father, pay thee plenteously:$_{40}$
My due from thee is this imperial crown,
Which, as immediate from thy place and blood,
Derives itself to me. Lo, here it sits,
Which God shall guard: and put the world's whole strength
Into one giant arm, it shall not force$_{45}$

This lineal honour from me: this from thee
Will I to mine leave, as 'tis left to me. *(Exit.)*
KING. Warwick! Gloucester! Clarence!
(RE-ENTER WARWICK, GLOUCESTER, CLARENCE, AND THE REST.)
CLAR. Doth the king call?
WAR. What would your majesty? How fares your grace?$_{50}$
KING. Why did you leave me here alone, my lords?
CLAR. We left the prince my brother here, my liege,
Who undertook to sit and watch by you.
KING. The Prince of Wales! Where is he? let me see him:
He is not here.$_{55}$
WAR. This door is open; he is gone this way.
GLOU. He came not through the chamber where we stay'd.
KING. Where is the crown? who took it from my pillow?
WAR. When we withdrew, my liege, we left it here.
KING. The prince hath ta'en it hence: go, seek him out.$_{60}$
Is he so hasty that he doth suppose
My sleep my death?
Find him, my Lord of Warwick; chide him hither.
(Exit Warwick.)
This part of his conjoins with my disease,
And helps to end me. See, sons, what things you are!$_{65}$
How quickly nature falls into revolt
When gold becomes her object!
For this the foolish over-careful fathers
Have broke their sleep with thoughts, their brains with care,
Their bones with industry;$_{70}$
For this they have engrossed and piled up
The canker'd heaps of strange-achieved gold;
For this they have been thoughtful to invest
Their sons with arts and martial exercises:
When, like the bee, culling from every flower$_{75}$
The virtuous sweets,
Our thighs pack'd with wax, our mouths with honey,
We bring it to the hive; and, like the bees,
Are murdered for our pains. This bitter taste
Yield his engrossments to the ending father.$_{80}$
(Re-enter WARWICK.)
Now, where is he that will not stay so long

Till his friend sickness hath determined me?
WAR. My lord, I found the prince in the next room,
Washing with kindly tears his gentle cheeks,
With such a deep demeanour in great sorrow$_{85}$
That tyranny, which never quaff'd but blood,
Would, by beholding him, have wash'd his knife
With gentle eye-drops. He is coming hither.
KING. But wherefore did he take away the crown?
(RE-ENTER PRINCE HENRY.)
Lo, where he comes. Come hither to me, Harry.$_{90}$
Depart the chamber, leave us here alone.
(Exeunt Warwick and the rest.)
PRINCE. I never thought to hear you speak again.
KING. Thy wish was father, Harry, to that thought:
I stay too long by thee, I weary thee.
Dost thou so hunger for mine empty chair$_{95}$
That thou wilt needs invest thee with my honours
Before thy hour be ripe? O foolish youth!
Thou seek'st the greatness that will overwhelm thee.
Stay but a little; for my cloud of dignity
Is held from falling with so weak a wind$_{100}$
That it will quickly drop: my day is dim.
Thou hast stolen that which after some few hours
Were thine without offence; and at my death
Thou hast seal'd up my expectation:
Thy life did manifest thou lovedst me not,$_{105}$
And thou wilt have me die assured of it.
Thou hidest a thousand daggers in thy thoughts,
Which thou hast whetted on thy stony heart,
To stab at half an hour of my life.
What! canst thou not forbear me half an hour?$_{110}$
Then get thee gone and dig my grave thyself,
And bid the merry bells ring to thine ear
That thou art crowned, not that I am dead.
Let all the tears that should bedew my hearse
Be drops of balm to sanctify thy head:$_{115}$
Only compound me with forgotten dust;
Give that which gave thee life unto the worms.
Pluck down my officers, break my decrees;

For now a time is come to mock at form:
Harry the fifth is crown'd: up, vanity!₁₂₀
Down, royal state! all you sage counsellors, hence!
And to the English court assemble now,
From every region, apes of idleness!
Now, neighbour confines, purge you of your scum:
Have you a ruffian that will swear, drink, dance,₁₂₅
Revel the night, rob, murder, and commit
The oldest sins the newest kind of ways?
Be happy, he will trouble you no more;
England shall double gild his treble guilt,
England shall give him office, honour, might;₁₃₀
For the fifth Harry from curb'd license plucks
The muzzle of restraint, and the wild dog
Shall flesh his tooth on every innocent.
O my poor kingdom, sick with civil blows!
When that my care could not withhold thy riots,₁₃₅
What wilt thou do when riot is thy care?
O, thou wilt be a wilderness again,
Peopled with wolves, thy old inhabitants!
PRINCE. O, pardon me, my liege! but for my tears,
The moist impediments unto my speech,₁₄₀
I had forestall'd this dear and deep rebuke
Ere you with grief had spoke and I had heard
The course of it so far. There is your crown;
And He that wears the crown immortally
Long guard it yours! If I affect it more₁₄₅
Than as your honour and as your renown,
Let me no more from this obedience rise,
Which my most inward true and duteous spirit
Teacheth, this prostrate and exterior bending.
God witness with me, when I here came in,₁₅₀
And found no course of breath within your majesty,
How cold it struck my heart! If I do feign,
O, let me in my present wildness die
And never live to show the incredulous world
The noble change that I have purposed!₁₅₅
Coming to look on you, thinking you dead,
And dead almost, my liege, to think you were,

I spake unto this crown as having sense,
And thus upbraided it: 'The care on thee depending
Hath fed upon the body of my father;$_{160}$
Therefore, thou best of gold art worst of gold:
Other, less fine in carat, is more precious,
Preserving life in medicine potable;
But thou, most fine, most honour'd, most renown'd,
Hast eat thy bearer up.' Thus, my most royal liege,$_{165}$
Accusing it, I put it on my head,
To try with it, as with an enemy
That had before my face murder'd my father,
The quarrel of a true inheritor.
But if it did infect my blood with joy,$_{170}$
Or swell my thoughts to any strain of pride;
If any rebel or vain spirit of mine
Did with the least affection of a welcome
Give entertainment to the might of it,
Let God for ever keep it from my head$_{175}$
And make me as the poorest vassal is
That doth with awe and terror kneel to it!
KING. O my son,
God put it in thy mind to take it hence,
That thou mightst win the more thy father's love,$_{180}$
Pleading so wisely in excuse of it!
Come hither, Harry, sit thou by my bed;
And hear, I think, the very latest counsel
That ever I shall breathe. God knows, my son,
By what by-paths and indirect crook'd ways$_{185}$
I met this crown; and I myself know well
How troublesome it sat upon my head.
To thee it shall descend with better quiet,
Better opinion, better confirmation;
For all the soil of the achievement goes$_{190}$
With me into the earth. It seem'd in me
But as an honour snatch'd with boisterous hand,
And I had many living to upbraid
My gain of it by their assistances;
Which daily grew to quarrel and to bloodshed,$_{195}$
Wounding supposed peace: all these bold fears

Thou see'st with peril I have answered;
For all my reign hath been but as a scene
Acting that argument: and now my death
Changes the mode; for what in me was purchased,$_{200}$
Falls upon thee in a more fairer sort;
So thou the garland wear'st successively.
Yet, though thou stand'st more sure than I could do,
Thou art not firm enough, since griefs are green;
And all my friends, which thou must make thy friends,$_{205}$
Have but their stings and teeth newly ta'en out;
By whose fell working I was first advanced
And by whose power I well might lodge a fear
To be again displaced: which to avoid,
I cut them off; and had a purpose now$_{210}$
To lead out many to the Holy Land,
Lest rest and lying still might make them look
Too near unto my state. Therefore, my Harry,
Be it thy course to busy giddy minds
With foreign quarrels; that action, hence borne out,$_{215}$
May waste the memory of the former days.
More would I, but my lungs are wasted so
That strength of speech is utterly denied me.
How I came by the crown, O God forgive;
And grant it may with thee in true peace live!$_{220}$
PRINCE. My gracious liege,
You won it, wore it, kept it, gave it me;
Then plain and right must my possession be:
Which I with more than with a common pain
'Gainst all the world will rightfully maintain.$_{225}$
(ENTER LORD JOHN OF LANCASTER.)
KING. Look, look, here comes my John of Lancaster.
LAN. Health, peace, and happiness to my royal father!
KING. Thou bring'st me happiness and peace, son John;
But health, alack, with youthful wings is flown
From this bare wither'd trunk: upon thy sight$_{230}$
My worldly business makes a period.
Where is my Lord of Warwick?
PRINCE. My Lord of Warwick!
(Enter WARWICK, and others.)

KING. Doth any name particular belong
Unto the lodging where I first did swoon?
WAR. 'Tis call'd Jerusalem, my noble lord.235
KING. Laud be to God! even there my life must end.
It hath been prophesied to me many years,
I should not die but in Jerusalem;
Which vainly I supposed the Holy Land:
But bear me to that chamber; there I'll lie;240
In that Jerusalem shall Harry die. *(Exeunt.)*

ACT V

SCENE I. GLOUCESTERSHIRE. SHALLOW'S HOUSE

(Enter Shallow, Falstaff, Bardolph, and Page.)

Shal. By cock and pie, sir, you shall not away to-night.
What, Davy, I say!
Fal. You must excuse me, Master Robert Shallow.
Shal. I will not excuse you; you shall not be excused;
excuses shall not be admitted; there is no excuse shall serve;₅
you shall not be excused. Why, Davy!
(Enter Davy.)
Davy. Here, sir.
Shal. Davy, Davy, Davy, Davy, let me see, Davy; let
me see, Davy; let me see: yea, marry, William cook, bid
him come hither. Sir John, you shall not be excused.₁₀
Davy. Marry, sir, thus; those precepts cannot be served:
and, again, sir, shall we sow the headland with wheat?
Shal. With red wheat, Davy. But for William cook:
are there no young pigeons?
Davy. Yes, sir. Here is now the smith's note for shoeing₁₅
and plough-irons.
Shal. Let it be cast and paid. Sir John, you shall not

be excused.

DAVY. Now, sir, a new link to the bucket must needs be had: and, sir, do you mean to stop any of William's wages, $_{20}$ about the sack he lost the other day at Hinckley fair?

SHAL. A' shall answer it. Some pigeons, Davy, a couple of short-legged hens, a joint of mutton, and any pretty little tiny kickshaws, tell William cook.

DAVY. Doth the man of war stay all night, sir? $_{25}$

SHAL. Yea, Davy. I will use him well: a friend i' the court is better than a penny in purse. Use his men well, Davy; for they are arrant knaves, and will backbite.

DAVY. No worse than they are backbitten, sir; for they have marvellous foul linen. $_{30}$

SHAL. Well conceited, Davy: about thy business, Davy.

DAVY. I beseech you, sir, to countenance William Visor of Woncot against Clement Perkes of the hill.

SHAL. There is many complaints, Davy, against that Visor: that Visor is an arrant knave, on my knowledge. $_{35}$

DAVY. I grant your worship that he is a knave, sir; but yet, God forbid, sir, but a knave should have some countenance

at his friend's request. An honest man, sir, is able to speak for himself, when a knave is not. I have served your worship truly, sir, this eight years; and if I cannot once $_{40}$ or twice in a quarter bear out a knave against an honest man, I have but a very little credit with your worship. The knave is mine honest friend, sir; therefore, I beseech your worship, let him be countenanced.

SHAL. Go to; I say he shall have no wrong. Look $_{45}$ about, Davy. *(Exit Davy)* Where are you, Sir John? Come, come, come, off with your boots. Give me your hand, Master Bardolph.

BARD. I am glad to see your worship.

SHAL. I thank thee with all my heart, kind Master $_{50}$ Bardolph: and welcome, my tall fellow *(to the Page.)* Come, Sir John.

FAL. I'll follow you, good Master Robert Shallow. *(Exit Shallow.)*

Bardolph, look to our horses. *(Exeunt Bardolph and Page.)*

If I were sawed into quantities, I should make$_{55}$
four dozen of such bearded hermits' staves as Master Shallow.
It is a wonderful thing to see the sembable coherence of
his men's spirits and his: they, by observing of him, do bear
themselves like foolish justices; he, by conversing with them,
is turned into a justice-like serving-man: their spirits are so$_{60}$
married in conjunction with the participation of society that
they flock together in consent, like so many wild-geese. If I
had a suit to Master Shallow, I would humour his men with
the imputation of being near their master: if to his men, I
would curry with Master Shallow that no man could better$_{65}$
command his servants. It is certain that either wise bearing
or ignorant carriage is caught, as men take diseases, one of
another: therefore let men take heed of their company. I
will devise matter enough out of this Shallow to keep Prince
Harry in continual laughter the wearing out of six fashions,$_{70}$
which is four terms, or two actions, and a' shall laugh
without intervallums. O, it is much that a lie with a slight
oath and a jest with a sad brow will do with a fellow that
never had the ache in his shoulders! O, you shall see
him laugh till his face be like a wet cloak ill laid up!$_{75}$
SHAL. *(Within)* Sir John!
FAL. I come, Master Shallow; I come, Master Shallow.
(Exit.)

SCENE II. WESTMINSTER. THE PALACE

(ENTER WARWICK AND THE LORD CHIEF JUSTICE, MEETING.)

WAR. How now, my lord chief justice! whither away?
CH. JUST. How doth the king?
WAR. Exceeding well; his cares are now all ended.
CH. JUST. I hope, not dead.
WAR. He's walk'd the way of nature;
And to our purposes he lives no more.$_{5}$
CH. JUST. I would his majesty had call'd me with him:
The service that I truly did his life
Hath left me open to all injuries.

WAR. Indeed I think the young king loves you not.

CH. JUST. I know he doth not, and do arm myself$_{10}$
To welcome the condition of the time,
Which cannot look more hideously upon me
Than I have drawn it in my fantasy.

*(ENTER LANCASTER, CLARENCE, GLOUCESTER, WESTMORELAND,
    AND OTHERS.)*

WAR. Here come the heavy issue of dead Harry:
O that the living Harry had the temper$_{15}$
Of him, the worst of these three gentlemen!
How many nobles then should hold their places,
That must strike sail to spirits of vile sort!

CH. JUST. O God, I fear all will be overturn'd!

LAN. Good morrow, cousin Warwick, good morrow.$_{20}$

GLOU. } Good morrow, cousin.
CLAR. }

LAN. We meet like men that had forgot to speak.

WAR. We do remember; but our argument
Is all too heavy to admit much talk.

LAN. Well, peace be with him that hath made us heavy!$_{25}$

CH. JUST. Peace be with us, lest we be heavier!

GLOU. O, good my lord, you have lost a friend indeed;
And I dare swear you borrow not that face
Of seeming sorrow, it is sure your own.

LAN. Though no man be assured what grace to find,$_{30}$
You stand in coldest expectation:
I am the sorrier; would 'twere otherwise.

CLAR. Well, you must now speak Sir John Falstaff fair;
Which swims against your stream of quality.

CH. JUST. Sweet princes, what I did, I did in honour,$_{35}$
Led by the impartial conduct of my soul;
And never shall you see that I will beg
A ragged and forestall'd remission.
If truth and upright innocency fail me,
I'll to the king my master that is dead,$_{40}$
And tell him who hath sent me after him.

WAR. Here comes the prince.

(Enter KING HENRY the fifth, attended.)

CH. JUST. Good morrow; and God save your majesty!

KING. This new and gorgeous garment, majesty,
Sits not so easy on me as you think. *45*
Brothers, you mix your sadness with some fear:
This is the English, not the Turkish court;
Not Amurath an Amurath succeeds,
But Harry. Yet be sad, good brothers,
For, by my faith, it very well becomes you: *50*
Sorrow so royally in you appears
That I will deeply put the fashion on
And wear it in my heart: why then, be sad;
But entertain no more of it, good brothers,
Than a joint burden laid upon us all. *55*
For me, by heaven, I bid you be assured,
I'll be your father and your brother too;
Let me but bear your love. I'll bear your cares:
Yet weep that Harry's dead; and so will I;
But Harry lives, that shall convert those tears *60*
By number into hours of happiness.
Princes. We hope no other from your majesty.
KING. You all look strangely on me: and you most;
You are, I think, assured I love you not.
CH. JUST. I am assured, if I be measured rightly, *65*
Your majesty hath no just cause to hate me.
KING. No!
How might a prince of my great hopes forget
So great indignities you laid upon me?
What! rate, rebuke, and roughly send to prison *70*
The immediate heir of England! Was this easy?
May this be wash'd in Lethe, and forgotten?
CH. JUST. I then did use the person of your father;
The image of his power lay then in me:
And, in the administration of his law, *75*
Whiles I was busy for the commonwealth,
Your highness pleased to forget my place,
The majesty and power of law and justice,
The image of the king whom I presented,
And struck me in my very seat of judgement; *80*
Whereon, as an offender to your father,
I gave bold way to my authority,

And did commit you. If the deed were ill,
Be you contented, wearing now the garland,
To have a son set your decrees at nought,$_{85}$
To pluck down justice from your awful bench.
To trip the course of law and blunt the sword
That guards the peace and safety of your person;
Nay, more, to spurn at your most royal image
And mock your workings in a second body.$_{90}$
Question your royal thoughts, make the case yours;
Be now the father and propose a son,
Hear your own dignity so much profaned,
See your most dreadful laws so loosely slighted,
Behold yourself so by a son disdain'd;$_{95}$
And then imagine me taking your part
And in your power soft silencing your son:
After this cold considerance, sentence me;
And, as you are a king, speak in your state
What I have done that misbecame my place,$_{100}$
My person, or my liege's sovereignty.
KING. You are right, justice, and you weigh this well;
Therefore still bear the balance and the sword:
And I do wish your honours may increase,
Till you do live to see a son of mine$_{105}$
Offend you, and obey you, as I did.
So shall I live to speak my father's words:
'Happy am I, that have a man so bold,
That dares do justice on my proper son;
And not less happy, having such a son,$_{110}$
That would deliver up his greatness so
Into the hands of justice.' You did commit me:
For which, I do commit into your hand
The unstained sword that you have used to bear;
With this remembrance, that you use the same$_{115}$
With the like bold, just, and impartial spirit
As you have done 'gainst me. There is my hand.
You shall be as a father to my youth:
My voice shall sound as you do prompt mine ear,
And I will stoop and humble my intents$_{120}$
To your well-practised wise directions.

And, princes all, believe me, I beseech you;
My father is gone wild into his grave,
For in his tomb lie my affections;
And with his spirit sadly I survive,₁₂₅
To mock the expectation of the world,
To frustrate prophecies and to raze out
Rotten opinion, who hath writ me down
After my seeming. The tide of blood in me
Hath proudly flow'd in vanity till now:₁₃₀
Now doth it turn and ebb back to the sea,
Where it shall mingle with the state of floods
And flow henceforth in formal majesty.
Now call we our high court of parliament:
And let us choose such limbs of noble counsel,₁₃₅
That the great body of our state may go
In equal rank with the best govern'd nation;
That war, or peace, or both at once, may be
As things acquainted and familiar to us;
In which you, father, shall have foremost hand.₁₄₀
Our coronation done, we will accite,
As I before remember'd, all our state:
And, God consigning to my good intents,
No prince nor peer shall have just cause to say,
God shorten Harry's happy life one day! *(Exeunt.)*

SCENE III. GLOUCESTERSHIRE. SHALLOW'S ORCHARD

(ENTER FALSTAFF, SHALLOW, SILENCE, DAVY, BARDOLPH, AND THE PAGE.)

SHAL. Nay, you shall see my orchard, where, in an
arbour, we will eat a last year's pippin of my own graffing,
with a dish of caraways, and so forth: come, cousin Silence:
and then to bed.
FAL. 'Fore God, you have here a goodly dwelling and₅
a rich.
SHAL. Barren, barren, barren; beggars all, beggars all,

Sir John: marry, good air. Spread, Davy; spread, Davy:
well said, Davy.

FAL. This Davy serves you for good uses; he is your
serving-man and your husband. [10]

SHAL. A good varlet, a good varlet, a very good varlet,
Sir John: by the mass, I have drunk too much sack at
supper: a good varlet. Now sit down, now sit down:
come, cousin. [15]

SIL. Ah, sirrah! quoth-a, we shall
Do nothing but eat, and make good cheer, *(Singing.)*
And praise God for the merry year;
When flesh is cheap and females dear,
And lusty lads roam here and there [20]
So merrily,
And ever among so merrily.

FAL. There's a merry heart! Good Master Silence,
I'll give you a health for that anon.

SHAL. Give Master Bardolph some wine, Davy. [25]

DAVY. Sweet sir, sit; I'll be with you anon; most
sweet sir, sit. Master page, good master page, sit. Proface!
What you want in meat, we'll have in drink: but
you must bear; the heart's all. *(Exit.)*

SHAL. Be merry, Master Bardolph; and, my little [30]
soldier there, be merry.

SIL. Be merry, be merry, my wife has all; *(Singing.)*
For women are shrews, both short and tall:
'Tis merry in hall when beards wag all,
And welcome merry Shrove-tide. [35]
Be merry, be merry.

FAL. I did not think Master Silence had been a man of
this mettle.

SIL. Who, I? I have been merry twice and once ere
now. [40]

(Re-enter DAVY.)

DAVY. There's a dish of leather-coats for you.
(To Bardolph.)

SHAL. Davy!

DAVY. Your worship! I'll be with you straight *(to Bardolph.)*
A cup of wine, sir?

SIL. A cup of wine that's brisk and fine, *(Singing.)* 45
And drink unto the leman mine;
And a merry heart lives long-a.
FAL. Well said, Master Silence.
SIL. An we shall be merry, now comes in the sweet
o' the night. 50
FAL. Health and long life to you, Master Silence.
SIL. Fill the cup, and let it come; *(Singing.)*
I'll pledge you a mile to the bottom.
SHAL. Honest Bardolph, welcome: if thou wantest any
thing, and wilt not call, beshrew thy heart. Welcome, my 55
little tiny thief *(to the Page)*, and welcome indeed too. I'll
drink to Master Bardolph, and to all the cavaleros about
London.
DAVY. I hope to see London once ere I die.
BARD. An I might see you there, Davy,— 60
SHAL. By the mass, you'll crack a quart together, ha!
will you not, Master Bardolph?
BARD. Yea, sir, in a pottle-pot.
SHAL. By God's liggens, I thank thee: the knave will
stick by thee, I can assure thee that. A' will not out; he 65
is true bred.
BARD. And I'll stick by him, sir.
SHAL. Why, there spoke a king. Lack nothing: be
merry. *(Knocking within.)* Look who's at door there, ho!
who knocks? *(Exit Davy.)* 70
FAL. Why, now you have done me right.
(To Silence, seeing him take off a bumper.)
SIL. Do me right. *(Singing.)*
And dub me knight:
Samingo.
Is't not so? 75
FAL. 'Tis so.
SIL. Is't so? Why then, say an old man can do somewhat.
(Re-enter DAVY.)
DAVY. An't please your worship, there's one Pistol
come from the court with news. 80
FAL. From the court! let him come in.
(ENTER PISTOL.)

How now, Pistol!

PIST. Sir John, God save you!

FAL. What wind blew you hither, Pistol?

PIST. Not the ill wind which blows no man to good.$_{85}$
Sweet knight, thou art now one of the greatest men in
this realm.

SIL. By'r lady, I think a' be, but goodman Puff of
Barson.

PIST. Puff!$_{90}$
Puff in thy teeth, most recreant coward base!
Sir John, I am thy Pistol and thy friend,
And helter-skelter have I rode to thee,
And tidings do I bring and lucky joys
And golden times and happy news of price.$_{95}$

FAL. I pray thee now, deliver them like a man of this
world.

PIST. A foutre for the world and worldlings base!
I speak of Africa and golden joys.

FAL. O base Assyrian knight, what is thy news?$_{100}$
Let King Cophetua know the truth thereof.

SIL. And Robin Hood, Scarlet, and John. *(Singing.)*

PIST. Shall dunghill curs confront the Helicons?
And shall good news be baffled?
Then, Pistol, lay thy head in Furies' lap.$_{105}$

SHAL. Honest gentleman, I know not your breeding.

PIST. Why then, lament therefore.

SHAL. Give me pardon, sir: if, sir, you come with news
from the court, I take it there's but two ways, either to
utter them, or to conceal them. I am, sir, under the king,$_{110}$
in some authority.

PIST. Under which king, Besonian? speak, or die.

SHAL. Under King Harry.

PIST. Harry the fourth? or fifth?

SHAL. Harry the fourth.

PIST. A foutre for thine office!
Sir John, thy tender lambkin now is king;$_{115}$
Harry the fifth's the man. I speak the truth:
When Pistol lies, do this; and fig me, like
The bragging Spaniard.

FAL. What, is the old king dead?

PIST. As nail in door: the things I speak are just.$_{120}$

FAL. Away, Bardolph! saddle my horse. Master
Robert Shallow, choose what office thou wilt in the land,
'tis thine. Pistol, I will double-charge thee with dignities.

BARD. O joyful day!
I would not take a knighthood for my fortune.$_{125}$

PIST. What! I do bring good news.

FAL. Carry Master Silence to bed. Master Shallow,
my Lord Shallow,—be what thou wilt; I am fortune's
steward—get on thy boots: we'll ride all night. O sweet
Pistol! Away, Bardolph! *(Exit Bard.)* Come, Pistol, utter$_{130}$
more to me; and withal devise something to do thyself
good. Boot, boot, Master Shallow: I know the young
king is sick for me. Let us take any man's horses; the
laws of England are at my commandment. Blessed are
they that have been my friends; and woe to my lord
chief-justice!$_{135}$

PIST. Let vultures vile seize on his lungs also!
'Where is the life that late I led?' say they:
Why, here it is; welcome these pleasant days! *(Exeunt.)*

SCENE IV. LONDON. A STREET

*(ENTER BEADLES, DRAGGING IN HOSTESS QUICKLY AND DOLL
TEARSHEET.)*

HOST. No, thou arrant knave; I would to God that I
might die, that I might have thee hanged: thou hast drawn
my shoulder out of joint.

FIRST BEAD. The constables have delivered her over to
me; and she shall have whipping-cheer enough, I warrant$_5$
her: there hath been a man or two lately killed about her.

DOL. Nut-hook, nut-hook, you lie. Come on; I'll tell
thee what, thou damned tripe-visaged rascal, an the child
I now go with do miscarry, thou wert better thou hadst
struck thy mother, thou paper-faced villain.$_{10}$

HOST. O the Lord, that Sir John were come! he would

make this a bloody day to somebody. But I pray God the
fruit of her womb miscarry!

FIRST BEAD. If it do, you shall have a dozen of cushions
again; you have but eleven now. Come, I charge you both$_{15}$
go with me; for the man is dead that you and Pistol beat
amongst you.

DOL. I'll tell you what, you thin man in a censer, I
will have you as soundly swinged for this,—you blue-bottle
rogue, you filthy famished correctioner, if you be not$_{20}$
swinged, I'll forswear half-kirtles.

FIRST BEAD. Come, come, you she knight-errant, come.

HOST. O God, that right should thus overcome might!
Well, of sufferance comes ease.

DOL. Come, you rogue, come; bring me to a justice.$_{25}$

HOST. Ay, come, you starved blood-hound.

DOL. Goodman death, goodman bones!

HOST. Thou atomy, thou!

DOL. Come, you thin thing; come, you rascal.

FIRST BEAD. *Very well. (Exeunt.)*

SCENE V. A PUBLIC PLACE NEAR WESTMINSTER ABBEY.

(ENTER TWO GROOMS, STREWING RUSHES.)

FIRST GROOM. More rushes, more rushes.

SEC. GROOM. The trumpets have sounded twice.

FIRST GROOM. 'Twill be two o'clock ere they come from
the coronation: dispatch, dispatch. *(Exeunt.)*

(ENTER FALSTAFF, SHALLOW, PISTOL, BARDOLPH AND PAGE.)

FAL. Stand here by me, Master Robert Shallow; I will$_5$
make the king do you grace: I will leer upon him as a'
comes by; and do but mark the countenance that he will
give me.

PIST. God bless thy lungs, good knight.

FAL. Come here, Pistol; stand behind me. O, if I had$_{10}$
had time to have made new liveries, I would have bestowed
the thousand pound I borrowed of you. But 'tis no matter;

this poor show doth better: this doth infer the zeal I had
to see him.

SHAL. It doth so.[15]

FAL. It shows my earnestness of affection,—

SHAL. It doth so.

FAL. My devotion,—

SHAL. It doth, it doth, it doth.

FAL. As it were, to ride day and night; and not to[20]
deliberate, not to remember, not to have patience to shift
me,—

SHAL. It is best, certain.

FAL. But to stand stained with travel, and sweating
with desire to see him; thinking of nothing else, putting[25]
all affairs else in oblivion, as if there were nothing else to
be done but to see him.

PIST. 'Tis 'semper idem,' for 'obsque hoc nihil est:'
'tis all in every part.

SHAL. 'Tis so, indeed.[30]

PIST. My knight, I will inflame thy noble liver,
And make thee rage.
Thy Doll, and Helen of thy noble thoughts,
Is in base durance and contagious prison;
Haled thither[35]
By most mechanical and dirty hand:
Rouse up revenge from ebon den with fell Alecto's snake,
For Doll is in. Pistol speaks nought but truth.

FAL. I will deliver her.

(Shouts within, and the trumpets sound.)

PIST. There roar'd the sea, and trumpet-clangor sounds.[40]

(Enter the KING and his train, the LORD CHIEF-JUSTICE among them.)

FAL. God save thy grace, King Hal! my royal Hal!

PIST. The heavens thee guard and keep, most royal
imp of fame!

FAL. God save thee, my sweet boy!

KING. My lord chief-justice, speak to that vain man.[45]

CH. JUST. Have you your wits? know you what 'tis you speak?

FAL. My king! my Jove! I speak to thee, my heart!

KING. I know thee not, old man: fall to thy prayers;
How ill white hairs become a fool and jester!

I have long dream'd of such a kind of man, 50
So surfeit-swell'd, so old, and so profane;
But, being awaked, I do despise my dream.
Make less thy body hence, and more thy grace;
Leave gormandizing; know the grave doth gape
For thee thrice wider than for other men. 55
Reply not to me with a fool-born jest:
Presume not that I am the thing I was;
For God doth know, so shall the world perceive,
That I have turn'd away my former self;
So will I those that kept me company. 60
When thou dost hear I am as I have been,
Approach me, and thou shalt be as thou wast,
The tutor and the feeder of my riots:
Till then, I banish thee, on pain of death,
As I have done the rest of my misleaders, 65
Not to come near our person by ten mile.
For competence of life I will allow you,
That lack of means enforce you not to evil:
And, as we hear you do reform yourselves,
We will, according to your strengths and qualities, 70
Give you advancement. Be it your charge, my lord,
To see perform'd the tenour of our word.
Set on. (Exeunt King, &c.)
FAL. Master Shallow, I owe you a thousand pound.
SHAL. Yea, marry, Sir John; which I beseech you to 75
let me have home with me.
FAL. That can hardly be, Master Shallow. Do not
you grieve at this; I shall be sent for in private to him:
look you, he must seem thus to the world: fear not your
advancements; I will be the man yet that shall make you 80
great.
SHAL. I cannot well perceive how, unless you should
give me your doublet, and stuff me out with straw. I beseech
you, good Sir John, let me have five hundred of my
thousand. 85
FAL. Sir, I will be as good as my word: this that you
heard was but a colour.
SHAL. A colour that I fear you will die in, Sir John.

FAL. Fear no colours: go with me to dinner: come,
Lieutenant Pistol; come, Bardolph: I shall be sent for soon₉₀
at night.
(RE-ENTER PRINCE JOHN, THE LORD CHIEF-JUSTICE; OFFICERS
  WITH THEM.)
CH. JUST. Go, carry Sir John Falstaff to the Fleet:
Take all his company along with him.
FAL. My lord, my lord,—
CH. JUST. I cannot now speak: I will hear you soon.₉₅
Take them away.
PIST. Si fortuna me tormenta, spero contenta.
(Exeunt all but Prince John and the Chief-Justice.)
LAN. I like this fair proceeding of the king's:
He hath intent his wonted followers
Shall all be very well provided for;₁₀₀
But all are banish'd till their conversations
Appear more wise and modest to the world.
CH. JUST. And so they are.
LAN. The king hath call'd his parliament, my lord.
CH. JUST. He hath.₁₀₅
LAN. I will lay odds that, ere this year expire,
We bear our civil swords and native fire
As far as France: I heard a bird so sing,
Whose music, to my thinking, pleased the king.
Come, will you hence? *(Exeunt.)*₁₁₀

EPILOGUE

(SPOKEN BY A DANCER.)

First my fear; then my courtesy; last my speech. My
fear is, your displeasure; my courtesy, my duty; and my
speech, to beg your pardons. If you look for a good speech
now, you undo me: for what I have to say is of mine own
making; and what indeed I should say will, I doubt, prove [5]
mine own marring. But to the purpose, and so to the
venture. Be it known to you, as it is very well, I was
lately here in the end of a displeasing play, to pray your
patience for it and to promise you a better. I meant
indeed to pay you with this; which, if like an ill venture [10]
it come unluckily home, I break, and you, my gentle
creditors, lose. Here I promised you I would be and
here I commit my body to your mercies: bate me some
and I will pay you some and, as most debtors do, promise
you infinitely. [15]
If my tongue cannot entreat you to acquit me, will you
command me to use my legs? and yet that were but light
payment, to dance out of your debt. But a good conscience
will make any possible satisfaction, and so would I. All
the gentlewomen here have forgiven me: if the gentlemen [20]
will not, then the gentlemen do not agree with the
    gentlewomen,
which was never seen before in such an assembly.

One word more, I beseech you. If you be not too
much cloyed with fat meat, our humble author will continue
the story, with Sir John in it, and make you merry[25]
with fair Katharine of France: where, for anything I know,
Falstaff shall die of a sweat, unless already a' be killed
with your hard opinions; for Oldcastle died a martyr, and
this is not the man. My tongue is weary; when my legs
are too, I will bid you good night: and so kneel down[30]
before you; but, indeed, to pray for the queen.

HENRY V

DRAMATIS PERSONÆ

KING HENRY the Fifth.
DUKE OF GLOUCESTER,
DUKE OF BEDFORD,
DUKE of EXETER, uncle to the King.
DUKE of YORK, cousin to the King.
EARLS OF SALISBURY, WESTMORELAND, AND WARWICK.
ARCHBISHOP OF CANTERBURY.
BISHOP OF ELY.
EARL OF CAMBRIDGE.
LORD SCROOP.
SIR THOMAS GREY.
SIR THOMAS ERPINGHAM, GOWER, FLUELLEN, MACMORRIS,
    JAMY, OFFICERS IN KING HENRY'S ARMY.
BATES, COURT, WILLIAMS, soldiers in the same.
PISTOL, NYM, BARDOLPH.
Boy.
A Herald.
CHARLES the Sixth, king of France.
LEWIS, the Dauphin.
DUKES OF BURGUNDY, ORLEANS, AND BOURBON.
The Constable of France.
RAMBURES and GRANDPRE, French Lords.
Governor of Harfleur.

MONTJOY, a French Herald.
Ambassadors to the King of England.
ISABEL, Queen of France.
KATHARINE, daughter to Charles and Isabel.
ALICE, a lady attending on her.
Hostess of a tavern in Eastcheap, formerly Mistress Quickly, and now married to Pistol.
Lords, Ladies, Officers, Soldiers, Citizens, Messengers, and Attendants.
Chorus.

SCENE: England; afterwards France.

PROLOGUE

CHOR. O for a Muse of fire, that would ascend
The brightest heaven of invention,
A kingdom for a stage, princes to act
And monarchs to behold the swelling scene!
Then should the warlike Harry, like himself,$_5$
Assume the port of Mars; and at his heels,
Leash'd in like hounds, should famine, sword and fire
Crouch for employment. But pardon, gentles all,
The flat unraised spirits that have dared
On this unworthy scaffold to bring forth$_{10}$
So great an object: can this cockpit hold
The vasty fields of France? or may we cram
Within this wooden O the very casques
That did affright the air at Agincourt?
O, pardon! since a crooked figure may$_{15}$
Attest in little place a million;
And let us, ciphers to this great accompt,
On your imaginary forces work.
Suppose within the girdle of these walls
Are now confined two mighty monarchies,$_{20}$
Whose high upreared and abutting fronts

The perilous narrow ocean parts asunder:
Piece out our imperfections with your thoughts;
Into a thousand parts divide one man,
And make imaginary puissance;$_{25}$
Think, when we talk of horses, that you see them
Printing their proud hoofs i' the receiving earth;
For 'tis your thoughts that now must deck our kings,
Carry them here and there; jumping o'er times,
Turning the accomplishment of many years$_{30}$
Into an hour-glass: for the which supply,
Admit me Chorus to this history;
Who prologue-like your humble patience pray,
Gently to hear, kindly to judge, our play. *(Exit.)*

ACT I

SCENE I. LONDON. AN ANTE-CHAMBER IN THE KING'S PALACE.

(ENTER THE ARCHBISHOP OF CANTERBURY, AND THE BISHOP OF ELY.)

CANT. My lord, I'll tell you; that self bill is urged,
Which in the eleventh year of the last king's reign
Was like, and had indeed against us pass'd,
But that the scambling and unquiet time
Did push it out of farther question.5
ELY. But how, my lord, shall we resist it now?
CANT. It must be thought on. If it pass against us,
We lose the better half of our possession:
For all the temporal lands which men devout
By testament have given to the church10
Would they strip from us; being valued thus:
As much as would maintain, to the king's honour,
Full fifteen earls and fifteen hundred knights,
Six thousand and two hundred good esquires;
And, to relief of lazars and weak age,15
Of indigent faint souls past corporal toil,
A hundred almshouses right well supplied;

And to the coffers of the king beside,
A thousand pounds by the year: thus runs the bill.
ELY. This would drink deep.
CANT. 'Twould drink the cup and all.₂₀
ELY. But what prevention?
CANT. The king is full of grace and fair regard.
ELY. And a true lover of the holy church.
CANT. The courses of his youth promised it not.
The breath no sooner left his father's body,₂₅
But that his wildness, mortified in him,
Seem'd to die too; yea, at that very moment
Consideration, like an angel, came
And whipp'd the offending Adam out of him,
Leaving his body as a paradise,₃₀
To envelope and contain celestial spirits.
Never was such a sudden scholar made;
Never came reformation in a flood,
With such a heady currance, scouring faults;
Nor never Hydra-headed wilfulness₃₅
So soon did lose his seat and all at once
As in this king.
ELY. We are blessed in the change.
CANT. Hear him but reason in divinity,
And all-admiring with an inward wish
You would desire the king were made a prelate:₄₀
Hear him debate of commonwealth affairs,
You would say it hath been all in all his study:
List his discourse of war, and you shall hear
A fearful battle render'd you in music:
Turn him to any cause of policy,₄₅
The Gordian knot of it he will unloose,
Familiar as his garter: that, when he speaks,
The air, a charter'd libertine, is still,
And the mute wonder lurketh in men's ears,
To steal his sweet and honey'd sentences;₅₀
So that the art and practic part of life
Must be the mistress to this theoric:
Which is a wonder how his grace should glean it,
Since his addiction was to courses vain,

His companies unletter'd, rude and shallow,$_{55}$
His hours fill'd up with riots, banquets, sports,
And never noted in him any study,
Any retirement, any sequestration
From open haunts and popularity.
ELY. The strawberry grows underneath the nettle$_{60}$
And wholesome berries thrive and ripen best
Neighbour'd by fruit of baser quality:
And so the prince obscured his contemplation
Under the veil of wildness; which, no doubt,
Grew like the summer grass, fastest by night,$_{65}$
Unseen, yet crescive in his faculty.
CANT. It must be so; for miracles are ceased;
And therefore we must needs admit the means
How things are perfected.
ELY. But, my good lord,
How now for mitigation of this bill$_{70}$
Urged by the commons? Doth his majesty
Incline to it, or no?
CANT. He seems indifferent,
Or rather swaying more upon our part
Than cherishing the exhibiters against us;
For I have made an offer to his majesty,$_{75}$
Upon our spiritual convocation
And in regard of causes now in hand,
Which I have open'd to his grace at large,
As touching France, to give a greater sum
Than ever at one time the clergy yet$_{80}$
Did to his predecessors part withal.
ELY. How did this offer seem received, my lord?
CANT. With good acceptance of his majesty;
Save that there was not time enough to hear,
As I perceived his grace would fain have done,$_{85}$
The severals and unhidden passages
Of his true titles to some certain dukedoms
And generally to the crown and seat of France
Derived from Edward, his great-grandfather.
ELY. What was the impediment that broke this off?$_{90}$
CANT. The French ambassador upon that instant

Craved audience; and the hour, I think, is come
To give him hearing: is it four o'clock?
ELY. It is.
CANT. Then go we in, to know his embassy;₉₅
Which I could with a ready guess declare,
Before the Frenchman speak a word of it.
ELY. I'll wait upon you, and I long to hear it. *(Exeunt.)*

SCENE II. THE SAME. THE PRESENCE CHAMBER

(ENTER KING HENRY, GLOUCESTER, BEDFORD, EXETER, WARWICK, WESTMORELAND, AND ATTENDANTS.)

K. HEN. Where is my gracious Lord of Canterbury?
EXE. Not here in presence.
K. HEN. Send for him, good uncle.
WEST. Shall we call in the ambassador, my liege?
K. HEN. Not yet, my cousin: we would be resolved,
Before we hear him, of some things of weight₅
That task our thoughts, concerning us and France.
(ENTER THE ARCHBISHOP OF CANTERBURY AND THE BISHOP OF ELY.)
CANT. God and his angels guard your sacred throne,
And make you long become it!
K. HEN. Sure, we thank you.
My learned lord, we pray you to proceed
And justly and religiously unfold₁₀
Why the law Salique that they have in France
Or should, or should not, bar us in our claim:
And God forbid, my dear and faithful lord,
That you should fashion, wrest, or bow your reading,
Or nicely charge your understanding soul₁₅
With opening titles miscreate, whose right
Suits not in native colours with the truth;
For God doth know how many now in health
Shall drop their blood in approbation
Of what your reverence shall incite us to.₂₀
Therefore take heed how you impawn our person,

How you awake our sleeping sword of war:
We charge you, in the name of God, take heed;
For never two such kingdoms did contend
Without much fall of blood; whose guiltless drops$_{25}$
Are every one a woe, a sore complaint
'Gainst him whose wrong gives edge unto the swords
That make such waste in brief mortality.
Under this conjuration speak, my lord;
For we will hear, note and believe in heart$_{30}$
That what you speak is in your conscience wash'd
As pure as sin with baptism.
CANT. Then hear me, gracious sovereign, and you peers,
That owe yourselves, your lives and services
To this imperial throne. There is no bar$_{35}$
To make against your highness' claim to France
But this, which they produce from Pharamond,
'In terram Salicam mulieres ne succedant:'
'No woman shall succeed in Salique land:'
Which Salique land the French unjustly gloze$_{40}$
To be the realm of France, and Pharamond
The founder of this law and female bar.
Yet their own authors faithfully affirm
That the land Salique is in Germany,
Between the floods of Sala and of Elbe;$_{45}$
Where Charles the Great, having subdued the Saxons,
There left behind and settled certain French;
Who, holding in disdain the German women
For some dishonest manners of their life,
Establish'd then this law; to wit, no female$_{50}$
Should be inheritrix in Salique land:
Which Salique, as I said, 'twixt Elbe and Sala,
Is at this day in Germany call'd Meisen.
Then doth it well appear the Salique law
Was not devised for the realm of France;$_{55}$
Nor did the French possess the Salique land
Until four hundred one and twenty years
After defunction of King Pharamond,
Idly supposed the founder of this law;
Who died within the year of our redemption$_{60}$

Four hundred twenty-six; and Charles the Great
Subdued the Saxons, and did seat the French
Beyond the river Sala, in the year
Eight hundred five. Besides, their writers say,
King Pepin, which deposed Childeric, $_{65}$
Did, as heir general, being descended
Of Blithild, which was daughter to King Clothair,
Make claim and title to the crown of France.
Hugh Capet also, who usurp'd the crown
Of Charles the duke of Lorraine, sole heir male $_{70}$
Of the true line and stock of Charles the Great,
To find his title with some shows of truth,
Though, in pure truth, it was corrupt and naught,
Convey'd himself as heir to the Lady Lingare,
Daughter to Charlemain, who was the son $_{75}$
To Lewis the emperor, and Lewis the son
Of Charles the Great. Also King Lewis the tenth,
Who was sole heir to the usurper Capet,
Could not keep quiet in his conscience,
Wearing the crown of France, till satisfied $_{80}$
That fair Queen Isabel, his grandmother,
Was lineal of the Lady Ermengare,
Daughter to Charles the foresaid duke of Lorraine:
By the which marriage the line of Charles the Great
Was re-united to the crown of France. $_{85}$
So that, as clear as is the summer's sun,
King Pepin's title and Hugh Capet's claim,
King Lewis his satisfaction, all appear
To hold in right and title of the female:
So do the kings of France unto this day; $_{90}$
Howbeit they would hold up this Salique law
To bar your highness claiming from the female,
And rather choose to hide them in a net
Than amply to imbar their crooked titles
Usurp'd from you and your progenitors. $_{95}$
K. HEN. May I with right and conscience make this claim?
CANT. The sin upon my head, dread sovereign!
For in the book of Numbers is it writ,
When the man dies, let the inheritance

Descend unto the daughter. Gracious lord,$_{100}$
Stand for your own; unwind your bloody flag;
Look back into your mighty ancestors:
Go, my dread lord, to your great-grandsire's tomb,
From whom you claim; invoke his warlike spirit,
And your great-uncle's, Edward the Black Prince,$_{105}$
Who on the French ground play'd a tragedy,
Making defeat on the full power of France,
Whiles his most mighty father on a hill
Stood smiling to behold his lion's whelp
Forage in blood of French nobility.$_{110}$
O noble English, that could entertain
With half their forces the full pride of France
And let another half stand laughing by,
All out of work and cold for action!
ELY. Awake remembrance of these valiant dead$_{115}$
And with your puissant arm renew their feats:
You are their heir; you sit upon their throne;
The blood and courage that renowned them
Runs in your veins; and my thrice-puissant liege
Is in the very May-morn of his youth,$_{120}$
Ripe for exploits and mighty enterprises.
EXE. Your brother kings and monarchs of the earth
Do all expect that you should rouse yourself,
As did the former lions of your blood.
WEST. They know your grace hath cause and means and
    might;$_{125}$
So hath your highness; never king of England
Had nobles richer and more loyal subjects,
Whose hearts have left their bodies here in England
And lie pavilion'd in the fields of France.
CANT. O, let their bodies follow, my dear liege,$_{130}$
With blood and sword and fire to win your right;
In aid whereof we of the spiritualty
Will raise your highness such a mighty sum
As never did the clergy at one time
Bring in to any of your ancestors.$_{135}$
K. HEN. We must not only arm to invade the French,
But lay down our proportions to defend

Against the Scot, who will make road upon us
With all advantages.
CANT. They of those marches, gracious sovereign, 140
Shall be a wall sufficient to defend
Our inland from the pilfering borderers.
K. HEN. We do not mean the coursing snatchers only,
But fear the main intendment of the Scot,
Who hath been still a giddy neighbour to us; 145
For you shall read that my great-grandfather
Never went with his forces into France
But that the Scot on his unfurnish'd kingdom
Came pouring, like the tide into a breach,
With ample and brim fulness of his force, 150
Galling the gleaned land with hot assays,
Girding with grievous siege castles and towns;
That England, being empty of defence,
Hath shook and trembled at the ill neighbourhood.
CANT. She hath been then more fear'd than harm'd, my
    liege; 155
For hear her but exampled by herself:
When all her chivalry hath been in France
And she a mourning widow of her nobles,
She hath herself not only well defended
But taken and impounded as a stray 160
The King of Scots; whom she did send to France,
To fill King Edward's fame with prisoner kings
And make her chronicle as rich with praise
As is the ooze and bottom of the sea
With sunken wreck and sumless treasuries. 165
WEST. But there's a saying very old and true,
'If that you will France win,
Then with Scotland first begin:'
For once the eagle England being in prey,
To her unguarded nest the weasel Scot 170
Comes sneaking and so sucks her princely eggs,
Playing the mouse in absence of the cat,
To tear and havoc more than she can eat.
EXE. It follows then the cat must stay at home:
Yet that is but a crush'd necessity, 175

Since we have locks to safeguard necessaries,
And pretty traps to catch the petty thieves.
While that the armed hand cloth fight abroad,
The advised head defends itself at home;
For government, though high and low and lower,$_{180}$
Put into parts, cloth keep in one consent,
Congreeing in a full and natural close,
Like music.
CANT. Therefore doth heaven divide
The state of man in divers functions,
Setting endeavour in continual motion;$_{185}$
To which is fixed, as an aim or butt,
Obedience: for so work the honey-bees,
Creatures that by a rule in nature teach
The act of order to a peopled kingdom.
They have a king and officers of sorts;$_{190}$
Where some, like magistrates, correct at home,
Others, like merchants, venture trade abroad,
Others, like soldiers, armed in their stings,
Make boot upon the summer's velvet buds,
Which pillage they with merry march bring home$_{195}$
To the tent-royal of their emperor;
Who, busied in his majesty, surveys
The singing masons building roofs of gold,
The civil citizens kneading up the honey,
The poor mechanic porters crowding in$_{200}$
Their heavy burdens at his narrow gate,
The sad-eyed justice, with his surly hum,
Delivering o'er to executors pale
The lazy yawning drone. I this infer,
That many things, having full reference$_{205}$
To one consent, may work contrariously:
As many arrows, loosed several ways,
Come to one mark; as many ways meet in one town;
As many fresh streams meet in one salt sea;
As many lines close in the dial's centre;$_{210}$
So may a thousand actions, once afoot,
End in one purpose, and be all well borne
Without defeat. Therefore to France, my liege.

Divide your happy England into four;
Whereof take you one quarter into France,$_{215}$
And you withal shall make all Gallia shake.
If we, with thrice such powers left at home,
Cannot defend our own doors from the dog,
Let us be worried and our nation lose
The name of hardiness and policy.$_{220}$
K. Hen. Call in the messengers sent from the Dauphin.
(Exeunt some Attendants.)
Now are we well resolved; and, by God's help,
And yours, the noble sinews of our power,
France being ours, we'll bend it to our awe,
Or break it all to pieces: or there we'll sit,$_{225}$
Ruling in large and ample empery
O'er France and all her almost kingly dukedoms,
Or lay these bones in an unworthy urn,
Tombless, with no remembrance over them:
Either our history shall with full mouth$_{230}$
Speak freely of our acts, or else our grave,
Like Turkish mute, shall have a tongueless mouth,
Not worshipp'd with a waxen epitaph.
(Enter Ambassadors of France.)
Now are we well prepared to know the pleasure
Of our fair cousin Dauphin; for we hear$_{235}$
Your greeting is from him, not from the king.
First Amb. May't please your majesty to give us leave
Freely to render what we have in charge;
Or shall we sparingly show you far off
The Dauphin's meaning and our embassy?$_{240}$
K. Hen. We are no tyrant, but a Christian king;
Unto whose grace our passion is as subject
As are our wretches fetter'd in our prisons:
Therefore with frank and with uncurbed plainness
Tell us the Dauphin's mind.
First Amb. Thus, then, in few.$_{245}$
Your highness, lately sending into France,
Did claim some certain dukedoms, in the right
Of your great predecessor, King Edward the third.
In answer of which claim, the prince our master

Says that you savour too much of your youth,$_{250}$
And bids you be advised there's nought in France
That can be with a nimble galliard won;
You cannot revel into dukedoms there.
He therefore sends you, meeter for your spirit,
This tun of treasure; and, in lieu of this,$_{255}$
Desires you let the dukedoms that you claim
Hear no more of you. This the Dauphin speaks.

K. HEN. What treasure, uncle?

EXE. Tennis-balls, my liege.

K. HEN. We are glad the Dauphin is so pleasant with us;
His present and your pains we thank you for:$_{260}$
When we have match'd our rackets to these balls,
We will, in France, by God's grace, play a set
Shall strike his father's crown into the hazard.
Tell him he hath made a match with such a wrangler
That all the courts of France will be disturb'd$_{265}$
With chaces. And we understand him well,
How he comes o'er us with our wilder days,
Not measuring what use we made of them.
We never valued this poor seat of England;
And therefore, living hence, did give ourself$_{270}$
To barbarous license; as 'tis ever common
That men are merriest when they are from home.
But tell the Dauphin I will keep my state,
Be like a king and show my sail of greatness
When I do rouse me in my throne of France:$_{275}$
For that I have laid by my majesty
And plodded like a man for working-days,
But I will rise there with so full a glory
That I will dazzle all the eyes of France,
Yea, strike the Dauphin blind to look on us.$_{280}$
And tell the pleasant prince this mock of his
Hath turn'd his balls to gun-stones; and his soul
Shall stand sore charged for the wasteful vengeance
That shall fly with them: for many a thousand widows
Shall this his mock mock out of their dear husbands;$_{285}$
Mock mothers from their sons, mock castles down;
And some are yet ungotten and unborn

That shall have cause to curse the Dauphin's scorn.
But this lies all within the will of God,
To whom I do appeal; and in whose name$_{290}$
Tell you the Dauphin I am coming on.
To venge me as I may and to put forth
My rightful hand in a well-hallow'd cause.
So get you hence in peace; and tell the Dauphin
His jest will savour but of shallow wit,$_{295}$
When thousands weep more than did laugh at it.
Convey them with safe conduct. Fare you well.
(Exeunt Ambassadors.)
Exe. This was a merry message.
K. Hen. We hope to make the sender blush at it.
Therefore, my lords, omit no happy hour$_{300}$
That may give furtherance to our expedition;
For we have now no thought in us but France,
Save those to God, that run before our business.
Therefore let our proportions for these wars
Be soon collected and all things thought upon$_{305}$
That may with reasonable swiftness add
More feathers to our wings; for, God before,
We'll chide this Dauphin at his father's door.
Therefore let every man now task his thought,
That this fair action may on foot be brought.$_{310}$
(Exeunt. Flourish.)

ACT II

PROLOGUE

(Enter Chorus.)

CHOR. Now all the youth of England are on fire,
And silken dalliance in the wardrobe lies:
Now thrive the armorers, and honour's thought
Reigns solely in the breast of every man:
They sell the pasture now to buy the horse, 5
Following the mirror of all Christian kings,
With winged heels, as English Mercuries.
For now sits Expectation in the air,
And hides a sword from hilts unto the point
With crowns imperial, crowns and coronets, 10
Promised to Harry and his followers.
The French, advised by good intelligence
Of this most dreadful preparation,
Shake in their fear and with pale policy
Seek to divert the English purposes. 15
O England! model to thy inward greatness,
Like little body with a mighty heart,
What mightst thou do, that honour would thee do,

Were all thy children kind and natural!
But see thy fault! France hath in thee found out$_{20}$
A nest of hollow bosoms, which he fills
With treacherous crowns; and three corrupted men,
One, Richard Earl of Cambridge, and the second,
Henry Lord Scroop of Masham, and the third,
Sir Thomas Grey, knight, of Northumberland,$_{25}$
Have, for the gilt of France,—O guilt indeed!—
Confirm'd conspiracy with fearful France;
And by their hands this grace of kings must die,
If hell and treason hold their promises,
Ere he take ship for France, and in Southampton.$_{30}$
Linger your patience on; and we'll digest
The abuse of distance; force a play:
The sum is paid; the traitors are agreed;
The king is set from London; and the scene
Is now transported, gentles, to Southampton;$_{35}$
There is the playhouse now, there must you sit:
And thence to France shall we convey you safe,
And bring you back, charming the narrow seas
To give you gentle pass; for, if we may,
We'll not offend one stomach with our play.$_{40}$
But, till the king come forth, and not till then,
Unto Southampton do we shift our scene. *(Exit.)*

SCENE I. LONDON. A STREET

(Enter Corporal Nym and Lieutenant Bardolph.)

BARD. Well met, Corporal Nym.
NYM. Good morrow, Lieutenant Bardolph.
BARD. What, are Ancient Pistol and you friends yet?
NYM. For my part, I care not: I say little; but when
time shall serve, there shall be smiles; but that shall be as$_5$
it may. I dare not fight; but I will wink and hold out
mine iron: it is a simple one; but what though? it will
toast cheese, and it will endure cold as another man's
sword will: and there's an end.

BARD. I will bestow a breakfast to make you friends;[10] and we'll be all three sworn brothers to France: let it be so, good Corporal Nym.

NYM. Faith, I will live so long as I may, that's the certain of it; and when I cannot live any longer, I will do as I may: that is my rest, that is the rendezvous[15] of it.

BARD. It is certain, corporal, that he is married to Nell Quickly: and, certainly, she did you wrong; for you were troth-plight to her.

NYM. I cannot tell: things must be as they may: men[20] may sleep, and they may have their throats about them at that time; and some say knives have edges. It must be as it may: though patience be a tired mare, yet she will plod. There must be conclusions. Well, I cannot tell.

(ENTER PISTOL AND HOSTESS.)

BARD. Here comes Ancient Pistol and his wife: good[25] corporal, be patient here. How now, mine host Pistol!

PIST. Base tike, call'st thou me host?

Now, by this hand, I swear, I scorn the term;

Nor shall my Nell keep lodgers.

HOST. No, by my troth, not long; for we cannot lodge[30] and board a dozen or fourteen gentlewomen that live honestly by the prick of their needles, but it will be thought we keep a bawdy house straight. *(Nym and Pistol draw.)* O well a day, Lady, if he be not drawn now! we shall see wilful adultery and murder committed.[35]

BARD. Good lieutenant! good corporal! offer nothing here.

NYM. Pish!

PIST. Pish for thee, Iceland dog! thou prick-ear'd cur of Iceland!

HOST. Good Corporal Nym, show thy valour, and put[40] up your sword.

NYM. Will you shog off? I would have you solus.

PIST. 'Solus,' egregious dog? O viper vile!

The 'solus' in thy most mervailous face;

The 'solus' in thy teeth, and in thy throat,[45]

And in thy hateful lungs, yea, in thy maw, perdy,

And, which is worse, within thy nasty mouth!
I do retort the 'solus' in thy bowels;
For I can take, and Pistol's cock is up,
And flashing fire will follow.$_{50}$

NYM. I am not Barbason; you cannot conjure me. I
have an humour to knock you indifferently well. If you
grow foul with me, Pistol, I will scour you with my rapier,
as I may, in fair terms: if you would walk off, I would
prick your guts a little, in good terms, as I may: and$_{55}$
that's the humour of it.

PIST. O braggart vile and damned furious wight!
The grave doth gape, and doting death is near;
Therefore exhale.

BARD. Hear me, hear me what I say: he that strikes the$_{60}$
first stroke, I'll run him up to the hilts, as I am a soldier.
(Draws.)

PIST. An oath of mickle might; and fury shall abate.
Give me thy fist, thy fore-foot to me give:
Thy spirits are most tall.

NYM. I will cut thy throat, one time or other, in fair$_{65}$
terms: that is the humour of it.

PIST. 'Couple a gorge!'
That is the word. I thee defy again.
O hound of Crete, think'st thou my spouse to get?
No; to the spital go,$_{70}$
And from the powdering-tub of infamy
Fetch forth the lazar kite of Cressid's kind,
Doll Tearsheet she by name, and her espouse:
I have, and I will hold, the quondam Quickly
For the only she; and—pauca, there's enough.
Go to.$_{75}$

(Enter the Boy.)

BOY. Mine host Pistol, you must come to my master,
and you, hostess: he is very sick, and would to bed.
Good Bardolph, put thy face between his sheets, and do
the office of a warming-pan. Faith, he's very ill.$_{80}$

BARD. Away, you rogue!

HOST. By my troth, he'll yield the crow a pudding one
of these days. The king has killed his heart. Good husband,

come home presently. (Exeunt Hostess and Boy.)

BARD. Come, shall I make you two friends? We must to France together: why the devil should we keep knives to cut one another's throats?

PIST. Let floods o'erswell, and fiends for food howl on!

NYM. You'll pay me the eight shillings I won of you at betting?

PIST. Base is the slave that pays.

NYM. That now I will have: that's the humour of it.

PIST. As manhood shall compound: push home.

(They draw.)

BARD. By this sword, he that makes the first thrust, I'll kill him; by this sword, I will.

PIST. Sword is an oath, and oaths must have their course.

BARD. Corporal Nym, an thou wilt be friends, be friends: an thou wilt not, why, then, be enemies with me too. Prithee, put up.

NYM. I shall have my eight shillings I won of you at betting?

PIST. A noble shalt thou have, and present pay;
And liquor likewise will I give to thee,
And friendship shall combine, and brotherhood:
I'll live by Nym, and Nym shall live by me;
Is not this just? for I shall sutler be
Unto the camp, and profits will accrue.
Give me thy hand.

NYM. I shall have my noble?

PIST. In cash most justly paid.

NYM. Well, then, that's the humour of 't.

(Re-enter HOSTESS.)

HOST. As ever you came of women, come in quickly to Sir John. Ah, poor heart! he is so shaked of a burning quotidian tertian, that it is most lamentable to behold. Sweet men, come to him.

NYM. The king hath run bad humours on the knight; that's the even of it.

PIST. Nym, thou hast spoke the right;
His heart is fracted and corroborate.

NYM. The king is a good king: but it must be as it

may; he passes some humours and careers.

PIST. Let us condole the knight; for, lambkins we will live.

SCENE II. SOUTHAMPTON. A COUNCIL-CHAMBER

(Enter Exeter, Bedford, and Westmoreland.)

BED. 'Fore God, his grace is bold, to trust these traitors.

EXE. They shall be apprehended by and by.

WEST. How smooth and even they do bear themselves!
As if allegiance in their bosoms sat,
Crowned with faith and constant loyalty.$_5$

BED. The king hath note of all that they intend,
By interception which they dream not of.

EXE. Nay, but the man that was his bedfellow,
Whom he hath dull'd and cloy'd with gracious favours,
That he should, for a foreign purse, so sell$_{10}$
His sovereign's life to death and treachery.

*(TRUMPETS SOUND. ENTER KING HENRY, SCROOP, CAMBRIDGE,
GREY, AND ATTENDANTS.)*

K. HEN. Now sits the wind fair, and we will aboard.
My Lord of Cambridge, and my kind Lord of Masham,
And you, my gentle knight, give me your thoughts:
Think you not that the powers we bear with us$_{15}$
Will cut their passage through the force of France,
Doing the execution and the act
For which we have in head assembled them?

SCROOP. No doubt, my liege, if each man do his best.

K. HEN. I doubt not that; since we are well persuaded$_{20}$
We carry not a heart with us from hence
That grows not in a fair consent with ours,
Nor leave not one behind that doth not wish
Success and conquest to attend on us.

CAM. Never was monarch better fear'd and loved$_{25}$
Than is your majesty: there's not, I think, a subject
That sits in heart-grief and uneasiness
Under the sweet shade of your government.

GREY. True: those that were your father's enemies
Have steep'd their galls in honey and do serve you$_{30}$
With hearts create of duty and of zeal.
K. HEN. We therefore have great cause of thankfulness;
And shall forget the office of our hand,
Sooner than quittance of desert and merit
According to the weight and worthiness.$_{35}$
SCROOP. So service shall with steeled sinews toil,
And labour shall refresh itself with hope,
To do your grace incessant services.
K. HEN. We judge no less. Uncle of Exeter,
Enlarge the man committed yesterday,$_{40}$
That rail'd against our person: we consider
It was excess of wine that set him on;
And on his more advice we pardon him.
SCROOP. That's mercy, but too much security:
Let him be punish'd, sovereign, lest example$_{45}$
Breed, by his sufferance, more of such a kind.
K. HEN. O, let us yet be merciful.
CAM. So may your highness, and yet punish too.
GREY. Sir,
You show great mercy, if you give him life,$_{50}$
After the taste of much correction.
K. HEN. Alas, your too much love and care of me
Are heavy orisons 'gainst this poor wretch!
If little faults, proceeding on distemper,
Shall not be wink'd at, how shall we stretch our eye$_{55}$
When capital crimes, chew'd, swallow'd and digested,
Appear before us? We'll yet enlarge that man,
Though Cambridge, Scroop and Grey, in their dear care
And tender preservation of our person,
Would have him punish'd. And now to our French causes:$_{60}$
Who are the late commissioners?
CAM. I one, my lord:
Your highness bade me ask for it to-day.
SCROOP. So did you me, my liege.
GREY. And I, my royal sovereign.$_{65}$
K. HEN. Then, Richard Earl of Cambridge, there is yours;
There yours, Lord Scroop of Masham; and, sir knight,

Grey of Northumberland, this same is yours:
Read them; and know, I know your worthiness.
My Lord of Westmoreland, and uncle Exeter,$_{70}$
We will aboard to night. Why, how now, gentlemen!
What see you in those papers that you lose
So much complexion? Look ye, how they change!
Their cheeks are paper. Why, what read you there,
That hath so cowarded and chased your blood$_{75}$
Out of appearance?
CAM. I do confess my fault;
And do submit me to your highness' mercy.
GREY & SCROOP. To which we all appeal.
K. HEN. The mercy that was quick in us but late,
By your own counsel is suppress'd and kill'd:$_{80}$
You must not dare, for shame, to talk of mercy;
For your own reasons turn into your bosoms,
As dogs upon their masters, worrying you.
See you, my princes and my noble peers,
These English monsters! My Lord of Cambridge here,$_{85}$
You know how apt our love was to accord
To furnish him with all appertinents
Belonging to his honour; and this man
Hath, for a few light crowns, lightly conspired,
And sworn unto the practices of France,$_{90}$
To kill us here in Hampton: to the which
This knight, no less for bounty bound to us
Than Cambridge is, hath likewise sworn. But, O,
What shall I say to thee, Lord Scroop? thou cruel,
Ingrateful, savage and inhuman creature!$_{95}$
Thou that didst bear the key of all my counsels,
That knew'st the very bottom of my soul,
That almost mightst have coin'd me into gold,
Wouldst thou have practised on me for thy use,
May it be possible, that foreign hire$_{100}$
Could out of thee extract one spark of evil
That might annoy my finger? 'tis so strange,
That, though the truth of it stands off as gross
As black and white, my eye will scarcely see it.
Treason and murder ever kept together,$_{105}$

As two yoke-devils sworn to either's purpose,
Working so grossly in a natural cause,
That admiration did not whoop at them:
But thou, 'gainst all proportion, didst bring in
Wonder to wait on treason and on murder:$_{110}$
And whatsoever cunning fiend it was
That wrought upon thee so preposterously
Hath got the voice in hell for excellence:
All other devils that suggest by treasons
Do botch and bungle up damnation$_{115}$
With patches, colours, and with forms being fetch'd
From glistering semblances of piety;
But he that temper'd thee bade thee stand up,
Gave thee no instance why thou shouldst do treason,
Unless to dub thee with the name of traitor.$_{120}$
If that same demon that hath gull'd thee thus
Should with his lion gait walk the whole world,
He might return to vasty Tartar back,
And tell the legions 'I can never win
A soul so easy as that Englishman's.'$_{125}$
O, how hast thou with jealousy infected
The sweetness of affiance! Show men dutiful?
Why, so didst thou: seem they grave and learned?
Why, so didst thou: come they of noble family?
Why, so didst thou: seem they religious?$_{130}$
Why, so didst thou: or are they spare in diet,
Free from gross passion or of mirth or anger,
Constant in spirit, not swerving with the blood,
Garnish'd and deck'd in modest complement,
Not working with the eye without the ear,$_{135}$
And but in purged judgement trusting neither?
Such and so finely bolted didst thou seem:
And thus thy fall hath left a kind of blot,
To mark the full-fraught man and best indued
With some suspicion. I will weep for thee;$_{140}$
For this revolt of thine, methinks, is like
Another fall of man. Their faults are open:
Arrest them to the answer of the law;
And God acquit them of their practices!

Exe. I arrest thee of high treason, by the name of$_{145}$
Richard Earl of Cambridge.
I arrest thee of high treason, by the name of Henry
Lord Scroop of Masham.
I arrest thee of high treason, by the name of Thomas
Grey, knight, of Northumberland.$_{150}$
Scroop. Our purposes God justly hath discover'd;
And I repent my fault more than my death;
Which I beseech your highness to forgive,
Although my body pay the price of it.
Cam. For me, the gold of France did not seduce;$_{155}$
Although I did admit it as a motive
The sooner to effect what I intended:
But God be thanked for prevention;
Which I in sufferance heartily will rejoice,
Beseeching God and you to pardon me.$_{160}$
Grey. Never did faithful subject more rejoice
At the discovery of most dangerous treason
Than I do at this hour joy o'er myself,
Prevented from a damned enterprise:
My fault, but not my body, pardon, sovereign.$_{165}$
K. Hen. God quit you in his mercy! Hear your sentence.
You have conspired against our royal person,
Join'd with an enemy proclaim'd and from his coffers
Received the golden earnest of our death;
Wherein you would have sold your king to slaughter,$_{170}$
His princes and his peers to servitude,
His subjects to oppression and contempt
And his whole kingdom into desolation.
Touching our person seek we no revenge;
But we our kingdom's safety must so tender,$_{175}$
Whose ruin you have sought, that to her laws
We do deliver you. Get you therefore hence,
Poor miserable wretches, to your death:
The taste whereof, God of his mercy give
You patience to endure, and true repentance$_{180}$
Of all your dear offences! Bear them hence.
(Exeunt Cambridge, Scroop, and Grey, guarded.)
Now, lords, for France; the enterprise whereof

Shall be to you, as us, like glorious.
We doubt not of a fair and lucky war,
Since God so graciously hath brought to light₁₈₅
This dangerous treason lurking in our way
To hinder our beginnings. We doubt not now
But every rub is smoothed on our way.
Then forth, dear countrymen: let us deliver
Our puissance into the hand of God,₁₉₀
Putting it straight in expedition.
Cheerly to sea; the signs of war advance:
No king of England, if not king of France, *(Exeunt.)*

SCENE III. LONDON. BEFORE A TAVERN
.

(Enter Pistol, Hostess, Nym, Bardolph, and Boy.)

HOST. Prithee, honey-sweet husband, let me bring thee
to Staines.
PIST. No; for my manly heart doth yearn.
Bardolph, be blithe: Nym, rouse thy vaunting veins:
Boy, bristle thy courage up; for Falstaff he is dead,₅
And we must yearn therefore.
BARD. Would I were with him, wheresome'er he is,
either in heaven or in hell!
HOST. Nay, sure, he's not in hell: he's in Arthur's bosom,
if ever man went to Arthur's bosom. A' made a₁₀
finer end and went away an it had been any christom
child; a' parted even just between twelve and one, even at
the turning o' the tide: for after I saw him fumble with
the sheets and play with flowers and smile upon his
fingers' ends, I knew there was but one way; for his nose₁₅
was as sharp as a pen, and a' babbled of green fields.
'How now, Sir John!' quoth I: 'what, man! be o' good
cheer.' So a' cried out 'God, God, God!' three or four
times. Now I, to comfort him, bid him a' should not
think of God; I hoped there was no need to trouble himself₂₀
with any such thoughts yet. So a' bade me lay more
clothes on his feet: I put my hand into the bed and felt

them, and they were as cold as any stone; then I felt to
his knees, and they were as cold as any stone, and so
upward and upward, and all was as cold as any stone.$_{25}$
NYM. They say he cried out of sack.
HOST. Ay, that a' did.
BARD. And of women.
HOST. Nay, that a' did not.
BOY. Yes, that a' did; and said they were devils$_{30}$
incarnate.
HOST. A' could never abide carnation; 'twas a colour
he never liked.
BOY. A' said once, the devil would have him about
women.$_{35}$
HOST. A' did in some sort, indeed, handle women; but
then he was rheumatic, and talked of the whore of Babylon.
BOY. Do you not remember, a' saw a flea stick upon
Bardolph's nose, and a' said it was a black soul burning in
hell-fire?$_{40}$
BARD. Well, the fuel is gone that maintained that fire:
that's all the riches I got in his service.
NYM. Shall we shog? the king will be gone from
Southampton.
PIST. Come, let's away. My love, give me thy lips.$_{45}$
Look to my chattels and my movables:
Let senses rule; the word is 'Pitch and Pay:'
Trust none;
For oaths are straws, men's faiths are wafer-cakes,
And hold-fast is the only dog, my duck:$_{50}$
Therefore, Caveto be thy counsellor.
Go, clear thy crystals. Yoke-fellows in arms,
Let us to France; like horse-leeches, my boys,
To suck, to suck, the very blood to suck!
BOY. And that's but unwholesome food, they say.$_{55}$
PIST. Touch her soft mouth, and march.
BARD. Farewell, hostess. *(Kissing her.)*
NYM. I cannot kiss, that is the humour of it; but, adieu.
PIST. Let housewifery appear: keep close, I thee command.
HOST. Farewell; adieu. *(Exeunt.)*$_{60}$

SCENE IV. FRANCE. THE KING'S PALACE

(Flourish. Enter the French King, the Dauphin, the Dukes of Berri and Bretagne, the Constable, and others.)

FR. KING. Thus comes the English with full power upon us;
And more than carefully it us concerns
To answer royally in our defences.
Therefore the Dukes of Berri and of Bretagne,
Of Brabant and of Orleans, shall make forth,5
And you, Prince Dauphin, with all swift dispatch,
To line and new repair our towns of war
With men of courage and with means defendant;
For England his approaches makes as fierce
As waters to the sucking of a gulf.10
It fits us then to be as provident
As fear may teach us out of late examples
Left by the fatal and neglected English
Upon our fields.
DAU. My most redoubted father,
It is most meet we arm us 'gainst the foe;15
For peace itself should not so dull a kingdom,
Though war nor no known quarrel were in question,
But that defences, musters, preparations,
Should be maintain'd, assembled and collected,
As were a war in expectation.20
Therefore, I say 'tis meet we all go forth
To view the sick and feeble parts of France:
And let us do it with no show of fear;
No, with no more than if we heard that England
Were busied with a Whitsun morris-dance:25
For, my good liege, she is so idly king'd,
Her sceptre so fantastically borne
By a vain, giddy, shallow, humorous youth,
That fear attends her not.
CON. O peace, Prince Dauphin!
You are too much mistaken in this king:30
Question your grace the late ambassadors,

With what great state he heard their embassy,
How well supplied with noble counsellors,
How modest in exception, and withal
How terrible in constant resolution,$_{35}$
And you shall find his vanities forespent
Were but the outside of the Roman Brutus,
Covering discretion with a coat of folly;
As gardeners do with ordure hide those roots
That shall first spring and be most delicate.$_{40}$
DAU. Well, 'tis not so, my lord high constable;
But though we think it so, it is no matter:
In cases of defence 'tis best to weigh
The enemy more mighty than he seems:
So the proportions of defence are fill'd;$_{45}$
Which of a weak and niggardly projection
Doth, like a miser, spoil his coat with scanting
A little cloth.
FR. KING. Think we King Harry strong;
And, princes, look you strongly arm to meet him.
The kindred of him hath been flesh'd upon us;$_{50}$
And he is bred out of that bloody strain
That haunted us in our familiar paths:
Witness our too much memorable shame
When Cressy battle fatally was struck,
And all our princes captived by the hand$_{55}$
Of that black name, Edward, Black Prince of Wales;
Whiles that his mountain sire, on mountain standing,
Up in the air, crown'd with the golden sun,
Saw his heroical seed, and smiled to see him,
Mangle the work of nature and deface$_{60}$
The patterns that by God and by French fathers
Had twenty years been made. This is a stem
Of that victorious stock; and let us fear
The native mightiness and fate of him.
(Enter a Messenger.)
MESS. Ambassadors from Harry King of England$_{65}$
Do crave admittance to your majesty.
FR. KING. We'll give them present audience. Go, and bring
them.

(Exeunt Messenger and certain Lords.)
You see this chase is hotly follow'd, friends.
DAU. Turn head, and stop pursuit; for coward dogs
Most spend their mouths when what they seem to threaten$_{70}$
Runs far before them. Good my sovereign,
Take up the English short, and let them know
Of what a monarchy you are the head:
Self-love, my liege, is not so vile a sin
As self-neglecting.
(Re-enter Lords, with EXETER and train.)
FR. KING. From our brother England?$_{75}$
EXE. From him; and thus he greets your majesty.
He wills you, in the name of God Almighty,
That you divest yourself, and lay apart
The borrow'd glories that by gift of heaven,
By law of nature and of nations, 'long$_{80}$
To him and to his heirs; namely, the crown
And all wide-stretched honours that pertain
By custom and the ordinance of times
Unto the crown of France. That you may know
'Tis no sinister nor no awkward claim,$_{85}$
Pick'd from the worm-holes of long-vanish'd days,
Nor from the dust of old oblivion raked,
He sends you this most memorable line,
In every branch truly demonstrative;
Willing you overlook this pedigree:$_{90}$
And when you find him evenly derived
From his most famed of famous ancestors,
Edward the third, he bids you then resign
Your crown and kingdom, indirectly held
From him the native and true challenger.$_{95}$
FR. KING. Or else what follows?
EXE. Bloody constraint; for if you hide the crown
Even in your hearts, there will he rake for it:
Therefore in fierce tempest is he coming,
In thunder and in earthquake, like a Jove,$_{100}$
That, if requiring fail, he will compel;
And bids you, in the bowels of the Lord,
Deliver up the crown, and to take mercy

On the poor souls for whom this hungry war
Opens his vasty jaws; and on your head[105]
Turning the widows' tears, the orphans' cries,
The dead men's blood, the pining maidens' groans,
For husbands, fathers and betrothed lovers,
That shall be swallow'd in this controversy.
This is his claim, his threatening and my message;[110]
Unless the Dauphin be in presence here,
To whom expressly I bring greeting too.
FR. KING. For us, we will consider of this further:
To-morrow shall you bear our full intent
Back to our brother England.
DAU. For the Dauphin,[115]
I stand here for him: what to him from England?
EXE. Scorn and defiance; slight regard, contempt,
And any thing that may not misbecome
The mighty sender, doth he prize you at.
Thus says my king; an if your father's highness[120]
Do not, in grant of all demands at large,
Sweeten the bitter mock you sent his majesty,
He'll call you to so hot an answer of it,
That caves and womby vaultages of France
Shall chide your trespass and return your mock[125]
In second accent of his ordnance.
DAU. Say, if my father render fair return,
It is against my will; for I desire
Nothing but odds with England: to that end,
As matching to his youth and vanity,[130]
I did present him with the Paris balls.
EXE. He'll make your Paris Louvre shake for it,
Were it the mistress-court of mighty Europe:
And, be assured, you'll find a difference,
As we his subjects have in wonder found,[135]
Between the promise of his greener days
And these he masters now: now he weighs time
Even to the utmost grain: that you shall read
In your own losses, if he stay in France.
FR. KING. To-morrow shall you know our mind at full.[140]
EXE. Dispatch us with all speed, lest that our king

Come here himself to question our delay;
For he is footed in this land already.
FR. KING. You shall be soon dispatch'd with fair conditions:
A night is but small breath and little pause₁₄₅
To answer matters of this consequence. *(Flourish. Exeunt.)*

ACT III

PROLOGUE

(Enter Chorus.)

CHOR. Thus with imagined wing our swift scene flies
In motion of no less celerity
Than that of thought. Suppose that you have seen
The well-appointed king at Hampton pier
Embark his royalty; and his brave fleet$_5$
With silken streamers the young Phœbus fanning:
Play with your fancies, and in them behold
Upon the hempen tackle ship-boys climbing;
Hear the shrill whistle which doth order give
To sounds confused; behold the threaden sails,$_{10}$
Borne with the invisible and creeping wind,
Draw the huge bottoms through the furrow'd sea,
Breasting the lofty surge: O, do but think
You stand upon the rivage and behold
A city on the inconstant billows dancing;$_{15}$
For so appears this fleet majestical,
Holding due course to Harfleur. Follow, follow:

Grapple your minds to sternage of this navy,
And leave your England, as dead midnight still,
Guarded with grandsires, babies and old women, [20]
Either past or not arrived to pith and puissance;
For who is he, whose chin is but enrich'd
With one appearing hair, that will not follow
These cull'd and choice-drawn cavaliers to France?
Work, work your thoughts, and therein see a siege; [25]
Behold the ordnance on their carriages,
With fatal mouths gaping on girded Harfleur.
Suppose the ambassador from the French comes back;
Tells Harry that the king doth offer him
Katharine his daughter, and with her, to dowry, [30]
Some petty and unprofitable dukedoms.
The offer likes not: and the nimble gunner
With linstock now the devilish cannon touches,
(Alarum, and chambers go off.)
And down goes all before them. Still be kind,
And eke out our performance with your mind. *(Exit.)* [35]

SCENE I. FRANCE. BEFORE HARFLEUR

(Alarum. Enter KING HENRY, EXETER, BEDFORD, GLOUCESTER, and Soldiers, with scaling-ladders.)

K. HEN. Once more unto the breach, dear friends, once
   more;
Or close the wall up with our English dead.
In peace there's nothing so becomes a man
As modest stillness and humility:
But when the blast of war blows in our ears, [5]
Then imitate the action of the tiger;
Stiffen the sinews, summon up the blood,
Disguise fair nature with hard-favour'd rage;
Then lend the eye a terrible aspect;
Let it pry through the portage of the head [10]
Like the brass cannon; let the brow o'erwhelm it

As fearfully as doth a galled rock
O'erhang and jutty his confounded base,
Swill'd with the wild and wasteful ocean.
Now set the teeth and stretch the nostril wide, [15]
Hold hard the breath and bend up every spirit
To his full height. On, on, you noblest English,
Whose blood is fet from fathers of war-proof!
Fathers that, like so many Alexanders,
Have in these parts from morn till even fought [20]
And sheathed their swords for lack of argument:
Dishonour not your mothers; now attest
That those whom you call'd fathers did beget you.
Be copy now to men of grosser blood,
And teach them how to war. And you, good yeomen, [25]
Whose limbs were made in England, show us here
The mettle of your pasture; let us swear
That you are worth your breeding; which I doubt not;
For there is none of you so mean and base,
That hath not noble lustre in your eyes. [30]
I see you stand like greyhounds in the slips,
Straining upon the start. The game's afoot:
Follow your spirit, and upon this charge
Cry 'God for Harry, England, and Saint George!'
(Exeunt. Alarum, and chambers go off.)

SCENE II. THE SAME

(Enter Nym, Bardolph, Pistol, and Boy.)

BARD. On, on, on, on, on! to the breach, to the breach!
NYM. Pray thee, corporal, stay: the knocks are too
hot; and, for mine own part, I have not a case of lives: the
humour of it is too hot, that is the very plain-song of it.
PIST. The plain-song is most just; for humours do [5]
abound:
Knocks go and come; God's vassals drop and die;
And sword and shield,

In bloody field,
Doth win immortal fame.

Boy. Would I were in an alehouse in London! I would give all my fame for a pot of ale and safety.

Pist. And I:
If wishes would prevail with me,
My purpose should not fail with me,
But thither would I hie.

Boy. As duly, but not as truly,
As bird doth sing on bough.

(Enter FLUELLEN.)

Flu. Up to the breach, you dogs! avaunt, you cullions!
(Driving them forward.)

Pist. Be merciful, great duke, to men of mould.
Abate thy rage, abate thy manly rage,
Abate thy rage, great duke!
Good bawcock, bate thy rage; use lenity, sweet chuck!

Nym. These be good humours! your honour wins bad
humours. *(Exeunt all but Boy.)*

Boy. As young as I am, I have observed these three
swashers. I am boy to them all three: but all they three,
though they would serve me, could not be man to me; for
indeed three such antics do not amount to a man. For
Bardolph, he is white-livered and red-faced; by the means
whereof a' faces it out, but fights not. For Pistol, he hath
a killing tongue and a quiet sword; by the means whereof
a' breaks words, and keeps whole weapons. For Nym, he
hath heard that men of few words are the best men; and
therefore he scorns to say his prayers, lest a' should be
thought a coward: but his few bad words are matched with
as few good deeds; for a' never broke any man's head but his
own, and that was against a post when he was drunk. They
will steal any thing, and call it purchase. Bardolph stole a
lute-case, bore it twelve leagues, and sold it for three
    half-pence.
Nym and Bardolph are sworn brothers in filching,
and in Calais they stole a fire-shovel: I knew by that piece
of service the men would carry coals. They would have me
as familiar with men's pockets as their gloves or their hand-

kerchers:
which makes much against my manhood, if I$_{45}$
should take from another's pocket to put into mine; for it
is plain pocketing up of wrongs. I must leave them, and
seek some better service: their villany goes against my weak
stomach, and therefore I must cast it up. *(Exit.)*
(Re-enter FLUELLEN, GOWER following.)

Gow. Captain Fluellen, you must come presently to$_{50}$
the mines; the Duke of Gloucester would speak with you.

FLU. To the mines! tell you the duke, it is not so good
to come to the mines; for, look you, the mines is not according
to the disciplines of the war: the concavities of it
is not sufficient; for, look you, th' athversary, you may discuss$_{55}$
unto the duke, look you, is digt himself four yard
under the countermines: by Cheshu, I think a' will plow
up all, if there is not better directions.

Gow. The Duke of Gloucester, to whom the order of
the siege is given, is altogether directed by an Irishman, a$_{60}$
very valiant gentleman, i' faith.

FLU. It is Captain Macmorris, is it not?

Gow. I think it be.

FLU. By Cheshu, he is an ass, as in the world: I will
verify as much in his beard: he has no more directions in$_{65}$
the true disciplines of the wars, look you, of the Roman
disciplines, than is a puppy-dog.
(ENTER MACMORRIS AND CAPTAIN JAMY.)

Gow. Here a' comes; and the Scots captain, Captain
Jamy, with him.

FLU. Captain Jamy is a marvellous falorous gentleman,$_{70}$
that is certain; and of great expedition and knowledge in
th' aunchient wars, upon my particular knowledge of his
directions: by Cheshu, he will maintain his argument as
well as any military man in the world, in the disciplines of
the pristine wars of the Romans.$_{75}$

JAMY. I say gud-day, Captain Fluellen.

FLU. God-den to your worship, good Captain James.

Gow. How now, Captain Macmorris! have you quit
the mines? have the pioners given o'er?

MAC. By Chrish, la! tish ill done: the work ish give$_{80}$

over, the trompet sound the retreat. By my hand, I swear,
and my father's soul, the work ish ill done; it ish give
over: I would have blowed up the town, so Chrish save
me, la! in an hour: O, tish ill done, tish ill done; by my
hand, tish ill done!₈₅

FLU. Captain Macmorris, I beseech you now, will you
voutsafe me, look you, a few disputations with you, as partly
touching or concerning the disciplines of the war, the Roman
wars, in the way of argument, look you, and friendly
communication; partly to satisfy my opinion, and partly₉₀
for the satisfaction, look you, of my mind, as touching the
direction of the military discipline; that is the point.

JAMY. It sall be vary gud, gud feith, gud captains
bath: and I sall quit you with gud leve, as I may pick
occasion; that sall I, marry.₉₅

MAC. It is no time to discourse, so Chrish save me: the
day is hot, and the weather, and the wars, and the king,
and the dukes: it is no time to discourse. The town is
     beseeched,
and the trumpet call us to the breach; and we
talk, and, be Chrish, do nothing: 'tis shame for us all: so₁₀₀
God sa' me, 'tis shame to stand still; it is shame, by my
hand: and there is throats to be cut, and works to be done;
and there ish nothing done, so Chrish sa' me, la!

JAMY. By the mess, ere theise eyes of mine take themselves
to slomber, ay'll de gud service, or ay'll lig i' the₁₀₅
grund for it; ay, or go to death; and ay'll pay 't as valorously
as I may, that sall I suerly do, that is the breff and
the long. Marry, I wad full fain hear some question 'tween
you tway.

FLU. Captain Macmorris, I think, look you, under your₁₁₀
correction, there is not many of your nation—

MAC. Of my nation! What ish my nation! Ish a villain,
and a bastard, and a knave, and a rascal. What ish
my nation? Who talks of my nation?

FLU. Look you, if you take the matter otherwise than₁₁₅
is meant, Captain Macmorris, peradventure I shall think
you do not use me with that affability as in discretion you
ought to use me, look you; being as good a man as yourself,

both in the disciplines of war, and in the derivation of
my birth, and in other particularities.$_{120}$

MAC. I do not know you so good a man as myself: so
Chrish save me, I will cut off your head.

GOW. Gentlemen both, you will mistake each other.

JAMY. A! that's a foul fault.

(A parley sounded.)

GOW. The town sounds a parley.$_{125}$

FLU. Captain Macmorris, when there is more better
opportunity to be required, look you, I will be so bold
as to tell you I know the disciplines of war; and there is
an end. *(Exeunt.)*

SCENE III. THE SAME. BEFORE THE GATES

*(The Governor and some Citizens on the walls; the English forces below. Enter
KING HENRY and his train.)*

K. HEN. How yet resolves the governor of the town?
This is the latest parle we will admit:
Therefore to our best mercy give yourselves;
Or like to men proud of destruction
Defy us to our worst: for, as I am a soldier,$_5$
A name that in my thoughts becomes me best,
If I begin the battery once again,
I will not leave the half-achieved Harfleur
Till in her ashes she lie buried.
The gates of mercy shall be all shut up,$_{10}$
And the flesh'd soldier, rough and hard of heart,
In liberty of bloody hand shall range
With conscience wide as hell, mowing like grass
Your fresh-fair virgins and your flowering infants.
What is it then to me, if impious war,$_{15}$
Array'd in flames like to the prince of fiends,
Do, with his smirch'd complexion, all fell feats
Enlink'd to waste and desolation?
What is't to me, when you yourselves are cause,
If your pure maidens fall into the hand$_{20}$

Of hot and forcing violation?
What rein can hold licentious wickedness
When down the hill he holds his fierce career?
We may as bootless spend our vain command
Upon the enraged soldiers in their spoil$_{25}$
As send precepts to the leviathan
To come ashore. Therefore, you men of Harfleur,
Take pity of your town and of your people,
Whiles yet my soldiers are in my command;
Whiles yet the cool and temperate wind of grace$_{30}$
O'erblows the filthy and contagious clouds
Of heady murder, spoil and villany.
If not, why, in a moment look to see
The blind and bloody soldier with foul hand
Defile the locks of your shrill-shrieking daughters;$_{35}$
Your fathers taken by the silver beards,
And their most reverend heads dash'd to the walls,
Your naked infants spitted upon pikes,
Whiles the mad mothers with their howls confused
Do break the clouds, as did the wives of Jewry$_{40}$
At Herod's bloody-hunting slaughtermen.
What say you? will you yield, and this avoid,
Or, guilty in defence, be thus destroy'd?
Gov. Our expectation hath this day an end:
The Dauphin, whom of succours we entreated,$_{45}$
Returns us that his powers are yet not ready
To raise so great a siege. Therefore, great king,
We yield our town and lives to thy soft mercy.
Enter our gates; dispose of us and ours;
For we no longer are defensible.$_{50}$
K. HEN. Open your gates. Come, uncle Exeter,
Go you and enter Harfleur; there remain,
And fortify it strongly 'gainst the French:
Use mercy to them all. For us, dear uncle,
The winter coming on and sickness growing$_{55}$
Upon our soldiers, we will retire to Calais.
To-night in Harfleur we will be your guest;
To-morrow for the march are we addrest.
(Flourish. The King and his train enter the town.)

SCENE IV. THE FRENCH KING'S PALACE

(Enter Katharine and Alice.)

KATH. Alice, tu as été en Angleterre, et tu parles bien
le langage.

ALICE. Un peu, madame.

KATH. Je te prie, m'enseignez; il faut que j'apprenne à
parler. Comment appelez-vous la main en Anglois? 5

ALICE. La main? elle est appelée de hand.

KATH. De hand. Et les doigts?

ALICE. Les doigts? ma foi, j'oublie les doigts; mais je
me souviendrai. Les doigts? je pense qu'ils sont appelés
de fingres; oui, de fingres. 10

KATH. La main, de hand; les doigts, de fingres. Je
pense que je suis le bon écolier; j'ai gagné deux mots
d'Anglois vîtement. Comment appelez-vous les ongles?

ALICE. Les ongles? nous les appelons de nails.

KATH. De nails. Ecoutez; dites-moi, si je parle bien: 15
de hand, de fingres, et de nails.

ALICE. C'est bien dit, madame; il est fort bon Anglois.

KATH. Dites-moi l'Anglois pour le bras.

ALICE. De arm, madame.

KATH. Et le coude? 20

ALICE. De elbow.

KATH. De elbow. Je m'en fais la répétition de tous
les mots que vous m'avez appris dès à présent.

ALICE. Il est trop difficile, madame, comme je pense.

KATH. Excusez-moi, Alice; écoutez: de hand, de fingres, 25
de nails, de arma, de bilbow.

ALICE. De elbow, madame.

KATH. O Seigneur Dieu, je m'en oublie! de elbow.
Comment appelez-vous le col?

ALICE. De neck, madame. 30

KATH. De nick. Et le menton?

ALICE. De chin.

KATH. De sin. Le col, de nick; le menton, de sin.

ALICE. Oui. Sauf votre honneur, en vérité, vous

prononcez les mots aussi droit que les natifs d'Angleterre.35

KATH. Je ne doute point d'apprendre, par la grace de
Dieu, et en peu de temps.

ALICE. N'avez vous pas déjà oublié ce que je vous ai
enseigné?

KATH. Non, je reciterai à vous promptement: de hand,40
de fingres, de mails,—

ALICE. De nails, madame.

KATH. De nails, de arm, de ilbow.

ALICE. Sauf votre honneur, de elbow.

KATH. Ainsi dis-je; de elbow, de nick, et de sin.45
Comment appelez-vous le pied et la robe?

ALICE. De foot, madame; et de coun.

KATH. De foot et de coun! O Seigneur Dieu! ce sont
mots de son mauvais, corruptible, gros, et impudique, et non
pour les dames d'honneur d'user: je ne voudrais prononcer50
ces mots devant les seigneurs de France pour tout le monde.
Foh! le foot et le coun! Néanmoins, je reciterai une autre
fois ma leçon ensemble: de hand, de fingres, de nails, de
arm, de elbow, de nick, de sin, de foot, de coun.

ALICE. Excellent, madame!55

KATH. C'est assez pour une fois: allons-nous à dîner.
(Exeunt.)

SCENE V. THE SAME

*(Enter the King of France, the Dauphin, the Duke of Bourbon, the Constable of
France, and others.)*

FR. KING. 'Tis certain he hath pass'd the river Somme.

CON. And if he be not fought withal, my lord,
Let us not live in France; let us quit all,
And give our vineyards to a barbarous people.

DAU. O Dieu vivant! shall a few sprays of us,5
The emptying of our fathers' luxury,
Our scions, put in wild and savage stock,
Spirt up so suddenly into the clouds,

And overlook their grafters?

BOUR. Normans, but bastard Normans, Norman bastards! $_{10}$
Mort de ma vie! if they march along
Unfought withal, but I will sell my dukedom,
To buy a slobbery and a dirty farm
In that nook-shotten isle of Albion.

CON. Dieu de batailles! where have they this mettle? $_{15}$
Is not their climate foggy, raw and dull,
On whom, as in despite, the sun looks pale,
Killing their fruit with frowns? Can sodden water,
A drench for sur-rein'd jades, their barley-broth,
Decoct their cold blood to such valiant heat? $_{20}$
And shall our quick blood, spirited with wine,
Seem frosty? O, for honour of our land,
Let us not hang like roping icicles
Upon our houses' thatch, whiles a more frosty people
Sweat drops of gallant youth in our rich fields!— $_{25}$
Poor we may call them in their native lords.

DAU. By faith and honour,
Our madams mock at us, and plainly say
Our mettle is bred out and they will give
Their bodies to the lust of English youth $_{30}$
To new-store France with bastard warriors.

BOUR. They bid us to the English dancing-schools,
And teach lavoltas high and swift corantos;
Saying our grace is only in our heels,
And that we are most lofty runaways. $_{35}$

FR. KING. Where is Montjoy the herald? speed him hence:
Let him greet England with our sharp defiance.
Up, princes! and, with spirit of honour edged
More sharper than your swords, hie to the field:
Charles Delabreth, high constable of France; $_{40}$
You Dukes of Orleans, Bourbon, and of Berri,
Alençon, Brabant, Bar, and Burgundy;
Jaques Chatillon, Rambures, Vaudemont,
Beaumont, Grandpré, Roussi, and Fauconberg,
Foix, Lestrale, Bouciqualt, and Charolois; $_{45}$
High dukes, great princes, barons, lords and knights,

For your great seats now quit you of great shames.
Bar Harry England, that sweeps through our land
With pennons painted in the blood of Harfleur:
Rush on his host, as doth the melted snow₅₀
Upon the valleys, whose low vassal seat
The Alps doth spit and void his rheum upon:
Go down upon him, you have power enough,
And in a captive chariot into Rouen
Bring him our prisoner.
CON. This becomes the great.₅₅
Sorry am I his numbers are so few,
His soldiers sick and famish'd in their march,
For I am sure, when he shall see our army,
He'll drop his heart into the sink of fear
And for achievement offer us his ransom.₆₀
FR. KING. Therefore, lord constable, haste on Montjoy,
And let him say to England that we send
To know what willing ransom he will give.
Prince Dauphin, you shall stay with us in Rouen.
DAU. Not so, I do beseech your majesty.₆₅
FR. KING. Be patient, for you shall remain with us.
Now forth, lord constable and princes all,
And quickly bring us word of England's fall. *(Exeunt.)*

SCENE VI. THE ENGLISH CAMP IN PICARDY

(Enter Gower and Fluellen, meeting.)

GOW. How now, Captain Fluellen! come you from the bridge?
FLU. I assure you, there is very excellent services
committed at the bridge.
GOW. Is the Duke of Exeter safe?₅
FLU. The Duke of Exeter is as magnanimous as Agamemnon;
and a man that I love and honour with my soul,
and my heart, and my duty, and my life, and my living,
and my uttermost power: he is not—God be praised and
blessed!—any hurt in the world; but keeps the bridge most₁₀

valiantly, with excellent discipline. There is an aunchient
lieutenant there at the pridge, I think in my very conscience
he is as valiant a man as Mark Antony; and he is
a man of no estimation in the world; but I did see him do
as gallant service.[15]

Gow. What do you call him?

Flu. He is called Aunchient Pistol.

Gow. I know him not.

(Enter Pistol.)

Flu. Here is the man.

Pist. Captain, I thee beseech to do me favours:[20]
The Duke of Exeter doth love thee well.

Flu. Ay, I praise God; and I have merited some love
at his hands.

Pist. Bardolph, a soldier, firm and sound of heart,
And of buxom valour, hath, by cruel fate,[25]
And giddy Fortune's furious fickle wheel,
That goddess blind,
That stands upon the rolling restless stone—

Flu. By your patience, Aunchient Pistol. Fortune is
painted blind, with a muffler afore her eyes, to signify to[30]
you that Fortune is blind; and she is painted also with a
wheel, to signify to you, which is the moral of it, that she is
turning, and inconstant, and mutability, and variation: and
her foot, look you, is fixed upon a spherical stone, which rolls,
and rolls, and rolls: in good truth, the poet makes a most[35]
excellent description of it: Fortune is an excellent moral.

Pist. Fortune is Bardolph's foe, and frowns on him;
For he hath stolen a pax, and hanged must a' be:
A damned death!
Let gallows gape for dog; let man go free[40]
And let not hemp his wind-pipe suffocate:
But Exeter hath given the doom of death
For pax of little price.
Therefore, go speak; the duke will hear thy voice;
And let not Bardolph's vital thread be cut[45]
With edge of penny cord and vile reproach:
Speak, captain, for his life, and I will thee requite.

Flu. Aunchient Pistol, I do partly understand your
meaning.

Pist. Why then, rejoice therefore.$_{50}$

Flu. Certainly, aunchient, it is not a thing to rejoice at:
for if, look you, he were my brother, I would desire the
duke to use his good pleasure, and put him to execution;
for discipline ought to be used.

Pist. Die and be damn'd! and figo for thy friendship!$_{55}$

Flu. It is well.

Pist. The fig of Spain! *(Exit.)*

Flu. Very good.

Gow. Why, this is an arrant counterfeit rascal; I remember
him now; a bawd, a cutpurse.$_{60}$

Flu. I'll assure you, a' uttered as brave words at the
bridge as you shall see in a summer's day. But it is very
well; what he has spoke to me, that is well, I warrant
you, when time is serve.

Gow. Why, 'tis a gull, a fool, a rogue, that now and$_{65}$
then goes to the wars, to grace himself at his return into
London under the form of a soldier. And such fellows are
perfect in the great commanders' names: and they will learn
you by rote where services were done; at such and such a
sconce, at such a breach, at such a convoy; who came off$_{70}$
bravely, who was shot, who disgraced, what terms the enemy
stood on; and this they con perfectly in the phrase of war,
which they trick up with new-tuned oaths: and what a
beard of the general's cut and a horrid suit of the camp
will do among foaming bottles and ale-washed wits, is
    wonderful$_{75}$
to be thought on. But you must learn to know such
slanders of the age, or else you may be marvellously mistook.

Flu. I tell you what, Captain Gower; I do perceive he
is not the man that he would gladly make show to the
world he is: if I find a hole in his coat, I will tell him$_{80}$
my mind. *(Drum heard.)* Hark you, the king is coming,
and I must speak with him from the pridge.

(Drum and Colours. Enter KING HENRY, GLOUCESTER, and Soldiers.)
God pless your majesty!

K. Hen. How now, Fluellen! camest thou from the

bridge?

FLU. Ay, so please your majesty. The Duke of Exeter[85]
has very gallantly maintained the pridge: the French is gone
off, look you; and there is gallant and most prave passages:
marry, th' athversary was have possession of the pridge; but
he is enforced to retire, and the Duke of Exeter is master of
the pridge: I can tell your majesty, the duke is a prave man.[90]

K. HEN. What men have you lost, Fluellen?

FLU. The perdition of th' athversary hath been very
great, reasonable great: marry, for my part, I think the
duke hath lost never a man, but one that is like to be
executed for robbing a church, one Bardolph, if your
      majesty[95]
know the man: his face is all bubukles, and whelks, and
knobs, and flames o' fire: and his lips blows at his nose,
and it is like a coal of fire, sometimes plue and sometimes
red; but his nose is executed, and his fire's out.

K. HEN. We would have all such offenders so cut off:[100]
and we give express charge, that in our marches through
the country, there be nothing compelled from the villages,
nothing taken but paid for, none of the French upbraided
or abused in disdainful language; for when lenity and
cruelty play for a kingdom, the gentler gamester is the[105]
soonest winner.

(Tucket. Enter MONTJOY.)

MONT. You know me by my habit.

K. HEN. Well then I know thee: what shall I know of thee?

MONT. My master's mind.

K. HEN. Unfold it.[110]

MONT. Thus says my king: Say thou to Harry of
England: Though we seemed dead, we did but sleep:
advantage is a better soldier than rashness. Tell him we could
have rebuked him at Harfleur, but that we thought not
good to bruise an injury till it were full ripe: now we[115]
speak upon our cue, and our voice is imperial: England
shall repent his folly, see his weakness, and admire our
sufferance. Bid him therefore consider of his ransom;
which must proportion the losses we have borne, the
subjects we have lost, the disgrace we have digested; which[120]

in weight to re-answer, his pettiness would bow under.
For our losses, his exchequer is too poor; for the effusion
of our blood, the muster of his kingdom too faint a
number; and for our disgrace, his own person, kneeling at our
feet, but a weak and worthless satisfaction. To this add $_{125}$
defiance: and tell him, for conclusion, he hath betrayed his
followers, whose condemnation is pronounced. So far my
king and master; so much my office.

K. HEN. What is thy name? I know thy quality.

MONT. Montjoy. $_{130}$

K. HEN. Thou dost thy office fairly. Turn thee back,
And tell thy king I do not seek him now;
But could be willing to march on to Calais
Without impeachment: for, to say the sooth,
Though 'tis no wisdom to confess so much $_{135}$
Unto an enemy of craft and vantage,
My people are with sickness much enfeebled,
My numbers lessened, and those few I have
Almost no better than so many French;
Who when they were in health, I tell thee, herald, $_{140}$
I thought upon one pair of English legs
Did march three Frenchmen. Yet, forgive me, God,
That I do brag thus! This your air of France
Hath blown that vice in me; I must repent.
Go therefore, tell thy master here I am; $_{145}$
My ransom is this frail and worthless trunk,
My army but a weak and sickly guard;
Yet, God before, tell him we will come on,
Though France himself and such another neighbour
Stand in our way. There's for thy labour, Montjoy. $_{150}$
Go, bid thy master well advise himself:
If we may pass, we will; if we be hinder'd,
We shall your tawny ground with your red blood
Discolour: and so, Montjoy, fare you well.
The sum of all our answer is but this: $_{155}$
We would not seek a battle, as we are;
Nor, as we are, we say we will not shun it:
So tell your master.

MONT. I shall deliver so. Thanks to your highness.

(Exit.)
GLOU. I hope they will not come upon us now.₁₆₀
K. HEN. We are in God's hand, brother, not in theirs.
March to the bridge; it now draws toward night:
Beyond the river we'll encamp ourselves,
And on to-morrow bid them march away. *(Exeunt.)*

SCENE VII. THE FRENCH CAMP, NEAR AGINCOURT

(Enter the Constable of France, the Lord Rambures, Orleans, Dauphin, with others.)

CON. Tut! I have the best armour of the world.
Would it were day!
ORL. You have an excellent armour; but let my horse
have his due.
CON. It is the best horse of Europe.₅
ORL. Will it never be morning?
DAU. My Lord of Orleans, and my lord high constable,
you talk of horse and armour?
ORL. You are as well provided of both as any prince in
the world.₁₀
DAU. What a long night is this! I will not change my
horse with any that treads but on four pasterns. Ça, ha!
he bounds from the earth, as if his entrails were hairs; le
cheval volant, the Pegasus, chez les narines de feu! When
I bestride him, I soar, I am a hawk: he trots the air; the₁₅
earth sings when he touches it; the basest horn of his hoof
is more musical than the pipe of Hermes.
ORL. He's of the colour of the nutmeg.
DAU. And of the heat of the ginger. It is a beast for
Perseus: he is pure air and fire; and the dull elements of₂₀
earth and water never appear in him, but only in patient
stillness while his rider mounts him: he is indeed a horse;
and all other jades you may call beasts.
CON. Indeed, my lord, it is a most absolute and
excellent horse.₂₅
DAU. It is the prince of palfreys; his neigh is like

the bidding of a monarch and his countenance enforces
homage.

ORL. No more, cousin.

DAU. Nay, the man hath no wit that cannot, from the[30]
rising of the lark to the lodging of the lamb, vary deserved
praise on my palfrey: it is a theme as fluent as the sea: turn
the sands into eloquent tongues, and my horse is argument
for them all: 'tis a subject for a sovereign to reason on, and
for a sovereign's sovereign to ride on; and for the world,[35]
familiar to us and unknown to lay apart their particular
functions and wonder at him. I once writ a sonnet in his
praise, and began thus: 'Wonder of nature,'—

ORL. I have heard a sonnet begin so to one's mistress.

DAU. Then did they imitate that which I composed to[40]
my courser, for my horse is my mistress.

ORL. Your mistress bears well.

DAU. Me well; which is the prescript praise and
perfection of a good and particular mistress.

CON. Nay, for methought yesterday your mistress[45]
shrewdly shook your back.

DAU. So perhaps did yours.

CON. Mine was not bridled.

DAU. O then belike she was old and gentle; and you
rode, like a kern of Ireland, your French hose off, and in[50]
your strait strossers.

CON. You have good judgement in horsemanship.

DAU. Be warned by me, then: they that ride so and
ride not warily, fall into foul bogs. I had rather have my
horse to my mistress.[55]

CON. I had as lief have my mistress a jade.

DAU. I tell thee, constable, my mistress wears his own
hair.

CON. I could make as true a boast as that, if I had a
sow to my mistress.[60]

DAU. 'Le chien est retourné à son propre vomissement,
et la truie lavée au bourbier:' thou makest use of any thing.

CON. Yet do I not use my horse for my mistress, or
any such proverb so little kin to the purpose.

RAM. My lord constable, the armour that I saw in[65]

your tent to-night, are those stars or suns upon it?

Con. Stars, my lord.

Dau. Some of them will fall to-morrow, I hope.

Con. And yet my sky shall not want.

Dau. That maybe, for you bear a many superfluously, and 'twere more honour some were away. [70]

Con. Even as your horse bears your praises; who would trot as well, were some of your brags dismounted.

Dau. Would I were able to load him with his desert! Will it never be day? I will trot to-morrow a mile, and my way shall be paved with English faces. [75]

Con. I will not say so, for fear I should be faced out of my way: but I would it were morning; for I would fain be about the ears of the English.

Ram. Who will go to hazard with me for twenty prisoners? [80]

Con. You must first go yourself to hazard, ere you have them.

Dau. 'Tis midnight; I'll go arm myself. *(Exit.)*

Orl. The Dauphin longs for morning. [85]

Ram. He longs to eat the English.

Con. I think he will eat all he kills.

Orl. By the white hand of my lady, he's a gallant prince.

Con. Swear by her foot, that she may tread out the oath.

Orl. He is simply the most active gentleman of France. [90]

Con. Doing is activity; and he will still be doing.

Orl. He never did harm, that I heard of.

Con. Nor will do none to-morrow: he will keep that good name still.

Orl. I know him to be valiant. [95]

Con. I was told that by one that knows him better than you.

Orl. What's he?

Con. Marry, he told me so himself; and he said he cared not who knew it. [100]

Orl. He needs not; it is no hidden virtue in him.

Con. By my faith, sir, but it is; never any body saw it but his lackey: 'tis a hooded valour; and when it appears, it will bate.

ORL. Ill will never said well. ₁₀₅

CON. I will cap that proverb with 'There is flattery in friendship.'

ORL. And I will take up that with, 'Give the devil his due.'

CON. Well placed: there stands your friend for the devil: have at the very eye of that proverb with 'A pox of ₁₁₀ the devil.'

ORL. You are the better at proverbs, by how much 'A fool's bolt is soon shot.'

CON. You have shot over.

ORL. 'Tis not the first time you were overshot. ₁₁₅

(Enter a Messenger.)

MESS. My lord high constable, the English lie within fifteen hundred paces of your tents.

CON. Who hath measured the ground?

MESS. The Lord Grandpré.

CON. A valiant and most expert gentleman. Would ₁₂₀ it were day! Alas, poor Harry of England! he longs not for the dawning as we do.

ORL. What a wretched and peevish fellow is this King of England, to mope with his fat-brained followers so far out of his knowledge! ₁₂₅

CON. If the English had any apprehension, they would run away.

ORL. That they lack; for if their heads had any intellectual armour, they could never wear such heavy head-
pieces.

RAM. That island of England breeds very valiant ₁₃₀ creatures; their mastiffs are of unmatchable courage.

ORL. Foolish curs, that run winking into the mouth of a Russian bear and have their heads crushed like rotten apples! You may as well say, that's a valiant flea that dare eat his breakfast on the lip of a lion. ₁₃₅

CON. Just, just; and the men do sympathize with the mastiffs in robustious and rough coming on, leaving their wits with their wives: and then give them great meals of beef and iron and steel, they will eat like wolves and fight like devils. ₁₄₀

ORL. Ay, but these English are shrewdly out of beef.

Con. Then shall we find to-morrow they have only stomachs to eat and none to fight. Now is it time to arm: come, shall we about it?

Orl. It is now two o'clock: but, let me see, by ten [145] We shall have each a hundred Englishmen. *(Exeunt.)*

ACT IV

PROLOGUE

(Enter Chorus.)

CHOR. Now entertain conjecture of a time
When creeping murmur and the poring dark
Fills the wide vessel of the universe.
From camp to camp through the foul womb of night
The hum of either army stilly sounds, 5
That the fixed sentinels almost receive
The secret whispers of each other's watch:
Fire answers fire, and through their paly flames
Each battle sees the other's umber'd face;
Steed threatens steed, in high and boastful neighs 10
Piercing the night's dull ear, and from the tents
The armourers, accomplishing the knights,
With busy hammers closing rivets up,
Give dreadful note of preparation:
The country cocks do crow, the clocks do toll, 15
And the third hour of drowsy morning name.
Proud of their numbers and secure in soul,
The confident and over-lusty French

Do the low-rated English play at dice;
And chide the cripple tardy-gaited night[20]
Who, like a foul and ugly witch, doth limp
So tediously away. The poor condemned English,
Like sacrifices, by their watchful fires
Sit patiently and inly ruminate
The morning's danger, and their gesture sad[25]
Investing lank-lean cheeks and war-worn coats
Presenteth them unto the gazing moon
So many horrid ghosts. O now, who will behold
The royal captain of this ruin'd band
Walking from watch to watch, from tent to tent,[30]
Let him cry 'Praise and glory on his head!'
For forth he goes and visits all his host,
Bids them good morrow with a modest smile
And calls them brothers, friends and countrymen.
Upon his royal face there is no note[35]
How dread an army hath enrounded him;
Nor doth he dedicate one jot of colour
Unto the weary and all-watched night,
But freshly looks and over-bears attaint
With cheerful semblance and sweet majesty;[40]
That every wretch, pining and pale before,
Beholding him, plucks comfort from his looks:
A largess universal like the sun
His liberal eye doth give to every one,
Thawing cold fear, that mean and gentle all,[45]
Behold, as may unworthiness define,
A little touch of Harry in the night.
And so our scene must to the battle fly;
Where—O for pity!—we shall much disgrace
With four or five most vile and ragged foils,[50]
Right ill-disposed in brawl ridiculous,
The name of Agincourt. Yet sit and see,
Minding true things by what their mockeries be. *(Exit.)*

SCENE I. THE ENGLISH CAMP AT AGINCOURT

(Enter King Henry, Bedford, and Gloucester.)

K. HEN. Gloucester, 'tis true that we are in great danger;
The greater therefore should our courage be.
Good morrow, brother Bedford. God Almighty!
There is some soul of goodness in things evil,
Would men observingly distil it out. 5
For our bad neighbour makes us early stirrers,
Which is both healthful and good husbandry:
Besides, they are our outward consciences,
And preachers to us all, admonishing
That we should dress us fairly for our end. 10
Thus may we gather honey from the weed,
And make a moral of the devil himself.
(ENTER ERPINGHAM.)
Good morrow, old Sir Thomas Erpingham:
A good soft pillow for that good white head
Were better than a churlish turf of France. 15
ERP. Not so, my liege: this lodging likes me better,
Since I may say 'Now lie I like a king.'
K. HEN. 'Tis good for men to love their present pains
Upon example; so the spirit is eased:
And when the mind is quicken'd, out of doubt, 20
The organs, though defunct and dead before,
Break up their drowsy grave and newly move,
With casted slough and fresh legerity.
Lend me thy cloak, Sir Thomas. Brothers both,
Commend me to the princes in our camp; 25
Do my good morrow to them, and anon
Desire them all to my pavilion.
GLOU. We shall, my liege.
ERP. Shall I attend your grace?
K. HEN. No, my good knight;
Go with my brothers to my lords of England: 30
I and my bosom must debate a while,
And then I would no other company.

ERP. The Lord in heaven bless thee, noble Harry!
(Exeunt all but King.)
K. HEN. God-a-mercy, old heart! thou speak'st cheerfully.
(ENTER PISTOL.)
PIST. Qui va lá? $_{35}$
K. HEN. A friend.
PIST. Discuss unto me; art thou officer?
Or art thou base, common, and popular?
K. HEN. I am a gentleman of a company.
PIST. Trail'st thou the puissant pike? $_{40}$
K. HEN. Even so. What are you?
PIST. As good a gentleman as the emperor.
K. HEN. Then you are a better than the king.
PIST. The king's a bawcock, and a heart of gold,
A lad of life, an imp of fame; $_{45}$
Of parents good, of fist most valiant:
I kiss his dirty shoe, and from heart-string
I love the lovely bully. What is thy name?
K. HEN. Harry le Roy.
PIST. Le Roy! a Cornish name: art thou of Cornish crew? $_{50}$
K. HEN. No, I am a Welshman.
PIST. Know'st thou Fluellen?
K. HEN. *Yes.*
PIST. Tell him, I'll knock his leek about his pate
Upon Saint Davy's day. $_{55}$
K. HEN. Do not you wear your dagger in your cap
that day, lest he knock that about yours.
PIST. Art thou his friend?
K. HEN. And his kinsman too.
PIST. The figo for thee, then! $_{60}$
K. HEN. I thank you: God be with you!
PIST. My name is Pistol call'd. *(Exit.)*
K. HEN. It sorts well with your fierceness.
(ENTER FLUELLEN AND GOWER.)
GOW. Captain Fluellen!
FLU. So! in the name of Jesu Christ, speak lower. It $_{65}$
is the greatest admiration in the universal world, when the
true and aunchient prerogatifes and laws of the wars is not
kept: if you would take the pains but to examine the wars

of Pompey the Great, you shall find, I warrant you, that
there is no tiddle taddle nor pibble pabble in Pompey's$_{70}$
camp; I warrant you, you shall find the ceremonies of the
wars, and the cares of it, and the forms of it, and the sobriety
of it, and the modesty of it, to be otherwise.

Gow. Why, the enemy is loud; you hear him all night.

Flu. If the enemy is an ass and a fool and a prating$_{75}$
coxcomb, is it meet, think you, that we should also, look
you, be an ass and a fool and a prating coxcomb? in your
own conscience, now?

Gow. I will speak lower.

Flu. I pray you and beseech you that you will.$_{80}$

(Exeunt Gower and Fluellen.)

K. Hen. Though it appear a little out of fashion,
There is much care and valour in this Welshman.

*(Enter three soldiers, John Bates, Alexander Court, and Michael
Williams.)*

Court. Brother John Bates, is not that the morning
which breaks yonder?

Bates. I think it be: but we have no great cause to$_{85}$
desire the approach of day.

Will. We see yonder the beginning of the day, but I
think we shall never see the end of it. Who goes there?

K. Hen. A friend.

Will. Under what captain serve you?$_{90}$

K. Hen. Under Sir Thomas Erpingham.

Will. A good old commander and a most kind
gentleman: I pray you, what thinks he of our estate?

K. Hen. Even as men wrecked upon a sand, that look
to be washed off the next tide.$_{95}$

Bates. He hath not told his thought to the king?

K. Hen. No; nor it is not meet he should. For, though
I speak it to you, I think the king is but a man, as I am: the
violet smells to him as it doth to me; the element shows to
him as it doth to me; all his senses have but human
conditions;$_{100}$
his ceremonies laid by, in his nakedness he appears
but a man; and though his affections are higher mounted
than ours, yet, when they stoop, they stoop with the like

wing. Therefore when he sees reason of fears, as we do, his
fears, out of doubt, be of the same relish as ours are: yet, in $_{105}$
reason, no man should possess him with any appearance
of fear, lest he, by showing it, should dishearten his army.

BATES. He may show what outward courage he will; but
I believe, as cold a night as 'tis, he could wish himself in
Thames up to the neck; and so I would he were, and I by $_{110}$
him, at all adventures, so we were quit here.

K. HEN. By my troth, I will speak my conscience of
the king: I think he would not wish himself any where but
where he is.

BATES. Then I would he were here alone; so should he $_{115}$
be sure to be ransomed, and a many poor men's lives saved.

K. HEN. I dare say you love him not so ill, to wish him
here alone, howsoever you speak this to feel other men's
minds: methinks I could not die any where so contented as
in the king's company; his cause being just and his quarrel $_{120}$
honourable.

WILL. That's more than we know.

BATES. Ay, or more than we should seek after; for we
know enough, if we know we are the king's subjects: if his
cause be wrong, our obedience to the king wipes the crime $_{125}$
of it out of us.

WILL. But if the cause be not good, the king himself
hath a heavy reckoning to make, when all those legs and
arms and heads, chopped off in a battle, shall join together
at the latter day and cry all 'We died at such a place;'
    some $_{130}$
swearing, some crying for a surgeon, some upon their wives
left poor behind them, some upon the debts they owe,
some upon their children rawly left. I am afeard there are
few die well that die in a battle; for how can they charitably
dispose of any thing, when blood is their argument? $_{135}$
Now, if these men do not die well, it will be a black matter
for the king that led them to it; whom to disobey were
against all proportion of subjection.

K. HEN. So, if a son that is by his father sent about
merchandise do sinfully miscarry upon the sea, the $_{140}$
imputation of his wickedness, by your rule, should be

imposed upon his father that sent him: or if a servant,
    under his
master's command transporting a sum of money, be assailed
by robbers and die in many irreconciled iniquities, you
may call the business of the master the author of the $_{145}$
servant's damnation: but this is not so: the king is not bound
to answer the particular endings of his soldiers, the father
of his son, nor the master of his servant; for they purpose
not their death, when they purpose their services. Besides,
there is no king, be his cause never so spotless, if it come to $_{150}$
the arbitrement of swords, can try it out with all unspotted
soldiers: some peradventure have on them the guilt of
    premeditated
and contrived murder; some, of beguiling virgins
with the broken seals of perjury; some, making the wars
their bulwark, that have before gored the gentle bosom of $_{155}$
peace with pillage and robbery. Now, if these men have
defeated the law and outrun native punishment, though they
can outstrip men, they have no wings to fly from God: war
is his beadle, war is his vengeance; so that here men are
punished for before-breach of the king's laws in now the $_{160}$
king's quarrel: where they feared the death, they have borne
life away; and where they would be safe, they perish: then
if they die unprovided, no more is the king guilty of their
damnation than he was before guilty of those impieties
for the which they are now visited. Every subject's duty is $_{165}$
the king's; but every subject's soul is his own. Therefore
should every soldier in the wars do as every sick man in his
bed, wash every mote out of his conscience: and dying so,
death is to him advantage; or not dying, the time was
blessedly lost wherein such preparation was gained: and in $_{170}$
him that escapes, it were not sin to think that, making God
so free an offer, He let him outlive that day to see His
greatness and to teach others how they should prepare.
WILL. 'Tis certain, every man that dies ill, the ill upon
his own head, the king is not to answer it. $_{175}$
BATES. I do not desire he should answer for me; and
yet I determine to fight lustily for him.
K. HEN. I myself heard the king say he would not be

ransomed.

WILL. Ay, he said so, to make us fight cheerfully: but$_{180}$ when our throats are cut, he may be ransomed, and we ne'er the wiser.

K. HEN. If I live to see it, I will never trust his word after.

WILL. You pay him then. That's a perilous shot out$_{185}$ of an elder-gun, that a poor and private displeasure can do against a monarch! you may as well go about to turn the sun to ice with fanning in his face with a peacock's feather. You'll never trust his word after! come, 'tis a foolish saying.$_{190}$

K. HEN. Your reproof is something too round: I should be angry with you, if the time were convenient.

WILL. Let it be a quarrel between us, if you live.

K. HEN. I embrace it.

WILL. How shall I know thee again?$_{195}$

K. HEN. Give me any gage of thine, and I will wear it in my bonnet: then, if ever thou darest acknowledge it, I will make it my quarrel.

WILL. Here's my glove: give me another of thine.

K. HEN. There.$_{200}$

WILL. This will I also wear in my cap: if ever thou come to me and say, after to-morrow, 'This is my glove,' by this hand, I will take thee a box on the ear.

K. HEN. If ever I live to see it, I will challenge it.

WILL. Thou darest as well be hanged.$_{205}$

K. HEN. Well, I will do it, though I take thee in the king's company.

WILL. Keep thy word: fare thee well.

BATES. Be friends, you English fools, be friends: we have French quarrels enow, if you could tell how to reckon.$_{210}$

K. HEN. Indeed, the French may lay twenty French crowns to one, they will beat us; for they bear them on their shoulders: but it is no English treason to cut French crowns, and to-morrow the king himself will be a clipper. *(Exeunt Soldiers.)*

Upon the king! let us our lives, our souls,$_{215}$
Our debts, our careful wives,

Our children and our sins lay on the king!
We must bear all. O hard condition,
Twin-born with greatness, subject to the breath
Of every fool, whose sense no more can feel$_{220}$
But his own wringing! What infinite heart's-ease
Must kings neglect, that private men enjoy!
And what have kings, that privates have not too,
Save ceremony, save general ceremony?
And what art thou, thou idol ceremony?$_{225}$
What kind of god art thou, that suffer'st more
Of mortal griefs than do thy worshippers?
What are thy rents? what are thy comings in?
O ceremony, show me but thy worth!
What is thy soul of adoration?$_{230}$
Art thou aught else but place, degree and form,
Creating awe and fear in other men?
Wherein thou art less happy being fear'd
Than they in fearing.
What drink'st thou oft, instead of homage sweet,$_{235}$
But poison'd flattery? O, be sick, great greatness,
And bid thy ceremony give thee cure!
Think'st thou the fiery fever will go out
With titles blown from adulation?
Will it give place to flexure and low bending?$_{240}$
Canst thou, when thou command'st the beggar's knee,
Command the health of it? No, thou proud dream,
That play'st so subtly with a king's repose;
I am a king that find thee, and I know
'Tis not the balm, the sceptre and the ball,$_{245}$
The sword, the mace, the crown imperial,
The intertissued robe of gold and pearl,
The farced title running 'fore the king,
The throne he sits on, nor the tide of pomp
That beats upon the high shore of this world,$_{250}$
No, not all these, thrice-gorgeous ceremony,
Not all these, laid in bed majestical,
Can sleep so soundly as the wretched slave,
Who with a body fill'd and vacant mind
Gets him to rest, cramm'd with distressful bread;$_{255}$

Never sees horrid night, the child of hell,
But, like a lackey, from the rise to set
Sweats in the eye of Phœbus and all night
Sleeps in Elysium; next day after dawn,
Doth rise and help Hyperion to his horse,$_{260}$
And follows so the ever-running year,
With profitable labour, to his grave:
And, but for ceremony, such a wretch,
Winding up days with toil and nights with sleep,
Had the fore-hand and vantage of a king.$_{265}$
The slave, a member of the country's peace,
Enjoys it; but in gross brain little wots
What watch the king keeps to maintain the peace,
Whose hours the peasant best advantages.
(ENTER ERPINGHAM.)
ERP. My lord, your nobles, jealous of your absence,$_{270}$
Seek through your camp to find you.
K. HEN. Good old knight,
Collect them all together at my tent:
I'll be before thee.
ERP. I shall do't, my lord. *(Exit.)*
K. HEN. O God of battles! steel my soldiers' hearts;
Possess them not with fear; take from them now$_{275}$
The sense of reckoning, if the opposed numbers
Pluck their hearts from them. Not to-day, O Lord,
O, not to-day, think not upon the fault
My father made in compassing the crown!
I Richard's body have interred new;$_{280}$
And on it have bestow'd more contrite tears
Than from it issued forced drops of blood:
Five hundred poor I have in yearly pay,
Who twice a-day their wither'd hands hold up
Toward heaven, to pardon blood; and I have built$_{285}$
Two chantries, where the sad and solemn priests
Sing still for Richard's soul. More will I do;
Though all that I can do is nothing worth,
Since that my penitence comes after all,
Imploring pardon.$_{290}$
(ENTER GLOUCESTER.)

Glou. My liege!

K. Hen. My brother Gloucester's voice? Ay;
I know thy errand, I will go with thee:
The day, my friends and all things stay for me.
(Exeunt.)

SCENE II. THE FRENCH CAMP

(Enter the Dauphin, Orleans, Rambures, and others.)

Orl. The sun doth gild our armour; up, my lords!
Dau. Montez à cheval! My horse! varlet! laquais! ha!
Orl. O brave spirit!
Dau. Via! les eaux et la terre.
Orl. Rien puis? l'air et le feu.$_5$
Dau. Ciel, cousin Orleans.
(Enter Constable.)
Now, my lord constable!
Con. Hark, how our steeds for present service neigh!
Dau. Mount them, and make incision in their hides,
That their hot blood may spin in English eyes,$_{10}$
And dout them with superfluous courage, ha!
Ram. What, will you have them weep our horses' blood?
How shall we, then, behold their natural tears?
(Enter Messenger.)
Mess. The English are embattled, you French peers.
Con. To horse, you gallant princes! straight to horse!$_{15}$
Do but behold yon poor and starved band,
And your fair show shall suck away their souls,
Leaving them but the shales and husks of men.
There is not work enough for all our hands;
Scarce blood enough in all their sickly veins$_{20}$
To give each naked curtle-axe a stain,
That our French gallants shall to-day draw out,
And sheathe for lack of sport: let us but blow on them,
The vapour of our valour will o'erturn them.
'Tis positive 'gainst all exceptions, lords,$_{25}$
That our superfluous lackeys and our peasants,

Who in unnecessary action swarm
About our squares of battle, were enow
To purge this field of such a hilding foe,
Though we upon this mountain's basis by$_{30}$
Took stand for idle speculation:
But that our honours must not. What's to say?
A very little little let us do,
And all is done. Then let the trumpets sound
The tucket sonance and the note to mount;$_{35}$
For our approach shall so much dare the field
That England shall couch down in fear and yield.
(Enter Grandpre.)
Grand. Why do you stay so long, my lords of France?
Yon island carrions, desperate of their bones,
Ill-favouredly become the morning field:$_{40}$
Their ragged curtains poorly are let loose,
And our air shakes them passing scornfully:
Big Mars seems bankrupt in their beggar'd host
And faintly through a rusty beaver peeps:
The horsemen sit like fixed candlesticks,$_{45}$
With torch-staves in their hand; and their poor jades
Lob down their heads, dropping the hides and hips,
The gum down-roping from their pale-dead eyes,
And in their pale dull mouths the gimmal bit
Lies foul with chew'd grass, still and motionless;$_{50}$
And their executors, the knavish crows,
Fly o'er them, all impatient for their hour.
Description cannot suit itself in words
To demonstrate the life of such a battle
In life so lifeless as it shows itself.$_{55}$
Con. They have said their prayers, and they stay for death.
Dau. Shall we go send them dinners and fresh suits
And give their fasting horses provender,
And after fight with them?
Con. I stay but for my guidon: to the field!$_{60}$
I will the banner from a trumpet take,
And use it for my haste. Come, come, away!
The sun is high, and we outwear the day. *(Exeunt.)*

SCENE III. THE ENGLISH CAMP

(Enter Gloucester, Bedford, Exeter, Erpingham, with all this host: Salisbury and Westmoreland.)

GLOU. Where is the king?
BED. The king himself is rode to view their battle.
WEST. Of fighting men they have full three score thousand.
EXE. There's five to one; besides, they all are fresh.
SAL. God's arm strike with us! 'tis a fearful odds.₅
God be wi' you, princes all; I'll to my charge:
If we no more meet till we meet in heaven,
Then, joyfully, my noble Lord of Bedford,
My dear Lord Gloucester, and my good Lord Exeter,
And my kind kinsman, warriors all, adieu!₁₀
BED. Farewell, good Salisbury; and good luck go with thee!
EXE. Farewell, kind lord; fight valiantly to-day:
And yet I do thee wrong to mind thee of it,
For thou art framed of the firm truth of valour.
(Exit Salisbury.)
BED. He is as full of valour as of kindness;₁₅
Princely in both.
(Enter the KING.)
WEST. O that we now had here
But one ten thousand of those men in England
That do no work to-day!
K. HEN. What's he that wishes so?
My cousin Westmoreland? No, my fair cousin:
If we are mark'd to die, we are enow₂₀
To do our country loss; and if to live,
The fewer men, the greater share of honour.
God's will! I pray thee, wish not one man more.
By Jove, I am not covetous for gold,
Nor care I who doth feed upon my cost;₂₅
It yearns me not if men my garments wear;
Such outward things dwell not in my desires:
But if it be a sin to covet honour,
I am the most offending soul alive.

No, faith, my coz, wish not a man from England:30
God's peace! I would not lose so great an honour
As one man more, methinks, would share from me
For the best hope I have. O, do not wish one more!
Rather proclaim it, Westmoreland, through my host,
That he which hath no stomach to this fight,35
Let him depart; his passport shall be made
And crowns for convoy put into his purse:
We would not die in that man's company
That fears his fellowship to die with us.
This day is call'd the feast of Crispian:40
He that outlives this day, and comes safe home,
Will stand a tip-toe when this day is named,
And rouse him at the name of Crispian.
He that shall live this day, and see old age,
Will yearly on the vigil feast his neighbours,45
And say 'To-morrow is Saint Crispian:'
Then will he strip his sleeve and show his scars,
And say 'These wounds I had on Crispin's day.'
Old men forget; yet all shall be forgot,
But he'll remember with advantages50
What feats he did that day: then shall our names,
Familiar in his mouth as household words,
Harry the king, Bedford and Exeter,
Warwick and Talbot, Salisbury and Gloucester,
Be in their flowing cups freshly remember'd.55
This story shall the good man teach his son;
And Crispin Crispian shall ne'er go by,
From this day to the ending of the world,
But we in it shall be remembered;
We few, we happy few, we band of brothers;60
For he to-day that sheds his blood with me
Shall be my brother; be he ne'er so vile,
This day shall gentle his condition:
And gentlemen in England now a-bed
Shall think themselves accursed they were not here,65
And hold their manhoods cheap whiles any speaks
That fought with us upon Saint Crispin's day.
(*RE-ENTER SALISBURY.*)

SAL. My sovereign lord, bestow yourself with speed:
The French are bravely in their battles set,
And will with all expedience charge on us.$_{70}$
K. HEN. All things are ready, if our minds be so.
WEST. Perish the man whose mind is backward now!
K. HEN. Thou dost not wish more help from England, coz?
WEST. God's will! my liege, would you and I alone,
Without more help, could fight this royal battle!$_{75}$
K. HEN. Why, now thou hast unwish'd five thousand men;
Which likes me better than to wish us one.
You know your places: God be with you all!
(Tucket. Enter MONTJOY.)
MONT. Once more I come to know of thee, King Harry,
If for thy ransom thou wilt now compound,$_{80}$
Before thy most assured overthrow:
For certainly thou art so near the gulf,
Thou needs must be englutted. Besides, in mercy,
The constable desires thee thou wilt mind
Thy followers of repentance; that their souls$_{85}$
May make a peaceful and a sweet retire
From off these fields, where, wretches, their poor bodies
Must lie and fester.
K. HEN. Who hath sent thee now?
MONT. The Constable of France.
K. HEN. I pray thee, bear my former answer back:$_{90}$
Bid them achieve me and then sell my bones.
Good God! why should they mock poor fellows thus?
The man that once did sell the lion's skin
While the beast lived, was killed with hunting him.
A many of our bodies shall no doubt$_{95}$
Find native graves; upon the which, I trust,
Shall witness live in brass of this day's work:
And those that leave their valiant bones in France,
Dying like men, though buried in your dunghills,
They shall be famed; for there the sun shall greet them,$_{100}$
And draw their honours reeking up to heaven;
Leaving their earthly parts to choke your clime,
The smell whereof shall breed a plague in France.
Mark then abounding valour in our English,

That being dead, like to the bullet's grazing, 105
Break out into a second course of mischief,
Killing in relapse of mortality.
Let me speak proudly: tell the constable
We are but warriors for the working-day;
Our gayness and our gilt are all besmirch'd 110
With rainy marching in the painful field;
There's not a piece of feather in our host—
Good argument, I hope, we will not fly—
And time hath worn us into slovenry:
But, by the mass, our hearts are in the trim; 115
And my poor soldiers tell me, yet ere night
They'll be in fresher robes, or they will pluck
The gay new coats o'er the French soldiers' heads
And turn them out of service. If they do this,—
As, if God please, they shall,—my ransom then 120
Will soon be levied. Herald, save thou thy labour;
Come thou no more for ransom, gentle herald:
They shall have none, I swear, but these my joints;
Which if they have as I will leave 'em them,
Shall yield them little, tell the constable. 125
Mont. I shall, King Harry. And so fare thee well:
Thou never shalt hear herald any more. *(Exit.)*
K. Hen. I fear thou'lt once more come again for ransom.
(Enter York.)
York. My lord, most humbly on my knee I beg
The leading of the vaward. 130
K. Hen. Take it, brave York. Now, soldiers, march away:
And how thou pleasest, God, dispose the day! *(Exeunt.)*

SCENE IV. THE FIELD OF BATTLE

(Alarum. Excursions. Enter Pistol, French Soldier, and Boy.)

Pist. Yield, cur!
Fr. Sol. Je pense que vous êtes gentilhomme de bonne qualité.
Pist. Qualtitie calmie custure me! Art thou a gentleman?

what is thy name? discuss.$_5$

FR. SOL. O Seigneur Dieu!

PIST. O, Signieur Dew should be a gentleman:
Perpend my words, O Signieur Dew, and mark;
O Signieur Dew, thou diest on point of fox,
Except, O signieur, thou do give to me$_{10}$
Egregious ransom.

FR. SOL. O, prenez miséricorde! ayez pitié de moi!

PIST. Moy shall not serve; I will have forty moys;
Or I will fetch thy rim out at thy throat
In drops of crimson blood.$_{15}$

FR. SOL. Est-il impossible d'échapper la force de ton
bras?

PIST. Brass, cur!
Thou damned and luxurious mountain goat,
Offer'st me brass?$_{20}$

FR. SOL. O pardonnez moi!

PIST. Say'st thou me so? is that a ton of moys?
Come hither, boy: ask me this slave in French
What is his name.

BOY. Écoutez: comment êtes-vous appelé?$_{25}$

FR. SOL. Monsieur le Fer.

BOY. He says his name is Master Fer.

PIST. Master Fer! I'll fer him, and firk him, and ferret
him: discuss the same in French unto him.

BOY. I do not know the French for fer, and ferret, and$_{30}$
firk.

PIST. Bid him prepare; for I will cut his throat.

FR. SOL. Que dit-il, monsieur?

BOY. Il me commande de vous dire que vous faites
vous prèt; car ce soldat ici est disposé tout à cette heure$_{35}$
de couper votre gorge.

PIST. Owy, cuppele gorge, permafoy,
Peasant, unless thou give me crowns, brave crowns;
Or mangled shalt thou be by this my sword.

FR. SOL. O, je vous supplie, pour l'amour de Dieu, me$_{40}$
pardonner! Je suis gentilhomme de bonne maison: gardez
ma vie, et je vous donnerai deux cents écus.

PIST. What are his words?

Boy. He prays you to save his life: he is a gentleman
of a good house; and for his ransom he will give you two⁴⁵
hundred crowns.

Pist. Tell him my fury shall abate, and I
The crowns will take.

Fr. Sol. Petit monsieur, que dit-il?

Boy. Encore qu'il est centre son jurement de pardonner⁵⁰
aucun prisonnier, néanmoins, pour les écus que vous
l'avez promis, il est content de vous donner la liberté, le
franchisement.

Fr. Sol. Sur mes genoux je vous donne mille remercîmens;
et je m'estime heureux que je suis tombé entre les⁵⁵
mains d'un chevalier, je pense, le plus brave, vaillant, et
très distingué seigneur d'Angleterre.

Pist. Expound unto me, boy.

Boy. He gives you, upon his knees, a thousand thanks;
and he esteems himself happy that he hath fallen into the⁶⁰
hands of one, as he thinks, the most brave, valorous, and
thrice-worthy signieur of England.

Pist. As I suck blood, I will some mercy show.
Follow me!

Boy. Suivez-vous le grand capitaine. *(Exeunt Pistol,*⁶⁵
and French Soldier.) I did never know so full a voice
issue from so empty a heart: but the saying is true, 'The
empty vessel makes the greatest sound.' Bardolph and
Nym had ten times more valour than this roaring devil i'
the old play, that every one may pare his nails with a⁷⁰
wooden dagger; and they are both hanged; and so would
this be, if he durst steal any thing adventurously. I must
stay with the lackeys, with the luggage of our camp: the
French might have a good prey of us, if he knew of it; for
there is none to guard it but boys. *(Exit.)*⁷⁵

SCENE V. ANOTHER PART OF THE FIELD

(Enter Constable, Orleans, Bourbon, Dauphin, and Rambures.)

Con. O diable!

ORL. O seigneur! le jour est perdu, tout est perdu!
DAU. Mort de ma vie! all is confounded, all!
Reproach and everlasting shame
Sits mocking in our plumes. O méchante fortune!₅
Do not run away. *(A short alarum.)*
CON. Why, all our ranks are broke.
DAU. O perdurable shame! let's stab ourselves.
Be these the wretches that we play'd at dice for?
ORL. Is this the king we sent to for his ransom?
BOUR. Shame and eternal shame, nothing but shame!₁₀
Let us die in honour: once more back again;
And he that will not follow Bourbon now,
Let him go hence, and with his cap in hand,
Like a base pander, hold the chamber-door
Whilst by a slave, no gentler than my dog,₁₅
His fairest daughter is contaminated.
CON. Disorder, that hath spoil'd us, friend us now!
Let us on heaps go offer up our lives.
ORL. We are enow yet living in the field
To smother up the English in our throngs,₂₀
If any order might be thought upon.
BOUR. The devil take order now! I'll to the throng:
Let life be short; else shame will be too long. *(Exeunt.)*

SCENE VI. ANOTHER PART OF THE FIELD

(Alarums. Enter KING HENRY and forces, EXETER, and others.)

K. HEN. Well have we done, thrice valiant countrymen:
But all's not done; yet keep the French the field.
EXE. The Duke of York commends him to your majesty.
K. HEN. Lives he, good uncle? thrice within this hour
I saw him down; thrice up again, and fighting;₅
From helmet to the spur all blood he was.
EXE. In which array, brave soldier, doth he lie,
Larding the plain; and by his bloody side,
Yoke-fellow to his honour-owing wounds,
The noble Earl of Suffolk also lies.₁₀

Suffolk first died: and York, all haggled over,
Comes to him, where in gore he lay insteep'd,
And takes him by the beard; kisses the gashes
That bloodily did yawn upon his face;
And cries aloud 'Tarry, dear cousin Suffolk!$_{15}$
My soul shall thine keep company to heaven;
Tarry, sweet soul, for mine, then fly abreast,
As in this glorious and well-foughten field
We kept together in our chivalry!'
Upon these words I came and cheer'd him up:$_{20}$
He smiled me in the face, raught me his hand,
And, with a feeble gripe, says 'Dear my lord,
Commend my service to my sovereign.'
So did he turn and over Suffolk's neck
He threw his wounded arm and kiss'd his lips;$_{25}$
And so espoused to death, with blood he seal'd
A testament of noble-ending love.
The pretty and sweet manner of it forced
Those waters from me which I would have stopp'd;
But I had not so much of man in me,$_{30}$
And all my mother came into mine eyes
and gave me up to tears.
K. Hen. I blame you not;
For, hearing this, I must perforce compound
With mistful eyes, or they will issue too. *(Alarum.)*
But, hark! what new alarum is this same?$_{35}$
The French have reinforced their scatter'd men:
Then every soldier kill his prisoners;
Give the word through. *(Exeunt.)*

SCENE VII. ANOTHER PART OF THE FIELD

(Enter Fluellen and Gower.)

Flu. Kill the poys and the luggage! 'tis expressly against
the law of arms: 'tis as arrant a piece of knavery, mark you
now, as can be offer't; in your conscience, now, is it not?
Gow. 'Tis certain there's not a boy left alive; and the

cowardly rascals that ran from the battle ha' done this$_5$
slaughter: besides, they have burned and carried away all
that was in the king's tent; wherefore the king, most worthily,
hath caused every soldier to cut his prisoner's throat.
O, 'tis a gallant king!

Flu. Ay, he was porn at Monmouth, Captain Gower.$_{10}$
What call you the town's name where Alexander the Pig
was born?

Gow. Alexander the Great.

Flu. Why, I pray you, is not pig great? the pig, or
the great, or the mighty, or the huge, or the magnanimous,$_{15}$
are all one reckonings, save the phrase is a little
variations.

Gow. I think Alexander the Great was born in Macedon:
his father was called Philip of Macedon, as I take it.

Flu. I think it is in Macedon where Alexander is porn.$_{20}$
I tell you, captain, if you look in the maps of the 'orld, I
warrant you sall find, in the comparisons between Macedon
and Monmouth, that the situations, look you, is both
alike. There is a river in Macedon; and there is also moreover
a river at Monmouth: it is called Wye at Monmouth;$_{25}$
but it is out of my prains what is the name of the other
river; but 'tis all one, 'tis alike as my fingers is to my fingers,
and there is salmons in both. If you mark Alexander's
life well, Harry of Monmouth's life is come after
it indifferent well; for there is figures in all things. Alexander,$_{30}$
God knows, and you know, in his rages, and his
furies, and his wraths, and his cholers, and his moods, and
his displeasures, and his indignations, and also being a
little intoxicates in his prains, did, in his ales and his angers,
look you, kill his best friend, Cleitus.$_{35}$

Gow. Our king is not like him in that: he never killed
any of his friends.

Flu. It is not well done, mark you now, to take the
tales out of my mouth, ere it is made and finished. I
speak but in the figures and comparisons of it: as Alexander$_{40}$
killed his friend Cleitus, being in his ales and his
cups; so also Harry Monmouth, being in his right wits and
his good judgements, turned away the fat knight with the

great belly-doublet: he was full of jests, and gipes, and
knaveries, and mocks; I have forgot his name.₄₅
Gow. Sir John Falstaff.
Flu. That is he: I'll tell you there is good men porn
at Monmouth.
Gow. Here comes his majesty.
(Alarum. Enter KING HENRY, and forces; WARWICK, GLOUCESTER,
*   EXETER, and others.)*
K. Hen. I was not angry since I came to France₅₀
Until this instant. Take a trumpet, herald;
Ride thou unto the horsemen on yon hill:
If they will fight with us, bid them come down,
Or void the field; they do offend our sight:
If they'll do neither, we will come to them,₅₅
And make them skirr away, as swift as stones
Enforced from the old Assyrian slings:
Besides, we'll cut the throats of those we have,
And not a man of them that we shall take
Shall taste our mercy. Go and tell them so.₆₀
(ENTER MONTJOY.)
Exe. Here comes the herald of the French, my liege.
Glo. His eyes are humbler than they used to be.
K. Hen. How now! what means this, herald? know'st
    thou not
That I have fined these bones of mine for ransom?
Comest thou again for ransom?
Mont. No, great king:₆₅
I come to thee for charitable license,
That we may wander o'er this bloody field
To look our dead, and then to bury them;
To sort our nobles from our common men.
For many of our princes—woe the while!—₇₀
Lie drown'd and soak'd in mercenary blood;
So do our vulgar drench their peasant limbs
In blood of princes; and their wounded steeds
Fret fetlock deep in gore and with wild rage
Yerk out their armed heels at their dead masters,₇₅
Killing them twice. O, give us leave, great king,
To view the field in safety and dispose

Of their dead bodies!

K. Hen. I tell thee truly, herald,
I know not if the day be ours or no;
For yet a many of your horsemen peer$_{80}$
And gallop o'er the field.

Mont. The day is yours.

K. Hen. Praised be God, and not our strength, for it!
What is this castle call'd that stands hard by?

Mont. They call it Agincourt.

K. Hen. Then call we this the field of Agincourt,$_{85}$
Fought on the day of Crispin Crispianus.

Flu. Your grandfather of famous memory, an't please
your majesty, and your great-uncle Edward the Plack
Prince of Wales, as I have read in the chronicles, fought a
most prave pattle here in France.$_{90}$

K. Hen. They did, Fluellen.

Flu. Your majesty says very true: if your majesties
is remembered of it, the Welshmen did good service in a
garden where leeks did grow, wearing leeks in their Monmouth
caps; which, your majesty know, to this hour is an$_{95}$
honourable badge of the service; and I do believe your majesty
takes no scorn to wear the leek upon Saint Tavy's day.

K. Hen. I wear it for a memorable honour;
For I am Welsh, you know, good countryman.

Flu. All the water in Wye cannot wash your majesty's$_{100}$
Welsh plood out of your pody, I can tell you that: God
pless it and preserve it, as long as it pleases his grace, and
his majesty too!

K. Hen. Thanks, good my countryman.

Flu. By Jeshu, I am your majesty's countryman, I$_{105}$
care not who know it; I will confess it to all the 'orld: I
need not to be ashamed of your majesty, praised be God,
so long as your majesty is an honest man.

K. Hen. God keep me so! Our heralds go with him:
Bring me just notice of the numbers dead$_{110}$
On both our parts. Call yonder fellow hither.
(Points to Williams. Exeunt Heralds with Montjoy.)

Exe. Soldier, you must come to the king.

K. Hen. Soldier, why wearest thou that glove in thy cap?

WILL. An't please your majesty, 'tis the gage of one
that I should fight withal, if he be alive.₁₁₅

K. HEN. An Englishman?

WILL. An't please your majesty, a rascal that swaggered
with me last night; who, if alive and ever dare to challenge
this glove, I have sworn to take him a box o' th' ear: or if I
can see my glove in his cap, which he swore, as he was a₁₂₀
soldier, he would wear if alive, I will strike it out soundly.

K. HEN. What think you, Captain Fluellen? is it fit
this soldier keep his oath?

FLU. He is a craven and a villain else, an't please your
majesty, in my conscience.₁₂₅

K. HEN. It may be his enemy is a gentleman of great
sort, quite from the answer of his degree.

FLU. Though he be as good a gentleman as the devil is,
as Lucifer and Belzebub himself, it is necessary, look your
grace, that he keep his vow and his oath: if he be perjured,₁₃₀
see you now, his reputation is as arrant a villain and a
Jacksauce, as ever his black shoe trod upon God's ground
and his earth, in my conscience, la!

K. HEN. Then keep thy vow, sirrah, when thou meetest
the fellow.₁₃₅

WILL. So I will, my liege, as I live.

K. HEN. Who servest thou under?

WILL. Under Captain Gower, my liege.

FLU. Gower is a good captain, and is good knowledge
and literatured in the wars.₁₄₀

K. HEN. Call him hither to me, soldier.

WILL. I will, my liege. *(Exit.)*

K. HEN. Here, Fluellen; wear thou this favour for me
and stick it in thy cap: when Alençon and myself were
down together, I plucked this glove from his helm: if any₁₄₅
man challenge this, he is a friend to Alençon, and an enemy
to our person; if thou encounter any such, apprehend him,
an thou dost me love.

FLU. Your grace doo's me as great honours as can be
desired in the hearts of his subjects: I would fain see the₁₅₀
man, that has but two legs, that shall find himself aggriefed
at this glove; that is all; but I would fain see it once,

an please God of his grace that I might see.
K. HEN. Knowest thou Gower?
FLU. He is my dear friend, an please you.₁₅₅
K. HEN. Pray thee, go seek him, and bring him to my
tent.
FLU. I will fetch him. *(Exit.)*
K. HEN. My Lord of Warwick, and my brother Gloucester,
Follow Fluellen closely at the heels:₁₆₀
The glove which I have given him for a favour
May haply purchase him a box o' th' ear;
It is the soldier's; I by bargain should
Wear it myself. Follow, good cousin Warwick:
If that the soldier strike him, as I judge₁₆₅
By his blunt bearing he will keep his word,
Some sudden mischief may arise of it;
For I do know Fluellen valiant
And, touched with choler, hot as gunpowder,
And quickly will return an injury:₁₇₀
Follow, and see there be no harm between them.
Go you with me, uncle of Exeter. *(Exeunt.)*

SCENE VIII. BEFORE KING HENRY'S PAVILION

(Enter Gower and Williams.)

WILL. I warrant it is to knight you, captain.
(ENTER FLUELLEN.)
FLU. God's will and his pleasure, captain, I beseech you
now, come apace to the king: there is more good toward
you peradventure than is in your knowledge to dream of.
WILL. Sir, know you this glove?₅
FLU. Know the glove! I know the glove is a glove.
WILL. I know this; and thus I challenge it.
(Strikes him.)
FLU. 'Sblood! an arrant traitor as any is in the universal
world, or in France, or in England!
GOW. How now, sir! you villain!₁₀
WILL. Do you think I'll be forsworn?

FLU. Stand away, Captain Gower; I will give treason
his payment into plows, I warrant you.

WILL. I am no traitor.

FLU. That's a lie in thy throat. I charge you in his$_{15}$
majesty's name, apprehend him: he's a friend of the Duke
Alençon's.

(ENTER WARWICK AND GLOUCESTER.)

WAR. How now, how now! what's the matter?

FLU. My Lord of Warwick, here is—praised be God for
it!—a most contagious treason come to light, look you, as$_{20}$
you shall desire in a summer's day. Here is his majesty.

(ENTER KING HENRY AND EXETER.)

K. HEN. How now! what's the matter?

FLU. My liege, here is a villain and a traitor, that, look
your grace, has struck the glove which your majesty is
take out of the helmet of Alençon.$_{25}$

WILL. My liege, this was my glove; here is the fellow
of it; and he that I gave it to in change promised to wear
it in his cap: I promised to strike him, if he did: I met
this man with my glove in his cap, and I have been as
good as my word.$_{30}$

FLU. Your majesty hear now, saving your majesty's
manhood, what an arrant, rascally, beggarly, lousy knave
it is: I hope your majesty is pear me testimony and witness,
and will avouchment, that this is the glove of Alençon,
that your majesty is give me; in your conscience, now?$_{35}$

K. HEN. Give me thy glove, soldier: look, here is the
fellow of it.
'Twas I, indeed, thou promised'st to strike;
And thou hast given me most bitter terms.

FLU. An please your majesty, let his neck answer for$_{40}$
it, if there is any martial law in the world.

K. HEN. How canst thou make me satisfaction?

WILL. All offences, my lord, come from the heart:
never came any from mine that might offend your majesty.

K. HEN. It was ourself thou didst abuse.$_{45}$

WILL. Your majesty came not like yourself: you appeared
to me but as a common man; witness the night, your
garments, your lowliness; and what your highness suffered

under that shape, I beseech you take it for your own fault
and not mine: for had you been as I took you for, I made$_{50}$
no offence; therefore, I beseech your highness, pardon me.

K. HEN. Here, uncle Exeter, fill this glove with crowns,
And give it to this fellow. Keep it, fellow;
And wear it for an honour in thy cap
Till I do challenge it. Give him the crowns:$_{55}$
And, captain, you must needs be friends with him.

FLU. By this day and this light, the fellow has mettle
enough in his belly. Hold, there is twelve pence for you;
and I pray you to serve Got, and keep you out of prawls,
and prabbles, and quarrels, and dissensions, and, I warrant$_{60}$
you, it is the better for you.

WILL. I will none of your money.

FLU. It is with a good will; I can tell you, it will serve
you to mend your shoes: come, wherefore should you be
so pashful? your shoes is not so good: 'tis a good silling, $_{65}$
I warrant you, or I will change it.

(Enter an English Herald.)

K. HEN. Now, herald, are the dead number'd?

Her. Here is the number of the slaughter'd French.

K. HEN. What prisoners of good sort are taken, uncle?

EXE. Charles Duke of Orleans, nephew to the king;$_{70}$
John Duke of Bourbon, and Lord Bouciqualt:
Of other lords and barons, knights and squires,
Full fifteen hundred, besides common men.

K. HEN. This note doth tell me of ten thousand French
That in the field lie slain: of princes, in this number,$_{75}$
And nobles bearing banners, there lie dead
One hundred twenty six: added to these,
Of knights, esquires, and gallant gentlemen,
Eight thousand and four hundred; of the which,
Five hundred were but yesterday dubb'd knights:$_{80}$
So that, in these ten thousand they have lost,
There are but sixteen hundred mercenaries;
The rest are princes, barons, lords, knights, squires,
And gentlemen of blood and quality.
The names of those their nobles that lie dead:$_{85}$
Charles Delabreth, high constable of France;

Jaques of Chatillon, admiral of France;
The master of the cross-bows, Lord Rambures;
Great Master of France, the brave Sir Guichard Dolphin,
John Duke of Alençon, Anthony Duke of Brabant, 90
The brother to the Duke of Burgundy,
And Edward Duke of Bar: of lusty earls,
Grandpré and Roussi, Fauconberg and Foix,
Beaumont and Marie, Vaudemont and Lestrale.
Here was a royal fellowship of death! 95
Where is the number of our English dead?
(Herald shews him another paper.)
Edward the Duke of York, the Earl of Suffolk,
Sir Richard Ketly, Davy Gam, esquire:
None else of name; and of all other men
But five and twenty. O God, thy arm was here; 100
And not to us, but to thy arm alone,
Ascribe we all! When, without stratagem,
But in plain shock and even play of battle,
Was ever known so great and little loss
On one part and on th' other? Take it, God, 105
For it is none but thine!
EXE. 'Tis wonderful!
K. HEN. Come, go we in procession to the village:
And be it death proclaimed through our host
To boast of this or take that praise from God
Which is his only. 110
FLU. Is it not lawful, an please your majesty, to tell
how many is killed?
K. HEN. Yes, captain; but with this acknowledgement,
That God fought for us.
FLU. Yes, my conscience, he did us great good. 115
K. HEN. Do we all holy rites;
Let there be sung 'Non nobis' and 'Te Deum;'
The dead with charity enclosed in clay:
And then to Calais; and to England then;
Where ne'er from France arrived more happy men. 120
(Exeunt.)

ACT V

PROLOGUE

(Enter Chorus.)

CHOR. Vouchsafe to those that have not read the story,
That I may prompt them: and of such as have,
I humbly pray them to admit the excuse
Of time, of numbers and due course of things,
Which cannot in their huge and proper life$_5$
Be here presented. Now we bear the king
Toward Calais: grant him there; there seen,
Heave him away upon your winged thoughts
Athwart the sea. Behold, the English beach
Pales in the flood with men, with wives and boys,$_{10}$
Whose shouts and claps out-voice the deep-mouth'd sea,
Which like a mighty whiffler 'fore the king
Seems to prepare his way: so let him land,
And solemnly see him set on to London.
So swift a pace hath thought that even now$_{15}$
You may imagine him upon Blackheath;
Where that his lords desire him to have borne
His bruised helmet and his bended sword

Before him through the city: he forbids it,
Being free from vainness and self-glorious pride; 20
Giving full trophy, signal and ostent
Quite from himself to God. But now behold,
In the quick forge and working-house of thought,
How London doth pour out her citizens!
The mayor and all his brethren in best sort, 25
Like to the senators of the antique Rome,
With the plebeians swarming at their heels,
Go forth and fetch their conquering Cæsar in:
As, by a lower but loving likelihood,
Were now the general of our gracious empress, 30
As in good time he may, from Ireland coming,
Bringing rebellion broached on his sword,
How many would the peaceful city quit,
To welcome him! much more, and much more cause,
Did they this Harry. Now in London place him; 35
As yet the lamentation of the French
Invites the King of England's stay at home;
The emperor's coming in behalf of France,
To order peace between them; and omit
All the occurrences, whatever chanced, 40
Till Harry's back-return again to France:
There must we bring him; and myself have play'd
The interim, by remembering you 'tis past.
Then brook abridgement, and your eyes advance,
After your thoughts, straight back again to France. 45 *(Exit.)*

SCENE I. FRANCE. THE ENGLISH CAMP

(Enter Fluellen and Gower.)

Gow. Nay, that's right; but why wear you your leek
to-day? Saint Davy's day is past.
Flu. There is occasions and causes why and wherefore
in all things: I will tell you, asse my friend, Captain Gower:
the rascally, scald, beggarly, lousy, pragging knave, Pistol, 5
which you and yourself and all the world know to be no

petter than a fellow, look you now, of no merits, he is
come to me and prings me pread and salt yesterday, look
you, and bid me eat my leek: it was in a place where I
could not breed no contention with him; but I will be so[10]
bold as to wear it in my cap till I see him once again, and
then I will tell him a little piece of my desires.
(ENTER PISTOL.)
GOW. Why, here he comes, swelling like a turkey-cock.
FLU. 'Tis no matter for his swellings nor his turkey-cocks.
God pless you, Aunchient Pistol! you scurvy, lousy knave,[15]
God pless you!
PIST. Ha! art thou bedlam? dost thou thirst, base Trojan,
To have me fold up Parca's fatal web?
Hence! I am qualmish at the smell of leek.
FLU. I peseech you heartily, scurvy, lousy knave, at[20]
my desires, and my requests, and my petitions, to eat, look
you, this leek: because, look you, you do not love it, nor
your affections and your appetites and your disgestions
doo's not agree with it, I would desire you to eat it.
PIST. Not for Cadwallader and all his goats.[25]
FLU. There is one goat for you. *(Strikes him.)* Will
you be so good, scauld knave, as eat it?
PIST. Base Trojan, thou shalt die.
FLU. You say very true, scauld knave, when God's will
is: I will desire you to live in the mean time, and eat your[30]
victuals: come, there is sauce for it. *(Strikes him.)* You
called me yesterday mountain-squire; but I will make you
to-day a squire of low degree. I pray you, fall to: if you
can mock a leek, you can eat a leek.
GOW. Enough, captain: you have astonished him.[35]
FLU. I say, I will make him eat some part of my leek,
or I will peat his pate four days. Bite, I pray you; it is
good for your green wound and your ploody coxcomb.
PIST. Must I bite?
FLU. Yes, certainly, and out of doubt and out of question[40]
too, and ambiguities.
PIST. By this leek, I will most horribly revenge: I eat
and eat, I swear—
FLU. Eat, I pray you: will you have some more sauce

to your leek? there is not enough leek to swear by.$_{45}$
PIST. Quiet thy cudgel; thou dost see I eat.
FLU. Much good do you, scauld knave, heartily. Nay,
pray you, throw none away; the skin is good for your
broken coxcomb. When you take occasions to see leeks
hereafter, I pray you, mock at 'em; that is all.$_{50}$
PIST. Good.
FLU. Ay, leeks is good: hold you, there is a groat to
heal your pate.
PIST. Me a groat!
FLU. Yes, verily and in truth, you shall take it; or I$_{55}$
have another leek in my pocket, which you shall eat.
PIST. I take thy groat in earnest of revenge.
FLU. If I owe you any thing, I will pay you in cudgels:
you shall be a woodmonger, and buy nothing of me
but cudgels. God b' wi' you, and keep you, and heal your$_{60}$
pate. *(Exit.)*
PIST. All hell shall stir for this.
GOW. Go, go; you are a counterfeit cowardly knave.
Will you mock at an ancient tradition, begun upon an
honourable respect, and worn as a memorable trophy of$_{65}$
predeceased valour and dare not avouch in your deeds
any of your words? I have seen you gleeking and galling
at this gentleman twice or thrice. You thought, because
he could not speak English in the native garb, he could not
therefore handle an English cudgel: you find it otherwise;$_{70}$
and henceforth let a Welsh correction teach you a good
English condition. Fare ye well. *(Exit.)*
PIST. Doth Fortune play the huswife with me now?
News have I, that my Doll is dead i' the spital
Of malady of France;$_{75}$
And there my rendezvous is quite cut off.
Old I do wax; and from my weary limbs
Honour is cudgelled. Well, bawd I'll turn,
And something lean to cutpurse of quick hand.
To England will I steal, and there I'll steal:$_{80}$
And patches will I get unto these cudgell'd scars,
And swear I got them in the Gallia wars. *(Exit.)*

SCENE II. FRANCE. A ROYAL PALACE

(Enter, at one door, King Henry, Exeter, Bedford, Gloucester, Warwick, Westmoreland, and other Lords; at another, the French King, Queen Isabel, the Princess Katharine, Alice and other Ladies; the Duke of Burgundy, and his train.)

K. HEN. Peace to this meeting, wherefore we are met!
Unto our brother France, and to our sister,
Health and fair time of day; joy and good wishes
To our most fair and princely cousin Katharine;
And, as a branch and member of this royalty, 5
By whom this great assembly is contrived,
We do salute you, Duke of Burgundy;
And, princes French, and peers, health to you all!
FR. KING. Right joyous are we to behold your face,
Most worthy brother England; fairly met: 10
So are you, princes English, every one.
Q. ISA. So happy be the issue, brother England,
Of this good day and of this gracious meeting,
As we are now glad to behold your eyes;
Your eyes, which hitherto have borne in them 15
Against the French, that met them in their bent,
The fatal balls of murdering basilisks:
The venom of such looks, we fairly hope,
Have lost their quality, and that this day
Shall change all griefs and quarrels into love. 20
K. HEN. To cry amen to that, thus we appear.
Q. ISA. You English princes all, I do salute you.
BUR. My duty to you both, on equal love,
Great Kings of France and England! That I have labour'd,
With all my wits, my pains and strong endeavours, 25
To bring your most imperial majesties
Unto this bar and royal interview,
Your mightiness on both parts best can witness.
Since then my office hath so far prevail'd
That, face to face and royal eye to eye, 30
You have congreeted, let it not disgrace me,
If I demand, before this royal view,

What rub or what impediment there is,
Why that the naked, poor and mangled Peace,
Dear nurse of arts, plenties and joyful births,$_{35}$
Should not in this best garden of the world
Our fertile France, put up her lovely visage?
Alas, she hath from France too long been chased,
And all her husbandry doth lie on heaps,
Corrupting in its own fertility.$_{40}$
Her vine, the merry cheerer of the heart,
Unpruned dies; her hedges even-pleach'd,
Like prisoners wildly overgrown with hair,
Put forth disorder'd twigs; her fallow leas
The darnel, hemlock and rank fumitory$_{45}$
Doth root upon, while that the coulter rusts
That should deracinate such savagery;
The even mead, that erst brought sweetly forth
The freckled cowslip, burnet and green clover,
Wanting the scythe, all uncorrected, rank,$_{50}$
Conceives by idleness and nothing teems
But hateful docks, rough thistles, kecksies, burs,
Losing both beauty and utility.
And as our vineyards, fallows, meads and hedges,
Defective in their natures, grow to wildness,$_{55}$
Even so our houses and ourselves and children,
Have lost, or do not learn for want of time,
The sciences that should become our country;
But grow like savages,—as soldiers will
That nothing do but meditate on blood,—$_{60}$
To swearing and stern looks, diffused attire
And every thing that seems unnatural,
Which to reduce into our former favour
You are assembled: and my speech entreats
That I may know the let, why gentle Peace$_{65}$
Should not expel these inconveniences
And bless us with her former qualities.
K. Hen. If, Duke of Burgundy, you would the peace,
Whose want gives growth to the imperfections
Which you have cited, you must buy that peace$_{70}$
With full accord to all our just demands;

Whose tenours and particular effects
You have enscheduled briefly in your hands.
BUR. The king hath heard them; to the which as yet
There is no answer made.
K. HEN. Well then the peace,$_{75}$
Which you before so urged, lies in his answer.
FR. KING. I have but with a cursorary eye
O'erglanced the articles: pleaseth your grace
To appoint some of your council presently
To sit with us once more, with better heed$_{80}$
To re-survey them, we will suddenly
Pass our accept and peremptory answer.
K. HEN. Brother, we shall. Go, uncle Exeter,
And brother Clarence, and you, brother Gloucester,
Warwick and Huntingdon, go with the king;$_{85}$
And take with you free power to ratify,
Augment, or alter, as your wisdoms best
Shall see advantageable for our dignity,
Any thing in or out of our demands;
And we'll consign thereto. Will you, fair sister,$_{90}$
Go with the princes, or stay here with us?
Q. ISA. Our gracious brother, I will go with them:
Haply a woman's voice may do some good,
When articles too nicely urged be stood on.
K. HEN. Yet leave our cousin Katharine here with us:$_{95}$
She is our capital demand, comprised
Within the fore-rank of our articles.
Q. ISA. She hath good leave.
(Exeunt all except Henry, Katharine, and Alice.)
K. HEN. Fair Katharine, and most fair,
Will you vouchsafe to teach a soldier terms
Such as will enter at a lady's ear$_{100}$
And plead his love-suit to her gentle heart?
KATH. Your majesty shall mock at me; I cannot speak
your England.
K. HEN. O fair Katharine, if you will love me soundly
with your French heart, I will be glad to hear you confess it$_{105}$
brokenly with your English tongue. Do you like me, Kate?
KATH. Pardonnez-moi, I cannot tell vat is 'like me.'

K. Hen. An angel is like you, Kate, and you are like
an angel.

Kath. Que dit-il? que je suis semblable à les anges? [110]

Alice. Oui, vraiment, sauf votre grace, ainsi dit-il.

K. Hen. I said so, dear Katharine; and I must not
blush to affirm it.

Kath. O bon Dieu! les langues des homines sont
pleines de tromperies. [115]

K. Hen. What says she, fair one? that the tongues of
men are full of deceits?

Alice. Oui, dat de tongues of de mans is be full of
deceits: dat is de princess.

K. Hen. The princess is the better Englishwoman. I' [120]
faith, Kate, my wooing is fit for thy understanding: I am
glad thou canst speak no better English; for, if thou couldst,
thou wouldst find me such a plain king that thou wouldst
think I had sold my farm to buy my crown. I know no
ways to mince it in love, but directly to say 'I love you:' [125]
then if you urge me farther than to say 'do you in faith?'
I wear out my suit. Give me your answer; i' faith, do:
and so clap hands and a bargain: how say you, lady?

Kath. Sauf votre honneur, me understand vell.

K. Hen. Marry, if you would put me to verses or to [130]
dance for your sake, Kate, why you undid me: for the one,
I have neither words nor measure, and for the other, I
have no strength in measure, yet a reasonable measure in
strength. If I could win a lady at leap-frog, or by vaulting
into my saddle with my armour on my back, under the [135]
correction of bragging be it spoken, I should quickly leap
into a wife. Or if I might buffet for my love, or bound my
horse for her favours, I could lay on like a butcher and
sit like a jack-an-apes, never off. But, before God, Kate,
I cannot look greenly nor gasp out my eloquence, nor I [140]
have no cunning in protestation; only downright oaths,
which I never use till urged, nor never break for urging.
If thou canst love a fellow of this temper, Kate, whose face
is not worth sun-burning, that never looks in his glass for
love of any thing he sees there, let thine eye be thy cook. [145]
I speak to thee plain soldier: if thou canst love me for this,

take me; if not, to say to thee that I shall die, is true; but
for thy love, by the Lord, no; yet I love thee too. And
while thou livest, dear Kate, take a fellow of plain and
     uncoined
constancy; for he perforce must do thee right,$_{150}$
because he hath not the gift to woo in other places: for
these fellows of infinite tongue, that can rhyme themselves
into ladies' favours, they do always reason themselves out
again. What! a speaker is but a prater; a rhyme is but a
ballad. A good leg will fall; a straight back will stoop; a$_{155}$
black beard will turn white; a curled pate will grow bald;
a fair face will wither; a full eye will wax hollow: but a
good heart, Kate, is the sun and the moon; or, rather, the
sun, and not the moon; for it shines bright and never
changes, but keeps his course truly. If thou would have$_{160}$
such a one, take me; and take me, take a soldier; take a
soldier, take a king. And what sayest thou then to my
love? speak, my fair, and fairly, I pray thee.

KATH. Is it possible dat I sould love de enemy of
France?$_{165}$

K. HEN. No; it is not possible you should love the
enemy of France, Kate: but, in loving me, you should love
the friend of France; for I love France so well that I will
not part with a village of it; I will have it all mine: and,
Kate, when France is mine and I am yours, then yours is$_{170}$
France and you are mine.

KATH. I cannot tell vat is dat.

K. HEN. No, Kate? I will tell thee in French; which
I am sure will hang upon my tongue like a new-married
wife about her husband's neck, hardly to be shook off. Je$_{175}$
quand sur le possession de France, et quand vous avez
le possession de moi,—let me see, what then? Saint Denis
be my speed!—done votre est France et vous êtes mienne.
It is as easy for me, Kate, to conquer the kingdom as
to speak so much more French: I shall never move thee in$_{180}$
French, unless it be to laugh at me.

KATH. Sauf votre honneur, le François que vous parlez,
il est meilleur que l'Anglois lequel je parle.

K. HEN. No, faith, is't not, Kate: but thy speaking of

my tongue, and I thine, most truly-falsely, must needs be$_{185}$
granted to be much at one. But, Kate, dost thou understand
thus much English, canst thou love me?

KATH. I cannot tell.

K. HEN. Can any of your neighbours tell, Kate? I'll
ask them. Come, I know thou lovest me: and at night,$_{190}$
when you come into your closet, you'll question this
    gentlewoman
about me; and I know, Kate, you will to her
dispraise those parts in me that you love with your heart:
but, good Kate, mock me mercifully; the rather, gentle
princess, because I love thee cruelly. If ever thou beest$_{195}$
mine, Kate, as I have a saving faith within me tells me
thou shalt, I get thee with scambling, and thou must
therefore needs prove a good soldier-breeder: shall not
thou and I, between Saint Denis and Saint George, compound
a boy, half French, half English, that shall go to$_{200}$
Constantinople and take the Turk by the beard? shall we
not? what sayest thou, my fair flower-de-luce?

KATH. I do not know dat.

K. HEN. No; 'tis hereafter to know, but now to promise:
do but now promise, Kate, you will endeavour for your$_{205}$
French part of such a boy; and for my English moiety take
the word of a king and a bachelor. How answer you, la plus
belle Katharine du monde, mon très cher et devin déesse?

KATH. Your majestee ave fausse French enough to
deceive de most sage demoiselle dat is en France.$_{210}$

K. HEN. Now, fie upon my false French! By mine
honour, in true English, I love thee, Kate: by which
honour I dare not swear thou lovest me; yet my blood
begins to flatter me that thou dost, notwithstanding the
poor and untempering effect of my visage. Now, beshrew$_{215}$
my father's ambition! he was thinking of civil wars
when he got me: therefore was I created with a stubborn
outside, with an aspect of iron, that, when I come to woo
ladies, I fright them. But, in faith, Kate, the elder I wax,
the better I shall appear: my comfort is, that old age, that$_{220}$
ill layer up of beauty, can do no more spoil upon my face:
thou hast me, if thou hast me, at the worst; and thou

shalt wear me, if thou wear me, better and better: and
therefore tell me, most fair Katharine, will you have me?
Put off your maiden blushes; avouch the thoughts of your$_{225}$
heart with the looks of an empress; take me by the hand,
and say 'Harry of England, I am thine:' which word thou
shalt no sooner bless mine ear withal, but I will tell thee
aloud 'England is thine, Ireland is thine, France is thine,
and Henry Plantagenet is thine;' who, though I speak it$_{230}$
before his face, if he be not fellow with the best king, thou
shalt find the best king of good fellows. Come, your
answer in broken music; for thy voice is music and thy
English broken; therefore, queen of all, Katherine, break
thy mind to me in broken English; wilt thou have me?$_{235}$

KATH. Dat is as it sall please de roi mon père.

K. HEN. Nay, it will please him well, Kate; it shall
please him, Kate.

KATH. Den it sail also content me.

K. HEN. Upon that I kiss your hand, and I call you$_{240}$
my queen.

KATH. Laissez, mon seigneur, laissez, laissez: ma foi, je
ne veux point que vous abaissiez votre grandeur en baisant
la main d'une de votre seigneurie indigne serviteur;
excusez-moi, je vous supplie, mon très-puissant seigneur.$_{245}$

K. HEN. Then I will kiss your lips, Kate.

KATH. Les dames et demoiselles pour être baisées
devant leur noces, il n'est pas la coutume de France.

K. HEN. Madam my interpreter, what says she?

ALICE. Dat it is not be de fashion pour les ladies of$_{250}$
France,—I cannot tell vat is baiser en Anglish.

K. HEN. To kiss.

ALICE. Your majesty entendre bettre que moi.

K. HEN. It is not a fashion for the maids in France to
kiss before they are married, would she say?$_{255}$

ALICE. Oui, vraiment.

K. HEN. O Kate, nice customs courtesy to great kings.
Dear Kate, you and I cannot be confined within the weak
list of a country's fashion: we are the makers of manners,
Kate; and the liberty that follows our places stops the$_{260}$
mouth of all find-faults; as I will do yours, for upholding

the nice fashion of your country in denying me a kiss:
therefore, patiently and yielding. *(Kissing her.)* You have
witchcraft in your lips, Kate: there is more eloquence in
a sugar touch of them than in the tongues of the French$_{265}$
council; and they should sooner persuade Harry of England
than a general petition of monarchs. Here comes
your father.

*(Re-enter the FRENCH KING and his QUEEN, BURGUNDY, and other
Lords.)*

BUR. God save your majesty! my royal cousin, teach
you our princess English?$_{270}$

K. HEN. I would have her learn, my fair cousin, how
perfectly I love her; and that is good English.

BUR. Is she not apt?

K. HEN. Our tongue is rough, coz, and my condition
is not smooth; so that, having neither the voice nor the$_{275}$
heart of flattery about me, I cannot so conjure up the spirit
of love in her, that he will appear in his true likeness.

BUR. Pardon the frankness of my mirth, if I answer
you for that. If you would conjure in her, you must make
a circle; if conjure up love in her in his true likeness, he$_{280}$
must appear naked and blind. Can you blame her then,
being a maid yet rosed over with the virgin crimson of
modesty, if she deny the appearance of a naked blind boy
in her naked seeing self? It were, my lord, a hard condition
for a maid to consign to.$_{285}$

K. HEN. Yet they do wink and yield, as love is blind
and enforces.

BUR. They are then excused, my lord, when they see
not what they do.

K. HEN. Then, good my lord, teach your cousin to$_{290}$
consent winking.

BUR. I will wink on her to consent, my lord, if you
will teach her to know my meaning: for maids, well summered
and warm kept, are like flies at Bartholomew-tide,
blind, though they have their eyes; and then they will$_{295}$
endure handling, which before would not abide looking on.

K. HEN. This moral ties me over to time and a hot
summer; and so I shall catch the fly, your cousin, in the

latter end and she must be blind too.

Bur. As love is, my lord, before it loves. _300_

K. Hen. It is so: and you may, some of you, thank
love for my blindness, who cannot see many a fair French
city for one fair French maid that stands in my way.

Fr. King. Yes, my lord, you see them perspectively,
the cities turned into a maid; for they are all girdled with _305_
maiden walls that war hath never entered.

K. Hen. Shall Kate be my wife?

Fr. King. So please you.

K. Hen. I am content; so the maiden cities you talk
of may wait on her: so the maid that stood in the way for _310_
my wish shall show me the way to my will.

Fr. King. We have consented to all terms of reason.

K. Hen. Is't so, my lords of England?

West. The king hath granted every article:
His daughter first, and then in sequel all, _315_
According to their firm proposed natures.

Exe. Only he hath not yet subscribed this:
Where your majesty demands, that the King of France,
having any occasion to write for matter of grant, shall name
your highness in this form and with this addition, in French, _320_
Notre très-cher fils Henri, Roi d'Angleterre, Hèritier de
France; and thus in Latin, Præclarissimus filius noster
Henricus, Rex Angliæ, et Hæres Franciæ.

Fr. King. Nor this I have not, brother, so denied,
But your request shall make me lot it pass. _325_

K. Hen. I pray you then, in love and dear alliance,
Let that one article rank with the rest;
And thereupon give me your daughter.

Fr. King. Take her, fair, son and from her blood raise up
Issue to me; that the contending kingdoms _330_
Of France and England, whose very shores look pale
With envy of each other's happiness,
May cease their hatred, and this dear conjunction
Plant neighbourhood and Christian-like accord
In their sweet bosoms, that never war advance _335_
His bleeding sword 'twixt England and fair France.

All. Amen!

K. HEN. Now, welcome, Kate: and bear me witness all,
That here I kiss her as my sovereign queen. *(Flourish.)*
Q. ISA. God, the best maker of all marriages,340
Combine your hearts in one, your realms in one!
As man and wife, being two, are one in love,
So be there 'twixt your kingdoms such a spousal,
That never may ill office, or fell jealousy,
Which troubles oft the bed of blessed marriage,345
Thrust in between the paction of these kingdoms,
To make divorce of their incorporate league;
That English may as French, French Englishmen,
Receive each other. God speak this Amen!
ALL. Amen!350
K. HEN. Prepare we for our marriage: on which day,
My Lord of Burgundy, we'll take your oath,
And all the peers', for surety of our leagues.
Then shall I swear to Kate, and you to me;
And may our oaths well kept and prosperous be!360
(Sennet. Exeunt.)

EPILOGUE

(Enter Chorus.)

CHOR. Thus far, with rough and all-unable pen,
Our bending author hath pursued the story,
In little room confining mighty men,
Mangling by starts the full course of their glory.
Small time, but in that small most greatly lived5
This star of England: Fortune made his sword;
By which the world's best garden he achieved,
And of it left his son imperial lord.
Henry the Sixth, in infant bands crown'd King
Of France and England, did this king succeed;10
Whose state so many had the managing,
That they lost France and made his England bleed:
Which oft our stage hath shown; and, for their sake,
In your fair minds let this acceptance take. *(Exit.)*

Made in the USA
Las Vegas, NV
27 August 2024

94527722R00225